BASIC BUSINESS APPRAISAL

RAYMOND C. MILES

Executive Director
The Institute of Business
Appraisers, Inc.

A WILEY-INTERSCIENCE PUBLICATION
JOHN WILEY & SONS
New York•Chichester•Brisbane•Toronto•Singapore

Library of Congress Cataloging in Publication Data:

Miles, Raymond C.
    Basic business appraisal.

    "A Wiley-Interscience publication."
    Includes bibliographies and index.
    1. Business enterprises—Valuation.   I. Title.
HF5681.V3M48 1984   657'.73   83-23368
ISBN 0-471-88555-X

Printed in the United States of America

10 9 8 7 6 5 4 3 2 1

To the memory
of my sons,

Stephen Raymond
and
Roy Christopher,

and to their mother

Preface

This book is intended for both the beginning business appraiser and the more experienced practitioner who may wish to refresh or expand his or her knowledge and skills.

The book consists of 16 chapters. The material follows a logical progression, beginning with basic concepts and continuing through the various steps of the appraisal process. Two chapters contain examples of actual appraisal reports, and the final chapter is a hypothetical appraisal assignment that the reader can use to test his or her knowledge of business appraising.

The individual chapters cover subjects as follows:

A table of contents for each chapter appears at the beginning of the chapter.

The beginning appraiser should preferably start his or her study of the book with Chapter 1 and proceed through each successive chapter until he or she has completed Chapter 13. The reader may then wish to return to some of the earlier chapters for review before actually undertaking the practice appraisal assignment of Chapter 16.

Although the experienced appraiser will find that some of the material in the book is already familiar, it is suggested that even a reader with appraisal experience go quickly through the entire sequence of the first thirteen chapters to familiarize himself or herself with the general content and arrangement of the material. This reader then may return to individual chapters for in-depth study of material that is of particular interest.

For both the beginner and the experienced appraiser, the book should be of permanent value as a reference source to return to from time to time as needs and circumstances indicate.

RAYMOND C. MILES

Boynton Beach, Florida
February 1984

Contents

1
Introduction to Business Appraising

1
Introduction
to Business Appraising

PURPOSE AND OBJECTIVE OF BOOK

This book is about *basic business appraisal*.

The objective of the book is to provide each reader with a working knowledge of the theory and techniques of business valuation and appraisal.

PREREQUISITES

Although this book will be useful to persons who may have prior experience in appraising real estate, businesses, or other kinds of property, it is also intended for readers who, at the outset, may know little or nothing about appraising.

The book assumes, however, that the reader has at least a basic understanding of businesses and how they operate. In particular, the book assumes that the reader understands the general functioning of a business, at least basic business economics, and that he or she has at least some understanding of business financial statements, including balance sheets and income/expense statements or, as they are sometimes called, profit/loss statements. However, it is not necessary for the reader to have extensive familiarity with business financial statements, as a discussion of such statements and their relationship to business valuation and appraisal is included in Chapters 6 and 7.

WHAT IS AN APPRAISAL?

The terms *valuation* and *appraisal* are essentially synonymous and interchangeable. Although Canadian usage seems to favor *valuation*, *valuator*, and their derivatives, while U.S. usage favors *appraisal* and *appraiser*, there is no significant difference in meaning. Both sets of terms are used in this book, without any intended distinction in meaning.

Several definitions of the word *appraisal* are pertinent in the present context.

One simple definition is that an appraisal (or a valuation) is "a judgment of the worth of something."

Another similar basic definition is that an appraisal is "a supportable opinion as to the value of something." The reader should note the presence of the word *supportable* in this definition.

Still another definition is found in *Black's Law Dictionary*, which defines *appraise* as "to fix or set a price or value upon, to fix or state the true value of a thing, usually in writing."

All of this leads to the following working definition that will be used in this book:

An **appraisal**: is an opinion as to value, usually in writing, or it is the process of estimating the cost or value, of an asset, asset group, or all of the assets of a business or investment.

In all of the foregoing definitions of *appraisal*, words like *judgment*, *opinion*, and *estimate* appear. The presence of these words in the definitions reflects the fact that appraising is not an exact science. It is almost never possible to measure value with exact, mathematical accuracy. Instead, the appraiser must exercise a certain amount of judgment, must make choices, and must arrive at estimates.

Some refer to appraising as an art rather than a science. However, the fact that the appraisal process is not exact does not necessarily mean that appraising is more artistic than scientific.

In fact, sound appraisals are based on the scientific method, which is (1) to define the problem, (2) to gather the pertinent facts, (3) to analyze the facts, and (4) therefrom to arrive at a conclusion.

The fact that the resulting conclusion may not eliminate all uncertainty does not mean that appraising is not a science. It is widely understood that when astronomers attempt to estimate the age of the universe, or to determine the composition of some distant galaxy, their conclusions are not exact. However, this does not deny scientific status to astronomy.

And this is true of appraising—it is a science, although seldom an exact one in the sense that mathematics, for example, is considered an exact science.

WHY BUSINESSES ARE APPRAISED

There are many possible reasons for appraising a business or a portion of a business, or for having the business appraised. Among the most common reasons are:

Contemplated sale of the business or a portion of thereof

Contemplated purchase of a business

Determination of values of individual assets within a group of assets (including a complete business) that has been purchased or otherwise acquired (allocation of assets)

Determination of loan value

Determination of insurable value

"Buy–sell" agreements between or among owners of a closely held business

Condemnation proceedings (eminent domain)

Property settlements (for example, dissolution of marriage)

Estate valuations (estate planning, estate tax returns)

Employee stock ownership plans (ESOPs)

CONTEMPLATED SALE OR PURCHASE OF A BUSINESS

When the owner of a business is considering selling it, he or she may decide to have the business appraised in order to help him or her decide what would be a reasonable price to ask for it, and to provide a basis for responding to offers from potential buyers.

Similarly, when a potential buyer is considering the purchase of a business, he or she should have some idea of what the business is worth, so that he or she can decide how much to offer for it.

ALLOCATION OF ASSETS ACQUIRED

When a business or other group of assets has been purchased or otherwise acquired, it is frequently desirable to have the various assets appraised as a basis for allocating the total acquisition cost among the individual assets. A major reason for the desirability of such an appraisal and resulting allocation of assets lies in the differences in tax treatment accorded to various categories of assets, as, for example, current assets, fixed (or long-term) assets, and certain kinds of intangible assets. The differences in tax treatment have a resulting effect on the taxable profits of an enterprise, and a sound allocation of assets appraisal frequently can be the means to substantial tax savings for the business owner or investor.

DETERMINATION OF LOAN VALUE

If a business or a portion of its assets is to be used or offered as collateral for a loan, an appraisal may be needed to determine the value of the business or assets for borrowing purposes. The lender almost always will wish to have such an appraisal before agreeing to the loan, and the potential borrower may find it desirable to have an appraisal made before applying for the loan, so that he or she can determine the size of the loan that could reasonably be requested.

DETERMINATION OF INSURABLE VALUE

An appraisal to determine the insurable value of an asset or group of assets may be made as a basis for determining what would be a reasonable amount for which to insure the business or assets, to provide an appropriate record of asset value in anticipation of a possible loss, or as a step in obtaining settlement for an actual loss of insured assets.

BUY–SELL AGREEMENTS

In the case of a closely held business or investment, either a partnership or a closely held corporation, there may be an agreement between or among some or all of the owners that in event of specified circumstances, such as the death or incapacity of one of them, one or more of the other owners will have certain priority rights to acquire the ownership interest of the deceased or incapacitated owner. Such agreements are commonly referred to as buy–sell agreements.

Some buy–sell agreements specify the actual price at which the ownership interest is to change hands given the specified circumstances. Other buy–sell agreements, instead of stating an actual price for the possible future change of ownership, specify the procedure by which a price is to be determined.

In either case, a professional appraisal is frequently the best way of determining the price for purposes of the buy–sell agreement.

CONDEMNATION PROCEEDINGS

Condemnation proceedings, such as those brought by governmental authorities under the right of eminent domain, frequently require determination of the value of a business, or a portion of a business, that will be lost or damaged as a result of the condemnation action. An appraisal provides an estimate of this value.

PROPERTY SETTLEMENTS

Appraisals are frequently required in connection with property settlements, such as in a dissolution of marriage or a division of property among heirs to a decedent's estate.

In the case of a dissolution of marriage, it may be necessary to determine the value of various kinds of property owned by one or the other party, or by the two of them together, in order to provide for division of property in connection with the divorce. For example, if the divorcing couple owns a home, a business, or any kind of property that is not readily subject to being actually divided, it is customary for one of the parties to take full title to the property, in effect buying the other's interest in it. An appraisal of the property usually will be required in order to determine the price (which may be either in money or in exchange for other property rights) that the party acquiring full title is to pay to the other.

Alternatively, property that is owned jointly by the divorcing parties may be sold to a third party, with the proceeds from the sale then being divided between the original owners. In such a case, an appraisal can help to determine what would be a reasonable price to ask for the property.

A similar situation exists in the case of property owned by an estate to which there are several heirs. That is, there may be property, such as a business or an interest in a business, in which one heir wishes to acquire full title by buying the interests of the other heirs. Here again, an appraisal of the property can provide the means for determining what price, whether in money or in exchange for other property, should be paid to the heirs who are surrendering their interests.

ESTATE VALUATIONS

Appraisals of businesses or other property may be needed for estate planning purposes, such as in determining the probable amount of gift or estate taxes as an aid in planning prior to the death of the owner.

In the case of the estate of a deceased person, appraisal of a business, business interest, or other property owned by the estate is frequently necessary in connection with the preparation and filing of an estate tax return.

EMPLOYEE STOCK OWNERSHIP PLANS

Employee stock ownership plans (ESOPs) are formal arrangements that offer employees the opportunity to purchase ownership shares in a closely held business. One advantage of such plans is that they offer tax benefits under certain circumstances, provided the plan complies with applicable federal requirements regarding the establishment and operation of the plan.

It will be apparent that an ESOP will require some means for determining the value of the company's stock for purposes of the plan. In most cases, this is done best by means of an appraisal performed by an independent party, someone who is not a member of the plan itself and who can therefore be expected to be totally objective in the appraisal.

OTHER REASONS FOR HAVING
BUSINESSES APPRAISED

In addition to the foregoing, there are a number of other possible reasons for appraising a business or business interest. Some of these include contemplated sale of specific business assets but not of the entire business, managerial determination of return on investment, appraisals required by or because of dissident owners of a business, possible liquidation of a business, a contemplated public offering of the capital stock of a business, and so on.

Still one more reason for appraising a business can be found in the viewpoint of a broker who hopes to help arrange the sale of the business and who needs to have at least a reasonably good estimate of what the business is worth, to assist in his or her efforts to find a buyer and bring about the sale.

IMPORTANCE OF REASON FOR APPRAISAL

It might seem at first that the reason for an appraisal is of no more than casual interest to the appraiser.

After all, value is value, is it not? The appraisal, the process of measuring or estimating value, is not affected by the reason for making the measurement or estimate.

Actually, this is not so.

The fact is that there are many kinds and varieties of value, and the reason for making an appraisal has a major influence on the appraiser's choice of the kind of value to be measured or estimated in a given situation.

Thus, an appraisal for insurance purposes will be based on a definition of value as given in the applicable insurance policy or as recognized by the insuror.

Likewise, an appraisal to determine the loan or collateral value of a business or of business assets will define value in a manner acceptable to lending agencies, who customarily consider value for lending purposes as being closely related to *liquidation* value.

Appraisals for a variety of other reasons, on the other hand, will need to be based on a value definition that is related in one way or another to the concept of *market* value.

In addition to affecting the appraiser's choice of the kind of value to be measured or estimated, the reason for the appraisal also affects the appraisal process in other ways, such as in the kind and amount of detail work that the appraiser performs in arriving at his or her value estimate and the manner in which the appraisal results are presented or reported.

For example, an appraisal whose function is to assist the owner of a business in arriving at a proposed selling price for the business does not require and therefore does not justify the additional cost of a highly detailed process of information gathering and analysis, as might be in order, for example, in the case of an appraisal related to a division of property in a hotly contested divorce action.

As for the manner in which the appraisal results are reported, an appraisal to arrive at an opinion about the value of a business for an owner who is considering selling it frequently can be reported in as simple a form as a one-page letter. On the other hand, an appraisal made to help support a tax appeal involving a large sum of money generally will need to be reported in great detail, complete with numerous exhibits, references to similar cases, and so on.

NEED FOR IMPARTIALITY AND OBJECTIVITY

The fact that the reason for an appraisal is important to the appraisal process does not imply that the appraiser should allow his or her objectivity or independence of judgment to be affected, or that he or she should bias the conclusions in such a manner, for example, as to be favorable to his or her client's interest.

On the contrary, both the appraiser's credibility (and therefore the ultimate value of the appraiser to his or her clients) and his or her professional status and reputation depend on the appraiser's being scrupulously objective at all times, never allowing judgment to be biased or conclusions to be influenced by what he or she may perceive as being in the selfish interest of the client, or even by pressure that some clients may attempt to exert on the appraiser.

2
Basic Appraisal Concepts

2

Basic
Appraisal Concepts

DEFINITION OF VALUE

In Chapter 1, *appraisal* was defined as "an opinion as to value, usually in writing, or the process of estimating the cost or value of an asset, asset group, or all of the assets of a business or investment."

A key word in the definition of appraisal is *value*, and it is necessary that we have as complete an understanding as possible of what is meant by the term *value*.

Of the several possible definitions, one that is especially pertinent from an appraisal standpoint is as follows:

Value: is that quality of a thing according to which it is thought of as being more or less desirable, useful, estimable, or important.

TYPES OF VALUE

The foregoing definition encompasses many types of value, not all of which are important in appraising.

There are religious value, philosophical value, social value, ethical value, moral value, sentimental value, and so on. In appraising, however, we are concerned almost exclusively with *economic* value, which is sometimes called *commercial* value.

Economic value is value that can be measured and expressed in economic, that is monetary, terms. More precisely:

Economic value: is that kind of value according to which a thing is capable of producing economic benefits for its owner or user.

Although economic value is usually the only type of value that is of direct concern in an appraisal, there are many kinds of economic value, of whose existence the appraiser needs to be aware and with many of which he needs to be familiar. Before proceeding to consideration of the various kinds of economic value, however, it is necessary to give some attention to three terms that represent related but somewhat different concepts, which are frequently confused. These three terms are *price*, *cost*, and *value*.

PRICE, COST, AND VALUE

Price, cost, value—although the three terms are closely related, they actually have different meanings.

Unfortunately, the meanings are often confused and the terms themselves are frequently used, incorrectly, as though they were synonymous and interchangeable.

As for *value*, it has already been said that value is that quality of a thing according to which it is thought of as being more or less desirable, useful, estimable, or important. It has also been said that economic value is that kind of value according to which a thing is capable of producing economic benefits for its owner or user. Value, then, is a quality or attribute of a thing. As a measure of amount, *value* refers to the true worth of something, according to some standard of worth. And the measurement or estimation of value, specifically economic value, is what appraising is about.

The term *price*, on the other hand, refers to the amount of some medium of exchange, frequently but not necessarily money, that is needed to acquire a thing or that has actually been expended to acquire it.

As for the relationship between price and value, it has been said that price is what you pay, and value is what you hope to get.

The third term, *cost*, refers to the amount of one or more commodities—such as money, labor, or material—that is needed or expended to create or acquire a thing.

Of the three terms, *price* and *cost* are closely related and may sometimes be identical. For example, if I purchase an article from a dealer, the sum of money that I pay him is the price for which I acquire the article and is also my cost of acquiring it. The price I pay the dealer is also the price he receives for the article. However, it is generally not the same as his cost of acquiring the article in the first place. Actually, the distinction between price and cost is not a difficult one to make, given an understanding of the definitions of the two terms, unless we become careless in using the two terms, as unfortunately tends to happen, at least among laypersons.

The relationship between price and value, and between price and cost, has been illustrated in the preceding paragraphs. As for the relationship between cost and value, consider the cost of an oil well wildcatting operation that has expended a considerable amount of money drilling what proves to be a dry hole. This is a situation in which the cost is great, but the value is very small or nonexistent.

KINDS OF ECONOMIC VALUE

We have said that of the many types of value that fall within the definition of value previously given, the one type of value that is of almost exclusive interest in appraising is economic or commercial value—that type of value according to which a thing is capable of producing economic benefits for its owner or user.

Within this one type of value, economic value, there are many subtypes or kinds of economic value. We hear many related terms, including:

Market value (or sometimes "fair market value")

Book value

Replacement value

Liquidation value

Going concern value

Loan value

Insurable value

These, and many others, are all kinds of economic value.

DEFINITIONS OF SOME KINDS OF ECONOMIC VALUE

Of the many kinds of economic value, several will be encountered in this book. Definitions of these value terms follow.*

Although the full significance of the following terms and definitions may not be apparent at this point to the reader who has little or no prior appraisal background, a review nevertheless will be of interest. As the various terms are mentioned in subsequent chapters, it will be helpful to refer again to the following definitions:

Book value: The value of an asset or group of assets (including a complete business) as stated in the owner's financial statements or accounting records. Book value frequently differs from other kinds of value, such as market value, for reasons that include tax considerations.

Fair market value: Variously defined by different sources and dependent to some extent on circumstances. One common definition that is especially

---

* A more extensive list of value terms and definitions appears in the publication *Glossary of "Value" Terms*, Boynton Beach, FL: Institute of Business Appraisers, Inc., 1981, publication RB-1.

useful for appraisal purposes is that fair market value is the price, in cash or equivalent, that a buyer could reasonably be expected to pay and a seller could reasonably be expected to accept, if the property were exposed for sale on the open market for a reasonable period of time, both buyer and seller being in possession of the pertinent facts, and neither being under compulsion to act.

Going concern value: Value of a business considered as an operating enterprise rather than as merely a collection of assets and liabilities. The term may be used to refer either to the total value of a going concern or to that portion of the total value that exceeds the value of the other identifiable assets of the business.

Goodwill value: (1) Value attributable to goodwill; (2) the value of the advantages that a business has developed as a result of intangibles applicable to the specific business itself, such as name, reputation, and so on; (3) that part of the total value of a going enterprise that is in excess of the capital investment; an ingredient of *going concern value.*

Insurable value: That portion of the value of an asset or asset group that is acknowledged or recognized under the provisions of an applicable loss insurance policy.

Investment value: (1) Value as determined or estimated in accordance with the investment value (income) approach; (2) the value of a thing that arises from its presumed ability to produce a profit or return on investment for its owner; (3) value to a particular investor based upon individual investment requirements, as distinguished from market value, which is value to a broader market than a single investor.

Liquidation value: The (estimated) proceeds, net after provision for applicable liabilities, if any, that would result from sale of an asset or a group of assets, if sold individually and not as part of the business enterprise of which they were originally a part. Sale may involve either forced liquidation or orderly disposal, with the amount of the net proceeds likely different for the two situations.

Market value: Same as *fair market value.*

Present value: In investment theory, the current monetary value, frequently in the sense of the current value of future benefits. Discounted value of aggregate future payments.

Replacement value: (1) The value of a business, asset, or asset group, as determined or estimated by the replacement cost approach; (2) value as determined on the basis of the estimated cost of replacing the assets in question with other items of like kind and condition, and capable of producing equivalent benefits (results) for the user. Replacement value can be either depreciated replacement value or replacement value new.

SEPARATING ECONOMIC VALUE FROM OTHER KINDS OF VALUE

It sometimes will be found that an asset or group of assets that is to be appraised may have one or more other kinds of value in addition to its economic value.

In such cases the appraiser must separate the economic value from the other types of value, since it is only the former that is of interest in an appraisal. Fortunately, this usually will not be difficult to do and will pose no special problems for the appraiser.

There will be some cases, however, in which the separation of economic value from one or more other types of value will be somewhat difficult. This tends to be true in particular when economic value is combined with sentimental value.

As a simple example, let us assume that I own an old pocketwatch that originally belonged to my grandfather. The case is of nickel-plated brass, the watch crystal is missing, and the movement no longer runs.

Although it might be possible to repair the watch, the cost of repair almost certainly would exceed its value as a timepiece after it was repaired. The watch is neither old enough nor rare enough to have value as an antique, and the materials it contains could not be sold for as much as it would cost to reclaim them.

Clearly, the watch has essentially no economic value.

However, the watch has value to me, solely because it once belonged to my grandfather. If, for some reason, I were offered $100 for it, I would not be willing to sell. Thus, it is apparent that the watch has a value to me of at least $100. However, this is sentimental—not economic—value and does not change the fact that, whatever sentimental value the watch has for me, it has essentially no economic value.

Not all situations in which sentimental value exists together with economic value are this simple, however.

As an example of a situation that is frequently encountered in practice, consider a small- to medium-sized business that was established several years ago by one man, who is still the owner and manager of the business. However, the founder–owner is looking forward to retiring at some time in the future, and for that reason he has decided to have his business appraised in order to get some idea of the price it might bring when sold.

During the years since he started the business, the owner has worked very hard to build it to what it is today, and he is understandably proud of his accomplishment. He also remembers the many times when he had to go to extraordinary lengths to overcome problems that threatened the continued success of the business, and the many worried days and sleepless nights that he devoted to working out solutions to difficult business problems.

One result of these and other circumstances is that the business has become almost a part of the founder–owner's life, and he perceives it—either consciously or subconsciously—as having a value that goes beyond its purely economic value. This additional value is, of course, sentimental value. The business is something the founder–owner created and nurtured, and he values it more highly than he would value an otherwise identical business that he had acquired with less effort, worry, and sustained personal commitment.

Unquestionably, a successful business like the one in this example has economic value, which can be measured or estimated by an appraiser using the principles and techniques described in this book. The point is, however, that this economic value may be only part of the total value that is perceived by the owner of the business. Provided only that the appraiser remains objective and does not allow himself or herself to be biased by the owner's feelings toward the business, the appraiser should have no special difficulty in arriving at an estimate of the economic value of the business. As for persuading the owner of the business to view it in such an objective manner, this is sometimes another matter.

THREE IMPORTANT PRINCIPLES OF APPRAISING

The theory of appraising incorporates a number of principles, three of which are especially important:

Principle of Alternatives
Principle of Substitution
Principle of Future Benefits

THE PRINCIPLE OF ALTERNATIVES

The Principle of Alternatives states that *in any contemplated transaction, each party has alternatives to consummating the transaction.*

For example, in the sale of a business, the owner of the business—the seller—has alternatives to consummating a transaction with a particular buyer at a particular price. In fact, the owner of the business has alternatives to consummating any transaction with any buyer—that is, he or she has alternatives to selling the business at all.

It may be that some of the owner's alternatives are not especially desirable; some of them may be as undesirable as liquidating the business. But the owner does have alternatives. And in the more general case, the owner who is considering selling at least has alternatives from the standpoint of the price he or she charges for the business and the potential buyer to whom he or she sells it. And the owner probably has other desirable alternatives that do not involve selling the business at all. For example, it may be feasible for him or her to continue to own and operate the business or to continue to own it while putting someone else in charge of its operation.

Similarly, in a situation involving the contemplated sale of a business, the potential buyer has alternatives to consummating a particular transaction at a particular price. For example, he or she can buy a business from some other seller, can start a whole new business, can invest available funds in some way other than purchasing or starting a business, and so on.

Of course, the Principle of Alternatives is obvious and hardly needs to be stated. However, because it is one of the fundamental principles that form the basis of almost all appraisals, including those under circumstances that do not actually involve a contemplated sale or other transaction, the appraiser needs to be aware of its existence.

THE PRINCIPLE OF SUBSTITUTION

The second principle underlying economic value is the Principle of Substitution. According to the Principle of Substitution, *the value of a thing tends to be determined by the cost of acquiring an equally desirable substitute.*

Simple as it is when stated, the Principle of Substitution is also quite profound. Even though you previously may not have been consciously aware of the Principle of Substitution, and may never have heard it stated, you will recognize that it does, indeed, play a key part in determining economic value under almost any circumstances.

To illustrate how the Principle of Substitution operates to determine value, let us assume that a new book has appeared on the best-seller lists, and because of what I have heard about the book I want very much to read it. Let us further assume that the book is available in both hard-cover and soft-cover editions, and, of course, the hard-cover edition is priced somewhat higher.

If my only interest in the book is to read it—that is, if I am not a book collector—the two editions are equally desirable from my standpoint. Thus, I will tend to place a value on the hard-cover edition that is no greater than the price of the soft-cover edition, which to me is an equally desirable substitute.

Thus, the value of the hard-cover edition is determined by the cost of the equally desirable substitute, namely the soft-cover edition of the same book.

ILLUSTRATION OF PRINCIPLE OF ALTERNATIVES AND PRINCIPLE OF SUBSTITUTION

As an example of how the Principle of Alternatives and the Principle of Substitution combine to determine economic value, assume that I am a potential buyer of a small business, from which I intend to earn my livelihood. My background is in restaurant management, and my preference is therefore to buy a restaurant.

I happen to know of a restaurant that impresses me favorably, and whose owner indicates that he might be willing to sell. My first impulse is to initiate negotiations with the owner with the objective of purchasing his restaurant.

Remembering the Principle of Alternatives, however, I decide to investigate other possibilities before actually starting to negotiate.

As a result of my investigation of alternatives, I discover that there are several other restaurants being offered for sale in the general area. A number of these restaurants are essentially similar from such standpoints as size, desirability of location, and, especially, profitability. Any one of these similar restaurants would serve my purpose by giving me a way to earn my livelihood in the restaurant business.

Accordingly, each of these restaurants is, in effect, an alternative to or a substitute for the others. My decision, other things being equal, will be to purchase the available restaurant that satisfies my requirements for the lowest price.

The reader will recognize here an application of the Principle of Substitution. From the standpoint of my purpose in buying a restaurant, each is equally desirable, and I will tend to establish a value for each restaurant that is determined by the price of the least expensive one.

This example of the Principle of Substitution is a relatively obvious one. However, the Principle of Substitution is not limited to things of the same kind or with similar characteristics, as was the case in the restaurant example. Instead, the Principle of Substitution applies to any two or more things that are equally desirable according to whatever standards of needs and wants apply in a given situation. This can be illustrated by an extension of the example.

If my background is in the restaurant business, it is likely that I also know something about the wholesale food distribution business. From my standpoint I would be willing to consider buying a wholesale food distribution business if one were available, as an alternative to buying a restaurant. If I am unable to find a restaurant that suits my requirements or at a price I can afford to pay, I will then turn my attention to any wholesale food distribution businesses that may be available.

My search for alternatives may encompass both restaurants and wholesale food distribution businesses, and in applying the Principle of Substitution to help me determine the value of businesses of either type that are available I will tend to base my value conclusions on the lowest-priced business that meets my requirements for earning a livelihood, essentially without regard to whether the business in question is a restaurant or a wholesale food distribution business.

It should be noted, however, that an example like the foregoing may be unique to a given person, in this case a potential buyer, and that some other potential buyer for a restaurant business might not consider a wholesale food distribution business a suitable alternative. This other buyer, then, might limit consideration of alternatives to available restaurants or might be willing to consider businesses of some other type, such as catering businesses.

Application of the Principle of Substitution to things that are different in nature—as in the example where a food distribution business is different in nature from a restaurant business—but of equal desirability according to whatever standards of desirability may apply, might be called the extended

Principle of Substitution. The extended Principle of Substitution can be very important in many appraisal situations, as will become apparent in the following discussion and in subsequent chapters of this book.

THE UNIVERSE OF EQUALLY DESIRABLE SUBSTITUTES

Depending on circumstances including the nature of the property to be appraised, the Principle of Substitution, and particularly the phrase "equally desirable substitute," may apply in either a narrow or a broad sense. In essence, the boundaries of the *universe of equally desirable substitutes* in a given situation are determined primarily by the needs or wants of the owner or buyer—actual or potential, real or hypothetical—of the property to be appraised.

For example, when the property to be appraised is a home in a residential community, it is reasonable to assume that potential buyers consist primarily of persons who, for one reason or another, need or desire to reside in the general geographic area where the home is located, and that their requirements are for a home that is at least roughly similar in size to the one being appraised. Thus, in applying the Principle of Substitution to determine the value of the home being appraised, the universe of equally desirable substitutes is assumed to consist of other homes of at least similar size and located in the same general geographic area.

On the other hand, when the property to be appraised is one whose primary economic purpose is to produce income for its owner, the phrase "equally desirable substitute" may take on a somewhat different meaning, and the search for such substitutes as a basis for comparison will not necessarily be limited to other property of similar kind, function, or geographic location. Instead, application of the Principle of Substitution in determining the economic value of income-producing assets potentially may encompass almost any form of asset that is similar to the one being appraised in amount of investment required, amount of income produced, degree of risk involved, and so on.

An example has previously been given of a restaurant business for which, in addition to other restaurant businesses, the universe of equally desirable substitutes might include, under some circumstances, wholesale food distribution businesses, catering businesses, and others.

As another example, consider a small one- or two-person business, such as a neighborhood grocery or delicatessen. If the method for identifying equally desirable substitutes for the neighborhood grocery is the same as for a home in a residential community, then the universe of equally desirable substitutes for the neighborhood grocery would be limited to other businesses, either of the same or somewhat different type, but in any event located in the same city or local community.

However, this is not necessarily a correct viewpoint on what constitutes the universe of equally desirable substitutes in such a case.

In addition to potential buyers who already reside in the community where the grocery is located, the grocery also may be of interest to potential buyers presently living elsewhere, even in other parts of the country. This is particularly likely to be the case with so-called "mom and pop" businesses in geographic areas that are considered particularly desirable for one reason or another, perhaps because they are in popular retirement areas.

Thus, the search for equally desirable substitutes (particularly businesses of similar type that have recently been sold, or in some instances are currently being offered for sale) should not necessarily be limited to the community or other local geographic area in which the business being appraised is located.

As still another example of an extended universe of equally desirable substitutes, consider property, such as a relatively large business or a so-called passive investment, whose economic purpose is primarily that of producing income for its owner, with the means of producing this income being of only secondary importance. That is, the fact that a given business may produce income for its owners by manufacturing and selling a certain line of products, or by offering a certain kind of service, may be less important than economic considerations including the amount of income produced, the amount of investment required, and the degree of risk involved.

Such situations, in which the means for producing income are secondary in importance to the other considerations mentioned, frequently exist with large, possibly publicly owned corporations and with some kinds of more or less passive investments.

It is apparent that, in such cases, the universe of equally desirable substitutes is not necessarily limited either to businesses of the same type as the one being appraised or to businesses located in the same geographic area.

Unfortunately, many appraisers overlook the fact that the universe of equally desirable substitutes for the business or other assets being appraised is not always limited to other assets of similar or identical type and located in the same geographic area. These appraisers tend to approach appraisals of businesses, small businesses in particular, in a manner that is not essentially different from appraising a home in a residential community. Needless to say, values estimated on such a basis may be seriously incorrect.

In every appraisal the appraiser needs to review carefully the facts of the situation, and particularly the nature of the business or other property to be appraised, to be able to select an appropriate set of boundaries and dimensions for the universe of equally desirable substitutes, within which boundaries and dimensions the search for information to be used in estimating the value of the property being appraised will be conducted.

THE PRINCIPLE OF FUTURE BENEFITS

The third important principle of appraising is the Principle of Future Benefits, which states that *economic value reflects anticipated future benefits*.

No one buys a business or other property simply because of what it has accomplished in the past or even what it consists of at present. Although these may be important considerations in determining what the business or other property is likely to do in the future, it is the anticipated future performance of a business that gives it economic value.

Because of the natural tendency to dwell on the past history and present status of a business or investment, the appraiser needs to be especially careful to remain aware of the fact that values are not reflections of the past, nor even of the present. Instead, as Justice Oliver Wendell Holmes put it, "All values are anticipations of the future."

This is not to say, of course, that the appraiser should not be greatly concerned with the past performance and present status of a business or other assets being appraised. On the contrary, the past performance and present status provide important clues, and frequently accurate ones, to probable future performance. If a business has exhibited a pattern of profitability and growth in the past, and if it is part of a growing industry where the future demand for goods and services is likely to remain strong, then it is likely that profitability and growth of the business will continue in the future.

On the other hand, if there are adverse circumstances affecting or likely to affect the business in the future, such as changing government regulations or increasingly severe competition, then a business with a good record of past performance may not perform nearly as well in the future. In such a case, an estimate of value based exclusively or primarily on past performance and present status may be seriously in error.

The appraiser must remain continually aware of the existence of the Principle of Future Benefits, and one of the most difficult parts of the task of appraising is to arrive at reasonable estimates of future circumstances and performance, without which estimates the appraiser cannot be confident of the validity of his or her results.

NATURE OF THE VALUATION PROCESS

The basic nature of the valuation process should now be apparent from the preceding discussion of the Principle of Alternatives and the Principle of Substitution, which, along with the Principle of Future Benefits, provide what might be considered the theoretical basis for appraising.

The valuation process consists, in essence, of searching for and identifying alternatives and then using the known or estimated cost of these alternatives as a basis for estimating the value of the thing, be it a business or something else, that is being appraised.

3

Steps in
the Appraisal Process

3

Steps in
the Appraisal Process

THE FIVE STEPS

The major concepts that provide much of the theoretical foundation for appraising have been covered in Chapter 2. Attention can now be turned to the practical question of how one makes an appraisal.

The actual appraisal process can be thought of as consisting of five steps:

1. Define the appraisal assignment.
2. Gather the pertinent facts.
3. Analyze the facts.
4. Determine the final estimate of value.
5. Prepare the appraisal report.

Each of these steps will be covered briefly in this chapter, and subsequent chapters will take up the steps individually and in detail.

DEFINING THE APPRAISAL ASSIGNMENT

When the appraiser defines the appraisal assignment, he or she is determining the parameters of the problem that he or she is expected to solve.

The various aspects of the definition of the assignment and the manner in which the necessary information is obtained are covered in detail in Chapter 4.

GATHERING THE PERTINENT FACTS

In the second step, gathering the facts, there are two broad areas of concern to the appraiser.

One of these areas involves facts relating to the business or other property to be appraised. These facts include the general nature of the business, details of its financial operation, its relationship with its customers, and so on.

The second broad area for fact gathering concerns influences that are external to the business or other property being appraised but that have an effect on its value. These external influences can include competition, general economic conditions, availability of labor, availability of materials, transportation facilities, and so on.

The process of gathering the facts for an appraisal is discussed in detail in Chapter 5.

ANALYZING THE FACTS

After the pertinent facts have been gathered, they must be studied, analyzed, and interpreted in order to determine or estimate the value of the property being appraised. This process of analysis consumes a substantial portion of the total time and effort that an appraiser expends on an appraisal, and it is the one step that, perhaps more than any of the others, demands a high degree of skill and insight from the appraiser.

A major part of this step in the appraisal process consists of organizing, studying, and interpreting financial information about the property being appraised—information that was gathered as part of step two. The interpretation and analysis of financial information are the subjects of Chapters 6 and 7.

Use of the information that has been gathered—not just the financial information but all of the information, both internal and external—to actually arrive at estimates of the value of the property involves one or more so-called approaches to estimating value.

Three of these approaches are similar to the three recognized approaches for appraising real property. They are the market data approach, the replacement cost approach, and the investment value approach (sometimes called the income approach). However, application of these three approaches to determining the value of businesses and business assets differs somewhat from their application in real estate appraising. As they apply to appraisal of businesses and business assets, these three approaches are covered in Chapters 8, 9, and 10.

In addition to these three counterparts to the three principal approaches in real estate appraising, appraisal of businesses and business assets frequently utilizes one or more other approaches. Some of these other approaches, which are seldom, if ever, used in real estate appraising, are covered in Chapter 11.

DETERMINING THE FINAL ESTIMATE OF VALUE

Once the pertinent facts have been gathered and analyzed and one or more approaches have been employed to arrive at estimates of the value of the property being appraised, it is still necessary for the appraiser to determine the final estimate of value. This is the fourth step in the appraisal process.

The necessity for making this final estimate of value, even after one or more of the approaches to estimating value has been used, may arise for any of several reasons.

In most cases, the appraiser will have used more than one approach to estimating the value of the property and as a result will have two or more estimates, which, although they presumably will be of at least similar magnitude, will not be exactly the same. It then becomes necessary to arrive at one figure for the value of the property being appraised (not necessarily any one of the individual estimates but possibly some sort of a consensus figure) that will be reported to the client as the appraiser's final estimate of value.

Also, there are some situations in which it may not be possible to estimate the total value of the property by any one of the available approaches. Instead, the appraiser may arrive at estimates of the value of the various separate parts of the total property, using different approaches for the different parts. It then becomes necessary to combine the value estimates for the individual parts of the total property into a single estimate of the value of the complete business or other property being appraised.

Even if the appraiser has used only one approach to estimating value and has applied this approach to the total property being appraised, so that there is but a single value estimate for the complete property, he or she will still, at a minimum, wish to apply his or her judgment to determine the reasonableness of the estimated value before deciding to use it as the basis for the report to the client.

Arriving at the final estimate of value is covered in Chapter 12.

PREPARING THE APPRAISAL REPORT

The fifth and final step in the appraisal process is to prepare the appraisal report.

Although most appraisal reports are in writing, the results of an appraisal are sometimes reported orally. For example, appraisal results may be reported orally when the appraiser serves as a witness in a legal proceeding. Also, there may be some other situations, as when the function of the appraisal is purely an advisory one in a limited situation, when an oral report to the client will suffice. In most cases, however, appraisal reports are in writing.

Written reports may range in length and complexity from a simple one- or two-page letter report to a formal narrative report containing a large number of pages and including detailed exhibits, references to sources, and other supplementary material.

This fifth step in the appraisal process, preparing the appraisal report, is covered in Chapter 13.

4

Defining the
Appraisal Assignment

4

Defining the
Appraisal Assignment

IMPORTANCE TO THE APPRAISER

Defining the appraisal assignment, which is the first step in the appraisal process, helps the appraiser in a number of ways.

First, a complete definition of the assignment assures the appraiser that he or she has an adequate understanding of the assignment—that is, that he or she has properly defined the problem to be solved, and that no important aspect of the assignment has been overlooked.

Second, the information contained in the definition of the assignment provides the appraiser with at least a rough plan for the work that will need to be done in actually performing the appraisal.

And, third, some of the information that the appraiser collects during the course of defining the assignment is information that will be incorporated subsequently into the appraisal report.

ELEMENTS TO BE DEFINED

The complete definition of an appraisal assignment involves determining the following:

Purpose and function of the appraisal

Definition of value to be estimated

Description of property appraised

Effective date of value estimate

Highest and best use of property

PURPOSE AND FUNCTION OF APPRAISAL

The purpose and function of an appraisal, although closely related, are not quite the same thing.

The term *purpose* refers to the objective of the appraisal process itself. This objective may be to determine the fair market value of appraised property as of a specified date. Or, in another situation, the purpose of the appraisal may be to determine the loan value or the insurable value of the property at a certain date.

The *function* of an appraisal, on the other hand, relates to the use that is to be made of the appraisal results after the appraisal has been completed. The function may be, for example, to assist the owner of a business in establishing an asking price for a contemplated sale. Or the function may be to estimate the value of property that is part of an estate in connection with preparation of an estate tax return, or to play a part in a property settlement in connection with a dissolution of marriage. Chapter 1 included a discussion of a number of common reasons for having a business appraised. Any one of these reasons, as well as some others, may represent the function of a given appraisal assignment.

In most cases, the appraiser will determine the function of the appraisal from discussion with the client at the time when the assignment is undertaken and will then determine the purpose by inference from the function.

Thus, if the request for an appraisal comes from the owner of a business who says that he or she is thinking of selling it, the function of the appraisal is to assist the owner in arriving at an asking price for the business, and its purpose is to estimate the fair market value. Similarly, if a bank official asks for an appraisal of business assets that are to be used as collateral for a requested loan, then the purpose of the appraisal is to estimate the loan value of the assets in question.

Once the function of an appraisal is known, the appraiser generally will be able to determine its purpose—that is, the type of value to be estimated—with little or no difficulty.

In this regard, Exhibit 1 lists the most common functions of appraisals, together with the corresponding purpose for each function. Although there occasionally may be an exception, the relationship between function and purpose as given in the exhibit will apply in the great majority of cases.

It will be noted from Exhibit 1 that there is a relatively large number of appraisal functions for which the desired type of value is fair market value. This includes functions that do not involve the actual sale of the property. It will also be noted that of the several kinds of value mentioned and defined in Chapter 2, there are some that do not occur ordinarily as type of value to be estimated. (This is not to imply, however, that these kinds of value are not of interest to appraisers of businesses and other property.)

Exhibit 1
RELATIONSHIP BETWEEN FUNCTION AND PURPOSE OF APPRAISAL

Function of (Reason for) Appraisal	Purpose of Appraisal (Type of Value to Be Estimated)
To assist potential seller of business in establishing asking price	Fair market value
To assist potential buyer of business in establishing offering price	Fair market value
To determine individual values of acquired assets (allocation of assets)	Fair market value
To support loan application (appraisal of assets offered as collateral)	Loan value
To determine amount of insurance coverage to be purchased	Insurable value

(Continued)

Exhibit 1 (*Continued*)

Function of (Reason for) Appraisal	Purpose of Appraisal (Type of Value to Be Estimated)
To support claim in connection with loss or damage of insured assets	Insurable value
To determine transfer price for purpose of buy–sell agreement	As determined through discussion with owners or their representatives; preferably fair market value but occasionally some other type of value, such as book value
Property settlement, dissolution of marriage	Fair market value, or as otherwise mutually agreeable to the parties or their representatives
Property settlement, division among heirs	Fair market value, or as otherwise mutually agreeable to heirs or their representatives
Condemnation proceedings (eminent domain)	As recognized, as result of statutory provisions or otherwise, by agency bringing condemnation action; preferably fair market value, but other kinds of value frequently take precedence because of circumstances of the individual situation
Estate valuation	Fair market value, or as otherwise recognized by cognizant taxing jurisdiction
Employee stock ownership plans	Fair market value
Possible liquidation (partial or complete) of business	Liquidation value

DEFINING VALUE TO BE ESTIMATED

Having determined the general kind of value to be estimated, either with the aid of Exhibit 1 or otherwise, the appraiser must still select the specific definition of the kind of value that is to be used in the appraisal. In so doing, the appraiser may wish to refer to established definitions, such as some of those given in Chapter 2.

If the function of the appraisal is likely to involve its coming under the scrutiny of governmental or similar authorities, then the appraiser should determine whether the reviewing authority may have its own definition of value, which it will be likely to apply. This is the case, for example, with appraisals to assist in determining tax liability and with many appraisals in connection with condemnation proceedings. The U.S. Internal Revenue Service has its own definition of fair market value, which it will tend to apply in preference to other possible definitions. Similarly, other governmental authorities, including other federal agencies and also many state and local agencies, will have their own definitions of value to be applied in given types of situations.

In cases in which the appraisal is likely to come under the scrutiny of a governmental or similar agency, the appraiser should determine whether the cognizant agency has its own definition of value (and possibly also its own preferred methods or techniques for estimating value) and should at least consider adopting such definition for the purpose of the appraisal.

A similar situation may exist in some judicial circumstances. Some court jurisdictions may have developed, through precedent or otherwise, value definitions and concepts that they will be inclined to apply in preference to others. Here again, the appraiser should determine whether this may be the case and should at least consider adopting whatever definition appears to be preferred by the jurisdiction that is expected to pass upon the case.

Most loss insurance policies contain one or more definitions of value for purposes of the policy. Although some of these definitions may not be as explicit as might be desired, the appraiser should at least take them into consideration when making an appraisal for insurance-related purposes.

Likewise, lending institutions tend to have their own definitions, or at least concepts, of what they consider value for collateral purposes, and the appraiser should be acquainted with these definitions or concepts when undertaking an appraisal for a loan-related function.

In the absence of required or preferred definitions on the part of outside agencies, the appraiser is, of course, at liberty to select—from the definitions given in Chapter 2 or otherwise—whatever definition of value he or she considers appropriate to the individual appraisal.

FAIR MARKET VALUE AND THE APPRAISAL ENVIRONMENT

As previously mentioned, there are a number of appraisal functions for which the appropriate kind of value to be estimated is fair market value. Because it is the kind of value that probably applies to the great majority of all appraisals, fair market value deserves special attention here.

There are many different definitions of fair market value, including some that have been approved or adopted by agencies such as the Internal Revenue Service and by various courts and state and local taxing and other authorities. Although almost all of these various definitions are similar in import, they differ in language, and the appraiser should be aware of such differences and should decide, in each situation in which fair market value is to be estimated, what specific definition applies.

Also, the terms *market value* and *fair value* are sometimes encountered. Although these terms are at least similar in general meaning to the various definitions of *fair market value*, there may be differences that will be important in given situations and of which the appraiser should therefore be aware.

Basic to the concept of market value is the assumption that there exists for the property an open market, in which there are a number of potential buyers for a given property and also including a number of potential sellers, each offering property more or less similar to the property being appraised.

In many cases, of course, the appraisal is being made for a function, such as determining tax liability or dividing property in connection with a dissolution of marriage, that does not involve actually putting the property on the market. In such cases, however, the assumption that the property is placed on the market is basic to the appraiser's effort to arrive at an estimate of the market value.

In other cases, the property to be appraised may be of unique nature or may be extremely large, such as a multi-billion-dollar business, the result in either case being that the number of potential buyers may be extremely limited, and the number of sellers offering comparable properties also may be quite limited. Here again, however, the assumption of an open (not necessarily huge) market is a necessary step toward arriving at an estimate of the value of the property.

In the case of a business or other property of such nature that the number of potential buyers and the number of sellers making competing offers is likely to be severely limited, it might be thought that the apparently limited dimensions of the market would so restrict competitive forces that any attempt to estimate the market value of the property would be moot. However, this is not necessarily the case; as explained in Chapter 2 in connection with the extended Principle of Substitution and the universe of equally desirable substitutes, the influences that determine the economic value of property extend far beyond the immediate market for the particular property itself.

In assuming the existence of an open market for the property being appraised, the appraiser is attempting to determine the value that such a market would place on the property—that is, the price at which the property would change ownership if it were offered for sale on the open market, or the price at which it will change ownership when offered for sale, as the case may be.

The assumed open market for the property being appraised, which the appraiser adopts as a frame of reference for efforts to estimate value, can be thought of as the *appraisal environment*. It is the hypothetical market environment that is the basis for the value estimate, as contrasted to the actual market that would determine the price at which the property would change ownership if it actually were offered for sale. In a sense, the figure for market value determined by an appraisal can be thought of as the price a buyer normally would be justified in paying for the property and for which the seller would be justified in selling it, as distinguished from the price that might actually be paid if the property were offered for sale.

The characteristics of the appraisal environment, or assumed open market, which provides a frame of reference for the appraiser's work, are described by the language of the applicable definition of market value.

In the language of the preferred definition of fair market value as given in Chapter 2:

Fair market value: is the price, in cash or equivalent, that a buyer could *reasonably* be expected to pay, and a seller could *reasonably* be expected to accept, if the property were exposed for sale on the *open market* for a *reasonable period of time,* both buyer and seller being in *possession of the pertinent facts* and *neither being under compulsion to act.*

In the definition, the italicized words and phrases help to determine and describe the appraisal environment.

Although these words and phrases describe circumstances and situations that do not always exist in real life, they are necessary parts of the hypothetical appraisal environment if the estimated value of the property is to represent fair value, rather than merely a price arrived at between a seller and a buyer under circumstances that may well be unique to the particular situation.

Thus, the appraisal environment used as a basis for estimating value assumes that both seller and buyer are reasonable even though this is not always the case in real life.

Similarly, the foregoing definition requires that the property be exposed for sale on the open market and that this be done for a reasonable period of time. That is, the value is to be estimated as though the property were offered for sale in such a manner that essentially all prospective buyers would be aware of its availability, rather than being offered on a limited basis or to only a few selected prospective buyers.

Further, the property should remain on the market, available for purchase, for a sufficient length of time to allow the action of market forces, including both competition among potential buyers and competition with the subject property from other offers, to have full effect. This is in contrast to some actual situations in which the property may be on the market only a short time before it is sold, possibly even being sold to the first potential buyer who makes an offer, at a price that may very well be lower than its actual open market value.

Some established definitions of fair market value fail to mention the length of time the property is to be considered as being exposed for sale. One such definition is promulgated by the Internal Revenue Service in its frequently quoted Revenue Ruling 59–60. This ruling defines fair market value as "the price at which the property would change hands between a willing buyer and a willing seller when the former is not under any compulsion to buy and the latter is not under any compulsion to sell, both parties having reasonable knowledge of relevant facts." It will be noted that, although this definition is generally similar in import to the preferred definition given in Chapter 2 and repeated in this chapter, the IRS definition makes no mention either of an open market or of the length of time the property is exposed for sale. Assuming that these omissions are not intentional, it can be argued that the open character of the market and the fact that a reasonable time is allowed to find a buyer and agree on a price are both implied. However, a definition that is as explicit as reasonably possible would certainly seem to be the preferable one.

The requirement in the preferred definition of fair market value that both buyer and seller be in possession of the pertinent facts is an obvious one, even though it is a requirement that is not always satisfied in actual practice. In real life, there are some situations in which the buyer of a business or other property does not have all the facts, as when some information has been deliberately withheld by the seller, and there are even cases in which the seller, because of his or her own negligence or otherwise, does not have all the facts pertinent to the value of the business or other property he or she is selling. For a value estimate to reflect fair market value, however, it necessarily must be based on assumptions including the assumption that both seller and buyer are aware of the pertinent facts.

The requirement in the definition of fair market value that neither buyer nor seller be under compulsion is also an obvious one. If the seller is under compulsion, perhaps because of an urgent need for funds or other personal reasons, he or she will be inclined to accept a lower price than otherwise—a price that may be substantially less than the fair market value of the property. Likewise, if the buyer is under compulsion, perhaps because he or she urgently needs to acquire a business so that he or she can earn a living from it, that buyer may be inclined to pay an unusually high price, which may exceed the fair market value of the property.

There is one other aspect of the preferred definition of fair market value that, although it does not play a part in establishing the appraisal environment, deserves special mention. This is the phrase "in cash or equivalent."

Many definitions of fair market value omit that phrase. They do not specify how the price of the property is to be paid, whether in cash, in the form of notes to come due at future dates, some combination of cash and notes, or even conceivably in some other manner, such as exchange for other property. The possibility that a definition that is silent regarding form of payment contemplates payment for the property in barter form can be ruled out as improbable. However, the fact remains that such a definition is ambiguous about whether payment is to be made all in cash at the time of sale or in some combination of cash and deferred payments.

Since terms of payment as agreed between seller and buyer may sometimes have a significant influence on the price at which the property changes hands, any ambiguity in the definition of fair market value as used for appraisal purposes is undesirable.

In interpreting definitions of fair market value that do not mention the form of payment, some appraisers assume that the definition intends payment all in cash at time of sale, while others take the viewpoint that the definition implies payment in whatever combination of immediate cash and deferred payments is customary.

It is a fact that a great many actual sales of businesses—possibly even the majority of all such sales—take place in the form of some combination of immediate cash and deferred payments, rather than all in cash at time of sale. However, there is an almost infinite number of possible combinations of cash and deferred payments, both concerning the portion of the total price paid in cash at time of sale and the schedule for subsequent payments, interest rate on the unpaid balance of the total price, type of collateral used to secure the unpaid balance of the price, and so on.

Accordingly, it seems apparent that if the applicable definition of fair market value is silent regarding form of payment, and if the silence is interpreted as implying that payment is to be made on the customary terms, the appraiser will be faced with an almost infinite variety of choices for what should be regarded as customary.

The preferable approach is to take the position, and preferably to state explicitly in the definition of fair market value, that the price for the property is to be paid in the form of all cash at the time of sale. When relating the value estimated on the basis of such an assumption to actual price that subsequently may be paid for the appraised property in a form other than all cash at time of sale, or to prices that have been paid for other comparable properties in combinations of cash and notes, both interest on the deferred portion of the price and any price differential that may be attributable to the deferred payment arrangement can be regarded by the appraiser as a cost of money.

DEFINITION OF PROPERTY TO BE APPRAISED

The third step in determining the parameters of the appraisal assignment is to define the property to be appraised. This must be done explicitly and with the least possible ambiguity about precisely what property is being appraised.

In appraisals of real property, defining the property to be appraised is almost always a straightforward and relatively simple matter. The property to be appraised may consist of the fee simple ownership of a certain parcel of land as described in a deed, recorded on a certain page, in a certain book, in the local town or county clerk or recorder's office, including existing improvements to the parcel in question. Or, the property may be described by a set of metes and bounds—an iron pipe here and a pile of stones there—and stated in the appraisal report. In other cases, an appraisal of real property may consist of a leasehold interest, as granted by a lease of stated date, entered into between named parties, and so on.

Thus, although defining real property to be appraised may involve descriptions that can sometimes become relatively lengthy and complex, arriving at an appropriate description of the property to be appraised does not ordinarily pose significant problems for the appraiser, who is usually able to copy the necessary descriptive information from other sources.

Defining the property to be appraised in a business appraisal, however, is not always such a simple or straightforward matter.

The first step in defining the property to be appraised in a business appraisal is to determine whether the business is a corporation, a proprietorship, or a partnership. This information, of course, is ordinarily obtained from the appraiser's client.

DEFINING PROPERTY TO BE APPRAISED—CORPORATIONS

If the business is incorporated, the question immediately arises about whether the property consists of the capital stock of the corporation or whether it is to be limited to some or all of the corporate assets. This information usually will be obtained from or in consultation with the client.

In some cases, it previously may not have occurred to the client that there is a significant difference between appraising the capital stock of a corporation and appraising its assets, and this is a matter that may need to be discussed with the client.

When large corporations change ownership, it is most often on the basis of a sale of capital stock. However, this is not necessarily the case with smaller corporations, especially closely held ones.

When an incorporated business is sold, there may be a number of reasons why the seller, the buyer, or both may prefer a sale of assets, with possible assumption by the buyer of some liabilities, in preference to a stock sale. For example, the seller may wish to retain ownership of the corporate shell, perhaps because of its relationship to other business activities that are not included in the sale, so as to be able to shelter, at least temporarily, profits arising from the sale of the business, and so on.

Likewise, there may be reasons why the buyer would prefer to acquire assets rather than a complete corporation including capital stock. For example, the buyer may be reluctant to assume possible unknown or contingent liabilities of the corporation, or he or she may wish to have the opportunity to revalue the various assets and thereby obtain tax advantages in connection with a completely new depreciation schedule. This latter is possible, of course, only if the assets are purchased as such, since, if the capital stock of the corporation is purchased, the depreciable assets have not changed legal ownership—they continue to be owned by the corporation—and the new owner of the corporation remains committed to the previously established depreciation schedule.

Thus, if the function of the appraisal relates to the potential or actual sale of the business, the question of whether the appraisal is to be based on an assumed sale of capital stock or a sale of assets must be resolved before the appraisal work can proceed effectively.

If the function of the appraisal does not involve an actual sale of the business, as, for example, when the function relates to determination of tax liability or a division of property, it will most often be the case that the appraisal should be approached from the viewpoint of the value of the capital stock—that is, including all assets of the corporation and giving effect to all of its liabilities.

If the capital stock of the corporation is to be appraised, then the appraisal ordinarily will include consideration of all the assets of the corporation, and all of its liabilities. Otherwise, the appraisal will encompass specific assets of the corporation—not necessarily all of its assets, however—and may possibly take into consideration some of its liabilities.

In the latter case, the appraiser will need to determine, in consultation with the client, which assets and which, if any, liabilities are to be included in the appraisal. For example, when an incorporated business is to be sold by means of a sale of assets, the corporation's cash on hand or on deposit in banks is usually excluded from the sale. The reasoning is that the amount of cash may fluctuate substantially from time to time, and, in any event, there is really not much point in selling cash. This may seem to be an obvious point, but it nevertheless needs to be settled as part of defining the property to be appraised.

And, of course, there also may be other assets owned by the corporation that are not to be included in an appraisal for a possible sale of assets. In the case of a closely held corporation, for example, assets to be excluded from the appraisal might consist of items to which the corporation holds title but which are in fact used by the owner for purposes that are partly or principally personal, such as automobiles.

If a corporation that is the subject of an appraisal owns real property, and if the appraisal is to be an appraisal of assets and liabilities rather than an appraisal of capital stock, it may be that the real property should not be included among the assets to be appraised.

This may be the case, for example, with a closely held corporation whose assets include the land and buildings where the business is located but which is to be sold under circumstances such that the land and buildings may continue to be owned by the present owner of the business, rather than being sold to the new owner. For example, the new owner may intend to move the business to a new location, in which case the existing real estate will not be needed. Alternatively, the new owner may intend to continue the business at its existing location, but by leasing the premises from the present owner rather than buying them as a part of the business.

As with other questions regarding which assets and which liabilities are to be included in an appraisal, questions concerning real estate must be resolved by consultation with the appraiser's client.

DEFINING PROPERTY TO BE APPRAISED—
PROPRIETORSHIPS AND PARTNERSHIPS

If a business that is the subject of an appraisal is not incorporated, then its legal form is that of either a proprietorship or a partnership.

In such a case, the business does not have its own separate identity from a legal standpoint, even thought it may have an established trade (fictitious) name, may be well known in the area where it does business, may have been established for many years, and so on. Rather, all of the assets of the business are owned and its liabilities are owed personally by the proprietor or partners.

An appraisal of a business whose legal form is that of a proprietorship or a partnership requires an item-by-item determination of which assets and which liabilities are to included in the appraisal. The situation is similar to that of an incorporated business that is to be appraised in anticipation of a sale of assets, except that, in the case of a partnership or a proprietorship, the appraiser may be dealing with a client whose general knowledge of business is somewhat less sophisticated and who therefore may require more assistance in understanding the necessity for making the detailed distinctions regarding which assets and liabilities are or are not to be included in the appraisal.

Specific problems may arise, as with items like tools, machinery, and motor vehicles that are used by the owner for both business and personal purposes. If the owner also owns the real estate used by the business, this can be another problem.

In the case of a business in the form of a partnership, the problem can be complicated by the necessity of getting all of the partners to understand and to agree on the resolution of questions concerning which items are to be included in the appraisal.

As with all questions concerning the definition of property to be included in an appraisal, the foregoing and similar questions are best resolved through discussion between the appraiser and the client.

EFFECTIVE DATE OF VALUE ESTIMATE

Because values tend to change with time, a necessary part of defining an appraisal assignment is to determine the effective date of the value estimate. This is the date as of which value will be estimated, sometimes referred to as the "as of" date of the appraisal, as distinguished from the date on which the appraisal work was actually performed or completed.

Depending on the function of the appraisal, the effective date of the value estimate may be dictated by circumstances, or it may be a matter of choice.

If the function of the appraisal is to estimate the value of property in the estate of a deceased person, the effective date will usually coincide with the date of death. (However, the U.S. estate tax laws at the time of this writing include provision for an optional effective date, which is at the election of the representative of the estate. In some cases this optional date can be advantageous from an estate tax standpoint. This matter needs to be discussed between the appraiser and the representative of the estate.)

Similarly, if the appraisal is in connection with a division of property between divorcing persons, then the effective date of the value estimate usually will be either the date on which the divorce becomes effective or some other date that may have been agreed on between the parties or their representatives for property distribution purposes.

If the appraisal is to determine asset values within a group of assets that has been acquired (allocation of assets), then the effective date of the value estimates will correspond with the date on which title to the assets passed to the new owner.

Appraisals to determine the value of a business in connection with an employee stock ownership plan usually will have their effective dates determined by the terms of the plan itself, which also may provide for periodic revaluations, such as on successive plan anniversary dates.

And, of course, there are many other situations in which the effective dates of the value estimates will be dictated by circumstances.

In other cases, however, such as when the appraisal is in connection with the contemplated sale or purchase of a business or is for the purpose of determining its loan or insurable value, the situation may call for a value estimate that is as up to date as possible, but without the exact effective date being otherwise important. In such cases, the effective date of the appraisal may be chosen to correspond with the date on which the appraiser completes his or her inspection of the business or assets or some other date related to the appraisal process itself.

A preferable practice, however, is to key the effective date in such situations to the effective date of the financial reports or similar information the appraiser uses as part of the basis for the estimate of value.

Financial reports for a business, as prepared by the owner or by someone else in his or her behalf and furnished by the owner to the appraiser, form an important part of the appraiser's total data base for almost all appraisals. Accordingly, it is reasonable that the effective date of the value estimates should be the same as the effective date of these financial reports.

Such an approach to selecting the effective date of the value estimate tends to protect the appraiser from the possibility of recent events that affect the value of the property but of which the appraiser may not be aware, while at the same time providing the client with a value estimate that is reasonably up to date for practical purposes.

If this approach, selecting an effective date to correspond with the date of the most recent available financial statements, is taken, the appraiser may include in his or her report a statement to the effect that he or she is not aware (if such is the case) of any changes or events subsequent to the effective date that would have a significant effect on the value of the property appraised.

HIGHEST AND BEST USE

It is an axiom of appraising that the value of property is estimated in anticipation of its highest and best use.

Highest and best use: can be defined as the legally permissible and reasonably feasible present use, or series of future uses, that will result in the greatest economic benefit to the owner of the property.

In many cases, of course, the highest and best use of property is the use that corresponds with its existing use. However, this is not always or necessarily the case.

For example, consider the hypothetical case of a tract of land in the downtown area of a city. The improvement to the land consists of an old, somewhat rundown building whose owner is leasing it to a tenant for use as a warehouse. Based on its existing use, this land with its building has a value that is related to the amount of rental income that it provides, less the owner's related expenses.

However, if the land in question is in an area where it is surrounded by establishments such as office buildings, retail stores, and the like, then it is quite likely that it would be more economically rewarding to the owner if the existing building were demolished and the land were used as the site for a new building more in character with its surroundings.

Similar examples can be found in the case of businesses and business assets.

An appraiser may be assigned to estimate the value of a business that manufactures a certain line of products for sale to a certain market. It is quite possible and will frequently prove to be the case that the business, or those of its assets that are to be included in the appraisal, are indeed being put to their highest and best use. However, this is not always the case, even though the business may be profitable to an adequate or more than adequate degree.

For example, a manufacturing or distribution business usually will have a substantial amount of inventory, which the business holds in anticipation of its eventually being sold or being used in products that will be sold.

However, it frequently happens that a portion of the inventory of a business is actually obsolete to the extent that it is not likely ever to be sold or to find its way into saleable products. Rather than continuing to keep this inventory on hand, a better solution might be to dispose of it, perhaps by selling it at a discount or even for scrap. To the extent that such obsolete inventory is included in the business, at least that portion of the business is not being put to its highest and best use.

As another example, consider a business that may have tools, equipment, or even buildings that, because of such circumstances as technological changes, shifting market or labor patterns, may no longer be as effective as they originally were for the purpose for which they are being used, but which might be more effective if put to some other use. Here again is an example of assets that are not being utilized in accordance with their highest and best use.

As still another example, consider a manufacturing or processing business that produces byproducts that are being discarded as worthless but which in fact might be sold or otherwise used for a purpose that will produce income. This could be the case, for example, with the scrap metal from a metal manufacturing business being disposed of at a dump rather than being sold to a scrap dealer. Other examples could include a butchering business that is discarding parts of the animal (such as bones, skin, and entrails) that could instead be put to some economic use, or a chemical processing operation that is discarding chemical byproducts when, in fact, they contain materials that could be recovered economically.

In extreme cases, an appraiser may sometimes be asked to appraise a business which, though profitable, is only marginally so, and rather than continuing as an operating business, might better be liquidated. The business would be discontinued, its assets being sold individually for whatever price they might bring, and the liabilities of the business would then be satisfied from the proceeds of the sale of assets.

In determining whether a business, business assets, or other property to be appraised is being utilized in accordance with its highest and best use—and, if not, what its value might be as determined by its highest and best use—the appraiser will need to become familiar with the business or other property to be appraised and then determine on the basis of this familiarity what, in fact, is the highest and best use of the business.

As previously stated, this frequently will lead to the conclusion that the highest and best use corresponds with the current actual use of the business. However, this is not always the case, and the appraiser needs to remain aware of this possibility and to be on guard against falling into the trap of simply assuming that the current use is also the highest and best use.

Although it is not a universal practice it is highly desirable for the appraisal report to include a statement about the highest and best use of the property. This includes cases in which the appraiser has determined that the current use is also the highest and best use. Unless such a statement is included in the appraisal report, there is room for suspicion that the appraiser may have failed to give adequate consideration to the question of highest and best use or may even have overlooked it entirely.

CHECKLIST FORM FOR DEFINING THE APPRAISAL ASSIGNMENT

Exhibit 2 illustrates a form that has been found useful in summarizing the definition of an appraisal assignment. The reader may wish to adopt it for his or her own use.

In addition to providing a summary of the assignment after it has been defined, the form also serves the function of a checklist, ensuring that no important aspect of defining the assignment is overlooked.

Exhibit 2
SUMMARY OF APPRAISAL ASSIGNMENT

Client _____   Proj./File no. _____

Purpose and function of appraisal
    Use to be made of appraisal results (function):

Type of value to be estimated (purpose):

Definition of value to be estimated:

(*Continued*)

Exhibit 2 (*Continued*)

Description of property to be appraised:

Effective date of value estimate:

Highest and best use:

5

Gathering the Facts for an Appraisal

5

Gathering the Facts
for an Appraisal

REQUIREMENTS FOR PERFORMING AN APPRAISAL

In order to perform an appraisal, the appraiser needs:

An understanding of appraisal theory and its practical application

An understanding of general business principles, including business economics and basic financial analysis

At least a rudimentary understanding of the functioning of the specific type of business (e.g., retail clothing store, metal products manufacturing, advertising agency, etc.) that is to be appraised

Detailed factual information about the business or other property that is to be appraised

Factual information about the business environment in which the business being appraised operates and in which it is expected to operate in the future

By the time this book has been completed, the reader should have a basic understanding of appraisal theory and its practical application, which is the first requirement. The reader who is interested in going beyond basic appraisal theory and techniques can do so with the help of the various books, periodical articles, and other sources of training and education that are available.

As was stated in Chapter 1, this book assumes that the reader has at least a basic understanding of how businesses operate, including at least basic business economics and business financial statements. However, the reader who feels that he or she may be weak in these areas will find that there are a number of good books and other study materials available, which he or she can use to strengthen an understanding of those weak areas. Information on some of these study aids will be found in the list of sources that appears at the end of Chapter 7.

The third requirement for performing an appraisal is an understanding, at least in broad terms, of the functioning of the specific kind of business that is to be appraised. This is necessary to permit the appraiser to identify the truly important aspects of the situation and to prevent the appraiser from falling victim, through ignorance or naivete, to the danger of producing an appraisal that, though apparently sound from a theoretical standpoint, does not properly reflect the real world in which the appraised business operates.

In many cases, the appraiser will have the necessary understanding at the time he or she undertakes the assignment, either as a result of having appraised similar businesses in the past or in some cases having previous personal experience, in some capacity other than as an appraiser, with businesses of the type in question.

Although such prior experience is the more desirable possibility, the appraiser who lacks previous experience with businesses of the type to be appraised, but who possesses a good understanding of business principles in general, should be able to acquire the necessary degree of familiarity with the operation of businesses such as the one being appraised while working on the appraisal assignment. Some ways to do this are suggested later in this chapter, particularly under "Sources of General Industry Information."

The remaining two requirements for performing an appraisal, namely factual information about the business or other property to be appraised and factual information about the business environment, are the principle subjects of this chapter.

In the following discussion the facts directly concerning the property being appraised are referred to as *internal facts*, while the facts concerning the environment in which it operates or exists are referred to as *external facts*.

IMPORTANCE OF FACT-GATHERING STEP

Gathering the pertinent facts, the second step in the appraisal process, is a crucial step and one fully deserving of the appraiser's effort and attention, because, regardless of how excellent an understanding the appraiser may have of appraisal theory and practice and regardless of the sophistication of the analytical techniques he or she may employ to arrive at a value conclusion, the result of the appraisal can be no better than the facts on which it is based.

KINDS OF INTERNAL INFORMATION

Factual information about the business or other property being appraised, or internal information, falls into three broad categories:

History of the business or other property to be appraised

Its present status

Its future outlook

The history of the business to be appraised includes both its general history from the time it was started and its financial history during the recent past, say for the past five years or so. Knowledge of the general history of the business provides the appraiser with background information and a frame of reference that will help him or her to put the other information about the business in proper context. Information about the recent financial history of the business provides the appraiser with a basis for understanding its economic aspects and, in the case of most appraisals, provides a major part of the basis for predicting future financial performance.

The importance of information on the present status of the business being appraised should be obvious. Like the information on the history of the business, information on its present status includes both general information and specific financial information.

The information on the future outlook for the business or other property being appraised is of special importance because, as expressed by the Principle of Future Benefits, it is this future outlook that determines the economic value.

More details about kinds of internal information needed for an appraisal will become apparent in the remainder of this chapter, including the "Internal Information Checklist."

SOURCES OF INTERNAL INFORMATION

Broadly speaking, there are three principal sources of internal information about the business or other property to be appraised:

Financial statements prepared by or on behalf of the business to be appraised

Interviews with persons who are acquainted with some or all aspects of the business

The appraiser's personal observation

SOURCES OF INTERNAL INFORMATION— FINANCIAL STATEMENTS

Financial statements are by far the best source of information about the financial history of the business. Such financial statements should include both annual income/expense (or profit/loss) statements and annual balance sheets and should cover a period of at least the last several years.

As a rule of thumb, the appraiser should obtain copies of financial statements covering a period of at least five years leading up to the date of appraisal. However, if the business exhibits an unstable or erratic pattern of sales or profits, statements covering a period of more than five years may be needed as part of the effort to identify whatever trends may exist. Of course, if the business has not been in existence for as long as five years, the appraiser must work from financial statements covering the shorter period.

In addition to annual income/expense statements and annual balance sheets, the appraiser may sometimes find it helpful to have available annual summaries of source and application of funds if such summaries are available.

The corporation income tax return contains essentially the same information as a conventional financial report, though in somewhat less detail. Accordingly, if the business to be appraised is a corporation, and if its tax returns are filed on the standard corporate form (Form 1120), tax returns can provide a direct substitute for formal financial statements if the latter are not available.

However, if the business is not incorporated—that is, if it is a proprietorship or partnership—tax returns are somewhat less helpful as a substitute for formal financial statements. This is because the income tax returns filed by the owner of a proprietorship or by the partners in a partnership are personal income tax returns and do not contain all of the information that is found in a corporation income tax return. (Partnerships are required, however, to file informational returns, even though the partnership is not taxed as such.)

When the business to be appraised is a proprietorship or a partnership and formal financial statements are not available, the appraiser usually will find it possible to reconstruct the equivalent of an income/expense statement for the business from the personal income tax returns of the owner or owners. However, the appraiser will need the help of the owner or owners in separating business-related income and expenses as shown on the tax return from other income and expenses shown on the return that are from sources not related to the business being appraised.

As for balance sheet or equivalent information on a proprietorship or partnership for which there are no formal financial statements, the appraiser frequently will find it necessary to be satisfied with an approximate balance sheet showing assets and liabilities as of the date of appraisal, prepared by the appraiser from information obtained through interviews with the owner or owners of the business and from such other sources as may be available.

In most appraisal assignments, financial statements and tax returns for the business to be appraised will be available from the appraiser's client or from the client's representative. This almost always will be the case when the appraiser's client is an owner of the business to be appraised.

In other cases, even though the appraisal is being performed for a client who has no direct connection with the business, it will be in the interest of the owner of the business to cooperate with the appraiser by supplying financial and other information. This will be the case, for example, with an appraisal that has been requested by a lending institution in connection with a loan application from the business or its owner.

In some cases, the owner of a business may not be cooperative in furnishing information to the appraiser. Problems that may be encountered by the appraiser in gathering information about a business to be appraised are discussed later in this chapter.

Of course, if the business to be appraised is a so-called public company, financial statements may be matters of public record and should be available to the appraiser through sources such as the company's public or stockholder relations office, libraries that maintain collections of corporation annual reports, the files of the Securities and Exchange Commission, and so on.

SOURCES OF INTERNAL INFORMATION—INTERVIEWS

The second principal source of internal information consists of interviews with persons who are associated with the business to be appraised or who are otherwise knowledgeable of it or of some aspect of its operation.

Such interviews are the best source of information, other than detailed financial information, about the past history of the business. In addition, interviews can provide the appraiser with answers to some of the questions he or she may have about financial operations and frequently will provide the principal basis for the appraiser's understanding of the present status of the business. Also, interviews with knowledgeable persons can provide the appraiser with important insights into the probable future outlook for the business.

In almost all cases, the appraiser will wish to schedule interviews with the owner or other executives of the business to be appraised. In some cases, it may be desirable to supplement interviews with the owner of the business with interviews with other key personnel, such as those in marketing, engineering, or manufacturing capacities, some of whom may have additional information or viewpoints that will be helpful to the appraiser.

It also may be useful to discuss the business being appraised with outsiders, such as the company's accountant, its banker, and possibly trade association executives who may be familiar with the business to be appraised.

In some cases, it may even be appropriate to discuss the business with some of its suppliers or competitors. Of course, any discussions with outsiders will require appropriate caution on the part of the appraiser so as not to disclose confidential or proprietary information or otherwise to harm the interests of the appraiser's client.

Suggestions for topics to be covered and specific questions to be asked during interviews with business owners, key executives, and others will be found in the "Internal Information Checklist" that appears later in this chapter.

SOURCES OF INTERNAL INFORMATION—PERSONAL OBSERVATION

The third major source of information about a business to be appraised is the appraiser's own personal observation. While not a substitute for either of the other two principal sources of internal information, personal observation by the appraiser can help flesh out his or her understanding of the business to be appraised and frequently will suggest additional investigations that should be pursued or additional questions to ask.

A tour of a manufacturing plant can help to fill out the appraiser's understanding of the operation of the business that he or she is appraising.

Similarly, a tour of the company's stockroom may disclose that some of the items stored are covered with a heavy layer of dust. Does this mean that some of the inventory is actually obsolete and therefore possibly unusable? If the stockroom presents a generally disorderly appearance, or if it appears that inventory is stored without particular regard for keeping similar items together, does this mean that the inventory record system is poor and that the amount of inventory shown on the company's books may not be a fair representation of what is actually on hand?

What about the front office and the engineering department, if there is one? Do they appear to be neat and orderly, staffed with persons who are attentive to their work and who at least give the appearance of knowing what they are doing?

Depending on the kind of business being appraised, personal observation can provide the appraiser with a wide variety of possible clues to subjects that should be investigated further. Here again, specific information to look for is suggested in the "Internal Information Checklist."

POSSIBLE PROBLEMS IN GATHERING INTERNAL INFORMATION

Occasionally, the appraiser may encounter unusual difficulties in obtaining the internal information needed for an adequate appraisal.

This may happen, for example, when the appraiser's client is other than the business or its owners, and when the circumstances of the appraisal involve a dispute or other adversary situation such that the owners of the business may believe that it would not be in their best interest to cooperate with the appraiser. In such a case, it still may be possible for the appraiser to obtain the needed information through such means as subpoenas or similar legal process, issued at the request of the appraiser's client or the client's attorney by a court having jurisdiction.

In other cases, the appraiser may suspect that the business owner or other source of information, while appearing to cooperate, is either withholding important information or is deliberately distorting key facts. In such a case, the appraiser must act something like a detective, using a combination of personal observation and judgment in an effort to get at the true facts.

For example, if the appraiser suspects that his or her client may be exaggerating the sales volume of the business in an effort to puff up its value before offering it for sale, the appraiser may wish to make an inspection of that part of the company's stockroom where finished goods are kept while awaiting shipment, or he or she may wish to tour the production area and shipping department. Is the quantity of product in the finished goods area consistent with the claimed sales volume, or does it appear to be too small or too great? Is the production area as busy as one would expect in a company with the claimed sales volume? Does the shipping area appear to be neat but busy, or does it appear to be relatively inactive?

Is there a sufficient number of employees in evidence to account for the claimed volume of business? (If it is difficult, because of plant layout or for other reasons, to make an actual count of employees, a count of automobiles in the company parking lot can provide a good alternative. Count the number of automobiles in the lot and then multiply by approximately 1.5 to account for normal car pooling. The result should be a reasonably good approximation of the total number of employees in the plant.)

To explore other areas of doubt or suspicion, the appraiser may wish to take such steps as checking the telephone book yellow pages to get an idea of the approximate number of competitors, examining the records of sales transactions or accounts receivable of the business as a means of verifying claims about number of customers or sales volume, and so on.

Although such situations are relatively infrequent, the appraiser occasionally will be unable to obtain the minimum amount of information that he or she considers necessary for a good appraisal, or the appraiser may become convinced that the information made available to him or her is seriously distorted or omits important information of a negative nature. In such cases, the appraiser must consider seriously whether he or she should proceed with the appraisal at all or withdraw from the assignment instead.

INTERNAL INFORMATION CHECKLIST

Following is a list of questions an appraiser may wish to ask about a business that he or she has been asked to appraise.

Not all of these questions will apply to all businesses or to all situations. However, many of the questions will apply in a given situation, and even those that do not apply directly may suggest other information the appraiser may wish to obtain.

Although no list of questions about a business can be exhaustive, the questions here cover many of the most important aspects of a business that should be scrutinized when the business is to be appraised. In addition to using it as a checklist, the appraiser may wish to use the list of questions to assist him or her in preparing for interviews with key personnel and others who may be able to contribute information for use in the appraisal.

About the Form of Organization of the Business

Is the business a sole proprietorship, partnership, or corporation?

If a partnership:

How many partners, and who are they?

What fractional interest in the business does each of them own?

If a corporation:

How many stockholders are there?

Who are the major stockholders, and what percentage of the total outstanding shares does each of them own?

Is the stock traded on a market?

What market?

What are recent prices for shares traded?

About the Products or Services of the Business

What are the principal products or services?

For what length of time has each been sold?

What has been the sales volume of each for each of the past five years?

What are the costs and gross profits for each of these products or services?

What portion of the total cost is for materials?

What portion is for labor?

What portion is for overhead?

Which of the products or services are proprietary?

Which products are purchased from others for resale?

What is the nature of agreements with suppliers of these products?

What features of the business's products or services distinguish them from competition?

What product or service warranties are given to customers?

What is the forecast of future sales and profits for each major product or service?

How do quality and price compare with similar products or services offered by competitors?

To what extent does the business rely on the services of outside vendors or subcontractors?

Who are the principal vendors or subcontractors?

What other products or services could be produced or furnished with the existing facilities?

About Markets and Marketing

What are the principal applications for each major product or service?

What are the principal markets for each major product or service?

To what extent are these markets already established, and to what extent must they still be developed?

What is the future outlook for growth, or lack of growth, of each of these markets?

Who are the principal customers?

What portion of the total sales volume does each of these customers represent?

Which major potential customers have not yet been secured as actual customers?

How do sales break down geographically?

What is the present backlog for each major product or service?

How has this backlog varied over the past three years?

Who are principal competitors?

What are the relative strengths and weaknesses of each of these competitors?

What is the estimated sales volume of each of these competitors?

What is this business's relative position among its competitors with regard to sales volume?

What is its relative position among its competitors with regard to reputation?

Has the business's past sales growth generally followed the industry trend, or has it been ahead of or behind this trend?

What is the forecast of future industrywide sales for each of the business's products or services?

What is the forecast of this business's future sales for each major product or service?

Does the business regularly use the services of any advertising or public relations firms?

Who are they?

Is the marketing aggressive and skillful?

Who is responsible for market research?

Who is responsible for advertising and sales promotion?

Who is responsible for product applications?

Who is responsible for exploiting new markets?

What is the nature of the direct selling organization (supervision, personnel, field offices, salary and other compensation)?

What is the nature of the distributor or sales representative organization (list of distributors or sales representatives, exclusive or nonexclusive nature of agreements, expiration dates of individual appointments, past performance of each distributor or representative, commission or discount rates, contract terms)?

What is the nature of the service organization (who is responsible for service, installation, maintenance, etc.)?

Are there any foreign operations?

Details?

Does the business use the services of any outside consultants for market research or similar activities?

Who are they?

What is their past record of accomplishment?

About the Financial Situation of the Business

What is the sales and earnings record of the business for each of the past five years?

What salaries or dividends have been paid to owners or stockholders during each of the past five years?

Are income/expense statements available for each of the past five years?

Are balance sheets available?

What are the details of the present accounts receivable (from whom receivable, amounts, age, etc.)?

What about inventory?

What is normal inventory level?

What is the actual inventory at present?

How does this inventory break down among raw material, work in process, and finished goods?

What is the condition (new, obsolete, damaged, etc.) of the existing inventory?

Is any portion of the inventory on consignment?

What portion?

Consigned to whom?

For how long?

On what terms?

What are the details of the accounts payable (to whom payable, amounts, age, any special circumstances, etc.)?

What loans are outstanding, to whom are they payable, and what are the terms of each loan (interest rate, payment schedule, collateral, etc.)?

What is the amount of accrued expenses payable?

What item does this include?

Are all federal and state taxes (including employee withholding taxes) current?

What is the present book value (net worth, invested capital plus retained earnings) of the business?

What is the amount of available working capital?

What is the business's depreciation policy for fixed assets?

What overhead (burden) rates are used in determining costs?

What are the various departmental budgets?

What is the advertising and sales promotion budget?

What is the total payroll?

Does the business own equity in any other businesses?

What liabilities, contingent or otherwise, exist in connection with product or service warranties?

Are there any existing claims or known contingent liabilities of any nature whatsoever?

Details?

Are there any contract disputes or renegotiations pending?

Are there any outstanding stock options, convertible notes, or the like?

Is there an existing forecast of future sales, profits, and capital requirements?

What does this forecast show?

About the Physical Facilities

Is a complete list of physical facilities and equipment available?

Is the real estate owned or leased?

If owned:

    What is the appraised value?

    When was this appraisal made?

    By whom?

If leased, what are the terms of the lease (period, rental, security deposit, restrictions on use of premises, renewal options, etc.)?

What are the zoning restrictions?

Are any of the other physical facilities or equipment leased rather than owned?

    Details?

Is there any excess or idle capacity?

    How much?

About Personnel and Organization

Is a complete organization chart available?

Are position descriptions available?

What are the functions of key executives and personnel?

What is the total personnel complement?

Are there established rates of pay or pay ranges for the various jobs?

How do these rates compare with those of other employers in the general area?

What is the wage and salary review policy?

What employee benefits exist (life insurance, hospitalization insurance, vacation, sick leave, pension, profit sharing, etc.)?

Is the cost of these benefits paid entirely by the business, or do the employees contribute part of the cost?

    What part?

Are the workers unionized?

Which ones?

What are the contract details?

Have there ever been any unsuccessful attempts to organize the workers?
Details?

Have there ever been any strikes?
Details?

What has been the experience with respect to employee turnover?

Are the employees given any formal training for their jobs?
Details?

Are written personnel policies or procedures available?

What is the general situation in the area with regard to availability of labor?

Is there a house organ, employee bulletin, or newsletter for employees?
Details?

Are copies available for review?

About Management

Is an organization chart available?

What are the backgrounds of key members of management?

What is the compensation of key members of management?

Are any members of management (or any other key employees) under contract to the business?

Details?

If the business were to be sold to a new owner, would the sale require any substantial reorganization of management?

Which members of management could be expected to remain with the business following its sale?

What are the management capabilities of the person in charge of each of the key departments?

How well is each of these departments staffed?

How capable is the second echelon of management?

Are there any strong differences of opinion among members of management?

Details?

Do separate departments cooperate willingly and effectively with one another, or are there cases where cooperation is grudging or nonexistent?

Is management progress-minded and willing to take reasonable risks?

Who dominates the organization?

If the business is a corporation:

What control do major stockholders exercise over the company's policies or activities?

About the Business in General

When was the business established?

For how long has it been owned by the present owner?

Does success of the business depend to an unusual degree on the capabilities, performance or contacts of one or more key persons?

Details?

What potentially dangerous situations exist, or might arise, in connection with the business's management, products, services, markets, finances, legal obligations, and so on?

How is the business regarded by its customers?

How is it regarded by its competitors?

How is it regarded by its suppliers?

How is it regarded by cognizant government agencies?

How is it regarded by its bank and by the financial community in general?

How is it regarded by its employees?

How is it regarded by the community in which it is located?

Has the business complied with applicable requirements of cognizant governmental regulatory agencies, such as the Occupational Safety and Health Administration (OSHA) and others?

What has been the past history of the business with regard to litigation?

Is the business involved in any joint ventures or similar undertakings?

What are the business's major accomplishments?

Where has the business failed to an appreciable degree?

KINDS OF EXTERNAL INFORMATION

Information about the environment in which a business operates provides the appraiser with a frame of reference for the business to be appraised, thus giving added significance to the internal information about the business itself. Information about the business environment is especially important to the appraiser in efforts to estimate the value of the business he or she is appraising according to the Principle of Future Benefits.

Information on the business environment, or external information, can be grouped into the following categories:

General information about the industry of which the business to be appraised is a part, including the future outlook for the industry

Information on individual companies within the industry

Information regarding any recent sales of other companies in the same industry as the company being appraised

Local or regional information about the geographic area in which the business to be appraised is located

GENERAL INDUSTRY INFORMATION

Information about the industry of which the business to be appraised is a part has several important functions in an appraisal:

By making a major contribution to the appraiser's understanding of the business environment in which the business operates, it helps to place the business being appraised in perspective and thus to arrive at value conclusions that take external considerations into proper account.

Because the future of any business is greatly influenced by the future of the industry of which it is a part, industry information is important to the appraiser's efforts to predict the future performance of the business being appraised and thus to arrive at an estimate of its value that includes the results of applying the Principle of Future Benefits.

In those instances in which the appraiser lacks previous familiarity with the kind of business to be appraised, industry information can make a valuable contribution to the appraiser's understanding of the operation of the business that he or she is to appraise.

Although the nature of the industry information to be gathered will vary to some extent from appraisal to appraisal, it usually will include most or all of the following:

Expectations with regard to future growth, or lack of growth, of the industry as a whole

A summary of the competitive situation within the industry, including the identity of those companies, if any, whose activities exert a major influence on the industry as a whole

General information on marketing methods within the industry, including any available information about likely future changes from existing marketing methods

Information on sources of materials used by companies within the industry, including any predictable future changes in the material supply situation

Recent or anticipated future technological developments that are likely to have a significant effect on the future of the industry and of individual companies within it

The relationship to the industry of federal (and in some cases state or local) regulatory activities, including probable future changes and the effect of these changes on companies within the industry

Other predictable changes in methods of doing business, such as in transportation, distribution, and other activities

SOURCES OF GENERAL INDUSTRY INFORMATION

Possible sources of general industry information include:

Trade associations

Trade publications, including trade periodicals

Various publications of the U.S. Bureau of the Census

Investors' information and reporting services, including both services available by subscription and those available without charge from sources such as stock brokerage firms

Compilations of industry financial data available from several sources

Publications of the U.S. Small Business Administration

Various specialized sources of industry information, such as the inquiry and information service operated by The Institute of Business Appraisers for the benefit of its members

Although not every industry has its own trade association, at least several hundred of the larger industries do have national trade associations. If one exists for the industry of interest, a trade association is an excellent source of industry information for the appraiser.

Most of the larger trade associations maintain some sort of information-gathering or research program to benefit the members of the industry. This information is frequently available in printed form such as annual surveys, and much of the information is available to nonmembers as well as members of the association.

Aside from information available in published form, executives of trade associations frequently can provide industry information that would not be available otherwise. This is also true of executives of the smaller trade associations, which may not conduct formal information-gathering or research programs.

There are several ways in which an appraiser can locate the trade association for a given industry, if one exists. Probably the most direct approach is to determine whether the business being appraised is a member of a trade association.

Also, there are bound directories of trade associations and similar organizations, which the appraiser should be able to find in a reasonably well-stocked public or university library. These directories include the *Encyclopedia of Associations* and *National Trade and Professional Associations of the United States and Canada and Labor Unions*, both of which are listed in the section on "Specific Information Sources" at the end of this chapter.

When other attempts fail, a trade association sometimes may be located by consulting telephone directories for some of the larger cities, particularly the directory for the District of Columbia, which is the home of a large proportion of all national trade organizations.

Another good source of general industry information consists of trade publications. These include some periodicals and other publications issued by trade associations, as well as trade publications from other publishers.

A review of several recent issues of a trade periodical will help to give the appraiser a general feeling for an industry with which he or she was not previously acquainted. Also, trade publications are a good source of clues regarding technological, legislative, regulatory, and other trends and developments that are considered important to the industry.

In many cases, the appraiser will find that the business to be appraised subscribes to one or more trade publications, and the appraiser may be able to borrow copies. Trade associations are another possible source of information about the existence of trade publications covering a given field.

Also, there are bound directories of publications, which the appraiser should be able to find in a library. Such directories include the *Ayer Directory of Publications* and *Publishers and Distributors of the United States*. (See "Specific Information Sources" at the end of this chapter.)

If the appraiser succeeds in identifying one or more trade periodicals but cannot find copies in a library or elsewhere, most publishers are willing to send sample issues on request.

The U.S. Bureau of the Census issues a variety of publications, some of which contain census information on individual industries. Some of the Census Bureau publications dealing with individual industries are listed at the end of this chapter.

Because the publications available from the Census Bureau change from time to time, the appraiser may wish to contact the bureau to inquire about the availability of information on a particular industry that is of interest to him or her at a given time.

Information on individual industries also can be found in publications such as some of the various investors' services that, although prepared primarily for the benefit of investors in the stock market, frequently contain information that will be helpful to appraisers. Because investors in the stock market are also concerned with the Principle of Future Benefits, these investors' services include information on future outlook for entire industries as well as for individual companies. Such investors' services include the *Investors Reference Service, Moody's Manuals, Standard and Poor's Industry Surveys*, and the *Value Line Investment Survey*. One or more of these investors' services usually can be found in a public library.

In addition to industry information in the various investors' services that are generally sold on a subscription basis, many of the larger stock brokerage firms publish industry reports from time to time. Such reports generally reflect the results of reasonably thorough research performed by specialists within the brokerage firm. These reports are prepared as a service to investors and are usually available free of charge. Although it is difficult to determine in advance just which stock brokerage firms may have information available on a given industry, the appraiser may find it helpful to telephone local offices of the larger stock brokerage firms to inquire about availability of information on the industry that is of interest to him or her.

In addition to general information on specific industries, there are also a number of sources of industry financial statistics. These sources include the *Annual Statement Studies* published by the Robert Morris Associates, the *Cost of Doing Business* surveys published by Dun and Bradstreet, and some others as listed at the end of this chapter.

The *Annual Statement Studies* publication issued by the Robert Morris Associates is one of the best sources of industry financial information for appraisal purposes. It contains composite income/expense, balance sheet, and other financial information for each of approximately 180 different industries. Within each industry, the financial data are further broken down into groups according to size of company. The information in these annual statement studies can be very useful to the appraiser, providing him or her with data to compare with the financial performance of the business being appraised.

The U.S. Small Business Administration offers a variety of publications, including some dealing with individual industries. Although the information in most of these publications is relatively rudimentary, they sometimes can provide an introduction to an industry with which the appraiser is not familiar. To determine whether such a publication exists for a specific industry, the appraiser can contact the local office of the Small Business Administration or request a copy of the SBA's list of available publications.

In addition, there are, of course, many other sources of general industry information, some of which are listed at the end of this chapter.

INFORMATION ON INDIVIDUAL COMPANIES

The appraiser sometimes may wish to obtain information on individual companies other than the company being appraised.

The other companies may be competitors with whom the appraiser wishes to compare the company being appraised, or they may be customers or suppliers.

Of course, the most direct source of information about a company is the company itself. If the company of interest is a publicly owned firm, a request to the company's public relations or stockholder relations office almost always will produce at least a copy of the latest annual report and possibly other information as well. The same sort of direct approach sometimes works with a closely held business, depending on the nature of the appraiser's need for the information and on the attitude of the company or individual to whom the request is made.

Annual reports on public companies are also available in some libraries, particularly large public libraries and college or university libraries where there is a school of business administration.

Another source of corporate financial information is the Securities and Exchange Commission, whose files contain information on literally tens of thousands of businesses, including many of relatively small size, which are required to file financial information with the SEC. The information filed with the SEC includes information similar to that found in corporate annual reports, along with more detailed information such as that contained in the so-called 10-K reports.

Lists of companies required to file financial information with the SEC appear in the *Directory of Companies Required to File Annual Reports with the Securities and Exchange Commission Under the Securities Exchange Act of 1934* and in *SEC Filing Companies*, both of which are listed at the end of this chapter. The list of information sources at the end of the chapter also includes two organizations that make a business of providing copies of 10-K reports and other information to requestors.

Relatively brief but still frequently useful information on several thousand of the larger businesses in the United States and Canada can be found in corporate directories such as the *Million Dollar Directory* and *Standard and Poor's Register of Corporations, Directors, and Executives*. These directories list companies alphabetically by name and contain information about each company, including its address, names and titles of key executives, members of the board of directors, brief descriptions of the company's lines of business, approximate sales volume, and additional information such as the names of the company's principal legal and accounting firms. Copies of these industrial directories can be found in many public and university libraries.

More complete information than that found in the industrial directories, and including detailed financial information as well as more general information about the company, can be found in the investors' reporting services previously mentioned, including the *Investors Reference Service, Moody's Manuals*, and the *Value Line Investment Survey*. However, these investors' reference services are generally limited to relatively large companies.

Industrial directories, such as *MacRae's Blue Book* and *Thomas's Register of American Manufacturers*, contain information on many companies, including some small ones that will not be found in other published sources. However, information in these directories is generally limited to the company's name, address, and a list of the products that the company produces.

In addition to national directories of business and industry, there are also state directories for almost every state. These contain information similar to that found in the national directories previously described but limited to companies located in the particular state and including many companies too small to be listed in any of the national directories.

In some states, directories of businesses are published by the state chamber of commerce or the state university. A major commercial publisher of such directories is State Industrial Directories Corporation, whose address appears in the list at the end of this chapter.

Copies of state industrial and business directories usually can be found in public libraries.

Finally, information on individual companies can be obtained from specialized reporting services, such as Dun and Bradstreet's credit reporting service, which is available on a subscription basis, and even from investigative and reporting services that, if the need warrants, can be hired to perform in-depth studies of designated companies.

INFORMATION ON ACTUAL SALES OF COMPANIES

In some cases, as when preparing to apply the market data approach that will be described in Chapter 8, the appraiser may need information on actual sales of companies, generally in the same industry as the business being appraised.

If the identity of the company that was sold is known, then the desired information usually can be obtained from the sources discussed above.

In most cases, however, the appraiser will need to learn first whether there have been any recent sales of companies in the industry, and then he or she will need certain information about these sales.

Other members of the industry, such as executives of the company being appraised or trade association personnel, may have information regarding recent sales of businesses in the industry. However, such information may be incomplete and also somewhat distorted.

There are some published sources of information on actual sales of companies. These include the comparability data file maintained by The Institute of Business Appraisers for the benefit of its members, together with other published sources listed at the end of this chapter.

Although they vary somewhat in both format and content, these sources of information on sales of companies generally include the names of both acquired and acquiring companies, a brief description of the line of business of each company, the sale price and date of sale, and a limited amount of additional information such as the annual sales volume and annual profits of the company that was sold.

A major limitation of these published sources of information on sales of companies is that, because they are themselves based primarily on published information, they tend to be limited to information on sales of relatively large businesses, containing little or no information on sales of the small- to medium-sized businesses with which most appraisers are concerned most of the time. This limitation applies to a lesser extent to the previously mentioned comparability data file of The Institute of Business Appraisers, which does contain some information on sales of smaller companies.

A further limitation of those sources consisting of periodicals is that the information is not in very convenient form. It is necessary to review several successive issues in detail in order to locate any sales that may be of interest. This limitation is not as serious, of course, with sources that are in non-periodical form.

INFORMATION ON GENERAL ECONOMIC ENVIRONMENT AND OUTLOOK

Information on the general economic environment (state, national, international), including the future economic outlook, is important in an appraisal for somewhat the same reasons as apply to general industry information. However, the general economic environment tends to affect all business and industry, not just the particular industry of which the business to be appraised is a part.

Interest in the general economic environment tends to be centered on the future outlook, expressed in such terms as growth (or lack of growth) in the so-called Gross National Product, anticipated future levels of employment and unemployment, expectations with regard to monetary inflation, and especially anticipated future interest rates. Because of the time frame in which the Principle of Future Benefits is applied in an appraisal, interest in economic outlook is in terms of the next several years rather than the shorter periods that are of interest for some other purposes.

The appraiser can keep generally informed about the economic outlook by reading such publications as *Barron's* and *The Wall Street Journal* and magazines such as *Business Week* or one of the news magazines. In addition to general economic news, such publications also will contain, from time to time, more specific information and forecasts.

There are also a number of other more formal sources of information on the general economic environment, some of which are listed at the end of this chapter.

Additional sources of information on the general economic environment include information services at the state level, many of which are operated as part of the state university systems, together with local sources such as local chambers of commerce.

On the national level, corresponding services include the Chamber of Commerce of the United States, the National Association of Manufacturers, and the National Federation of Independent Business.

In attempting to interpret information on the general economic outlook as it relates to his appraisal assignment, the appraiser frequently will find that there are conflicts within the available information. It seems that, at any given time, there are at least two (and sometimes more) very different schools of thought, each of which has its quota of prominent adherents, which have very different expectations regarding the economic outlook for the future. Even recognizing that some of the persons whose opinions find their way into print may be politically motivated, and accordingly discarding or modifying their opinions, the appraiser will still be faced with conflicting opinions from individuals or organizations who have no apparent reasons for bias.

Fortunately, the appraiser is not required to be an economic seer; it is not necessary to be able to discern truth amid the morass of conflicting claims and opinions. Instead, the appraiser's job is to try to determine the economic expectations that influence the market, since it is the expectation of the market, whether or not correct, that produces the expectation of economic benefits on which the Principle of Future Benefits is based. How the appraiser determines what the market is thinking is still a somewhat difficult matter, but fortunately it is not as difficult as attempting to distinguish truth from the conflicting opinions of the economic "experts."

LOCAL AND REGIONAL INFORMATION

The final kind of information needed by the appraiser is information about the local environment—city, county, state, or region. This information is important at least from such standpoints as future supply of labor, local regulatory requirements, and cost of doing business as affected by such influences as local taxes, real estate values, and the like.

Depending on the nature of the business and its products or services, local or regional information also may be important from such standpoints as the future market for the products or services of the business and the future availability of goods or services it requires for its operations.

The state chamber of commerce almost always will have information of value to the appraiser. This also may be true of local chambers of commerce, depending on their size and the nature of the local program.

Another good source of state and regional information might be a business research service such as those operated by state development offices or state universities.

Utility companies are frequently excellent sources of local or regional information. Because they need it for their own planning purposes, most utility companies go to some lengths to gather information such as expected future population levels, growth of industry, and so on. Most utility companies are willing to share this information with interested persons.

Publications that are possible sources of local and regional information include the local or area newspaper and various publications of the U.S. Bureau of the Census as listed at the end of this chapter.

In the case of appraisals requiring information about foreign countries, consular officials of the country in question are a possible source of information for the appraiser. The Canadian government publishes a variety of publications, generally similar in content to publications of the U.S. Bureau of the

Census and other U.S. government publications. Many of these Canadian publications are available from Statistics Canada, whose address is given at the end of this chapter.

SOME SPECIFIC INFORMATION SOURCES

General Industry Information

Almanac of Business and Industrial Financial Ratios. Prentice-Hall, Inc., Englewood Cliffs, NJ 07632. Annual.

Annual Statement Studies. Robert Morris Associates, 1616 Philadelphia National Bank Building, Philadelphia, PA 19107. Annual. Approximately 380 pages.

Census of Business. U.S. Department of Commerce, Superintendent of Documents, U.S. Government Printing Office, Washington, DC 20401. Quinquennial.

Census of Construction Industries. U.S. Department of Commerce, Bureau of the Census, Washington, DC 20233. 1977.

Census of Mineral Industries. U.S. Department of Commerce, Bureau of the Census, Washington, DC 20233. Quadrennial.

Census of Retail Trade—Final Report, Subject Series. U.S. Department of Commerce, Bureau of the Census, Washington, DC 20233. 1977.

Census of Retail Trade—Major Retail Center Series. U.S. Department of Commerce, Bureau of the Census, Washington, DC 20233. 1977.

Census of Service Industries. U.S. Department of Commerce, Bureau of the Census, Washington, DC 20233. 1977.

Census of Transportation. U.S. Department of Commerce, Bureau of the Census, Washington, DC 20233. Quinquennial.

Census of Wholesale Trade. U.S. Department of Commerce, Bureau of the Census, Washington, DC 20233. 1977.

Consolstat. W. T. Grimm and Company, 135 LaSalle St., Chicago, IL 60603. Reporting service.

Cost of Doing Business—Corporations. Dun and Bradstreet, Inc., 99 Church St., New York, NY 10007.

Cost of Doing Business—Partnerships and Proprietorships. Dun and Bradstreet, Inc., 99 Church St., New York, NY 10007

Expenses in Retail Business. NCR Corporate Education—Learning Systems, Dayton, OH 45479. 1981. 56 pages.

Fact Book on Small Business. National Federation of Independent Business, 150 W. 20th Ave., San Mateo, CA 94403. 1979. 74 pages.

F & S Index United States. Predicasts, Inc., 11001 Cedar Ave., Cleveland, OH 44106. Monthly.

Industry Studies. Predicasts, Inc., 11001 Cedar Ave., Cleveland, OH 44106. Custom studies to order.

Investors Reference Service. Arnold Bernhard and Company, 711 Third Ave., New York, NY 10017. Approximately 2400 pages.

Key Business Ratios in 800 Lines. Dun and Bradstreet, Inc., 99 Church St., New York, NY 10007. Annual.

List of Industry Analysts in the Federal Government. Washington Research, 918 16th St. NW, Washington, DC 20006. 1978.

Mahon's Industry Guides, edited by James J. Mahon, et al. Warren, Gorham and Lamont, Inc., 210 South St., Boston, MA 02111. Set of 18 individual guides.

Management Assistance Series. U.S. Small Business Administration, P.O. Box 15434, Ft. Worth, TX 76119.

Market Reports. Predicasts, Inc., 11001 Cedar Ave., Cleveland, OH 44106. Custom reports to order.

M/B Financial Weekly. Media General Financial Services, P.O. Box 26991, Richmond, VA 23261. Weekly.

Moody's Manuals—Industrial, Financial, and Over-the-Counter. Moody's Investors Service, Inc., 99 Church St., New York, NY 10007. Annual.

Operating Ratios for Business and Income Properties. International Association of Assessing Officers, 1313 E. 60th St., Chicago, IL 60637. 1978. 2 pages.

Predi-Briefs. Predicasts, Inc., 11001 Cedar Ave., Cleveland, OH 44106. Monthly.

Predicasts Overview of Markets and Technology (PROMT). Predicasts, Inc., 11001 Cedar Ave., Cleveland, OH 44106. Monthly.

Quarterly Financial Report for Manufacturing, Mining, and Trade Corporations. Federal Trade Commission, Superintendent of Documents, U.S. Government Printing Office, Washington, DC 20402. Quarterly. Approximately 90 pages.

Small Business Bibliography Series. U.S. Small Business Administration, P.O. Box 15434, Ft. Worth, TX 76119.

Standard and Poor's Industry Surveys. Standard and Poor's Corporation, 25 Broadway, New York, NY 10004.

The Value Line Investment Survey. Arnold Bernhard and Company, 711 Third Ave., New York, NY 10017. Weekly.

Wholesaling. U.S. Small Business Administration, P.O. Box 15434, Ft. Worth, TX 76119. 1973. 8 pages.

Information on Individual Companies

Bishop's Service, Inc., 41 E. 42nd St., New York, NY 10017. Investigative and reporting service.

Directory of Companies Required to File Annual Reports with the Securities and Exchange Commission Under the Securities Exchange Act of 1934. Securities and Exchange Commission, Superintendent of Documents, U.S. Government Printing Office, Washington, DC 20402. Annual.

Investors Reference Service. Arnold Bernhard and Co., 711 Third Ave., New York, NY 10017. Approximately 2400 pages.

MacRae's Blue Book. MacRae's Blue Book Company, 100 Shore Dr., Hinsdale, IL 60521. Annual.

Million Dollar Directory. Dun's Marketing Services, 3 Century Dr., Parsippany, NJ 07054. Annual. 2 volumes.

Moody's Handbook of Common Stocks. Moody's Investors Service, Inc., 99 Church St., New York, NY 10007.

SEC Filing Companies. Disclosure Incorporated, 5161 River Rd., Washington, DC 20016. 1980. 83 pages.

Sources of State Information on Corporations. Washington Researchers, 918 16th St. NW, Washington, DC 20006. 1978.

Standard and Poor's Industry Surveys. Standard and Poor's Corporation, 25 Broadway, New York, NY 10004.

Standard and Poor's Register of Corporations, Directors, and Executives. Standard and Poor's Corporation, 25 Broadway, New York, NY 10004. Annual. 3 volumes.

State Industrial Directories Corporation, 2 Penn Plaza, New York, NY 10001.

10-K Reports. Disclosure Incorporated, 5161 River Rd., Washington, DC 20016.

10-K Reports. National Investment Library, 80 Wall St., New York, NY 10016.

Thomas Register of American Manufacturers and Thomas Register Catalog File. Thomas Publishing Company, One Penn Plaza, New York, NY 10001. Annual. Multivolume.

The Value Line Investment Survey. Arnold Bernhard and Company, 711 Third Ave., New York, NY 10017. Weekly.

Information on Actual Sales of Companies

Comparability Data File. The Institute of Business Appraisers, Inc., P.O. Box 1447, Boynton Beach, FL 33435. Data service.

Directory of Acquisitions. Quality Services, Inc., 3887 State St., Santa Barbara, CA 93105.

Mergers and Acquisitions—The Journal of Corporate Venture. Information for Industry, Inc., 1621 Brookside Rd., McLean, VA 22101. Quarterly.

Mergers and Corporate Policy. Cambridge Corporation Publishers, P.O. Box 64, Ipswich, MA 01938. Biweekly.

Merger Summary. W. T. Grimm and Company, 135 S. LaSalle St., Chicago, IL 60603. Semiannual.

The National Review of Corporate Acquisitions, by J. J. Mahoney. Tweed Publishing Co., 23 Main St., Tiburon, CA 94920.

Retail Business Goodwill: Survey of Prices Paid. Valuation Press, Inc., P.O. Box 1080, Marina del Rey, CA 90291. 1979. 15 pages.

Statistical Report on Mergers and Acquisitions. U.S. Federal Trade Commission, 6th and Pennsylvania Aves. NW, Room 130, Washington, DC 20580.

10-K Reports. Disclosure Incorporated, 5161 River Rd., Washington, DC 20016.

10-K Reports. National Investment Library, 80 Wall St., New York, NY 10005.

Valudata. W. T. Grimm and Company, 135 LaSalle St., Chicago, IL 60603. Custom reporting service.

Yearbook of Merger Activity to January 1, 1980, by editorial staff of Mergers and Federal Policy. Cambridge Corporation Publishers, P.O. Box 64, Ipswich, MA 01938.

Yearbook on Corporate Mergers, Joint Ventures, and Corporate Policy. Cambridge Corporation Publishers, P.O. Box 64, Ipswich, MA 01938. 1981.

Information on General Economic Environment

Barron's. Dow Jones and Company, 200 Burnett Rd., Chicopee, MA 01021. Weekly.

Business Conditions Digest. U.S. Department of Commerce, Bureau of Economic Analysis, Superintendent of Documents, U.S. Government Printing Office, Washington, DC 20402. Monthly.

Census of Population. U.S. Department of Commerce, Social and Economic Statistics Administration, Washington, DC 20233. Decennial.

Chamber of Commerce of the United States, 1615 H St. NW, Washington, DC 20062.

ICC World Economic Yearbook—1980. ICC Publishing Corporation, Inc., 1212 Avenue of the Americas, New York, NY 10036. 1980.

International Economic Indicators. Superintendent of Documents, U.S. Government Printing Office, Washington, DC 20402. Quarterly.

National Federation of Independent Business, 150 W. 20th Ave., San Mateo, CA 94403.

Office of Business Economics and Economic Research Service (OBERS) Projections. Office of Business Economics and Economic Research Service, U.S. Water Resources Council and Departments of Commerce and Agriculture, Superintendent of Documents, U.S. Government Printing Office, Washington, DC 20402. 1974.

Population of the United States, Trends and Prospects. U.S. Department of Commerce, Bureau of the Census, Washington, DC 20233.

Predicasts Basebook. Predicasts, Inc., 11001 Cedar Ave., Cleveland, OH 44106. Annual.

Predicasts Forecasts. Predicasts, Inc., 11001 Cedar Ave., Cleveland, OH 44106. Quarterly; annual edition available.

Quarterly Economic Reports for Small Business. National Federation of Independent Business, 150 W. 20th Ave., San Mateo, CA 94403. Quarterly. Approximately 32 pages.

Survey of Current Business. U.S. Department of Commerce, Bureau of Economic Analysis, Superintendent of Documents, U.S. Government Printing Office, Washington, DC 20402. Monthly.

U.S. Industrial Outlook. U.S. Department of Commerce, Bureau of Domestic Commerce, Superintendent of Documents, U.S. Government Printing Office, Washington, DC 20402. Annual. Approximately 500 pages.

Weekly Business Statistics. U.S. Department of Commerce, Bureau of Economic Analysis, Superintendent of Documents, U.S. Government Printing Office, Washington, DC 20402. Weekly.

The World Almanac and Book of Facts, edited by George E. Delury. Newspaper Enterprise Association, Inc., 200 Park Ave., New York, NY 10017. Annual.

Worldcasts. Predicasts, Inc., 11001 Cedar Ave., Cleveland, OH 44106. Separate editions by region and by product.

World Economic Development Projections from 1978 to the Year 2000, by Herman Kahn. ICC Publishing Corporation, Inc., 1212 Avenue of the Americas, New York, NY 10036.

Local and Regional Information

Area Economic Projections 1990. Bureau of Economic Analysis, Department of Commerce, Superintendent of Documents, U.S. Government Printing Office, Washington, DC 20402. 1974.

Census of Agriculture. U.S. Department of Commerce, Bureau of the Census, Superintendent of Documents, U.S. Government Printing Office, Washington, DC 20402. Quinquennial.

Census of Business. U.S Department of Commerce, Bureau of the Census, Superintendent of Documents, U.S. Government Printing Office, Washington, DC 20402. Quinquennial.

Census of Construction Industries. U.S. Department of Commerce, Bureau of the Census, Washington, DC 20233. 1977.

Census of Governments. U.S. Department of Commerce, Bureau of the Census, Superintendent of Documents, U.S. Government Printing Office, Washington, DC 20402. Decennial.

Census of Housing. U.S. Department of Commerce, Bureau of the Census, Superintendent of Documents, U.S. Government Printing Office, Washington, DC 20233. Decennial.

Census of Retail Trade—Final Report, Subject Series. U.S. Department of Commerce, Bureau of the Census, Washington, DC 20233. 1977.

Census of Retail Trade—Major Retail Center Series. U.S. Department of Commerce, Bureau of the Census, Washington, DC 20233. 1977.

Census of Service Industries. U.S. Department of Commerce, Bureau of the Census, Washington, DC 20233. 1977.

Census of Wholesale Trade. U.S. Department of Commerce, Bureau of the Census, Washington, DC 20233. 1977.

Commercial Atlas and Marketing Guide. Rand McNally and Company, 10 E. 53rd St., New York, NY 10022. Annual.

County and City Data Book. U.S. Department of Commerce, Bureau of the Census, Washington, DC 20233. 1977. 1011 pages.

County Business Patterns. U.S Department of Commerce, Bureau of the Census, Superintendent of Documents, U.S. Government Printing Office. Washington, DC 20402. Annual.

Directory of Federal Statistics for Local Areas, Urban Update, 1977–1978, A Guide to Sources. U.S. Department of Commerce, Bureau of the Census, Superintendent of Documents, U.S. Government Printing Office, Washington, DC 20402. Annual.

Statistics Canada Catalogue. Statistics Canada, Ottawa, Ontario K1A 0V7, Canada.

Sources of Additional Information

Ayer Directory of Publications. Ayer Press, One Bala Ave., Bala Cynwyd, PA 19004. 1980. 1272 pages.

Basic Library Reference Sources. U.S. Small Business Administration, P.O. Box 15434, Ft. Worth, TX 76119. 1978. 12 pages.

Business Organizations and Agencies Directory, edited by Anthony T. Kruzas and Robert C. Thomas. Gale Research Company, Book Tower, Detroit, MI 48226. 1980. 890 pages.

Business Services and Information: The Guide to the Federal Government, edited by Timothy C. Weckesser, Joseph R. Whaley, and Miriam Whaley. John Wiley and Sons, Inc., 605 Third Ave., New York, NY 10016. 1978. 392 pages.

Consultants and Consulting Organizations Directory, edited by Paul Wasserman and Janice McLean. Gale Research Company, Book Tower, Detroit, MI 48226. 1979. 1136 pages.

Directory of Business and Financial Services, edited by Mary McNierney Grant and Norma Cote. Special Libraries Association, 235 Park Ave. South, New York, NY 10003. 1967. 232 pages.

Directory of Directories, edited by James M. Ethridge. Gale Research Company, Book Tower, Detroit, MI 48226.

Directory of Federal Statistics for Local Areas, Urban Update, 1977–1978, A Guide to Sources. U.S. Department of Commerce, Bureau of the Census, Superintendent of Documents, U.S. Government Printing Office, Washington, DC 20402. 1979.

Directory of Information Resources in the United States, compiled by National Referral Center, Library of Congress. Superintendent of Documents, U.S. Government Printing Office, Washington, DC 20402.

Directory of Special Libraries and Information Centers, by Margaret Labash Young and Harold Chester Young. Gale Research Company, Book Tower, Detroit, MI 48226. 1979. 1279 pages.

Encyclopedia of Associations, edited by Nancy Yakes and Denise Akey. Gale Research Company, Book Tower, Detroit, MI 48226. Annual. Approximately 1600 pages.

Free research service. Library of Congress, Reference Section, Science and Technology Division, 10 1st St. SE, Washington, DC 20540.

Government Market Studies. Washington Researchers, 918 16th St. NW, Washington, DC 20006. 1979.

How to Find Information About Companies, edited by Donna M. Jablonski. Washington Researchers, 918 16th St. NW, Washington, DC 20006. 1979. 284 pages.

The Inside Source, by Bruce M. Spence and Joseph D. Adams Jr., with Peter J. deLuca. Quad International Corporation, Box 711, Ridgewood, NJ 07450. 1977. 495 pages.

Names and Numbers: A Journalist's Guide to the Most Needed Information Sources and Contacts, by Rod Norland. John Wiley and Sons, Inc., 605 Third Ave., New York, NY 10016. 1978. 560 pages.

National Directories for Use in Marketing. U.S. Small Business Administration, Publications Department, 1030 15th St. NW, Washington, DC 20540.

National Referral Center, Library of Congress, 10 1st St. SE, Washington, DC 20540.

National Trade and Professional Associations of the United States and Canada and Labor Unions, edited by Craig Colgate Jr. Colombia Books, Inc., 734 15th St. NW, Washington, DC 20005.

Out of print publications available from University Microfilms International, Books Editorial Department, 300 N. Zeeb Rd., Ann Arbor, MI 48106.

Publishers and Distributors of the United States. R. R. Bowker Company, 1180 Avenue of the Americas, New York, NY 10036. 1979. 233 pages.

Sources of Composite Financial Data—A Bibliography. Robert Morris Associates, 1616 Philadelphia National Bank Building, Philadelphia, PA 19107. Annual. 14 pages.

Sources of State Information on Corporations. Washington Researchers, 918 16th St. NW, Washington, DC 20006. 1978.

Where to Find Business Information: A Worldwide Guide for Everyone Who Needs the Answers to Business Questions, by David M. Brownstone and Gordon Carruth. John Wiley and Sons, Inc., 605 Third Ave., New York, NY 10016. 1979. 616 pages.

6
Using Financial Statements in Appraising

6
Using Financial Statements in Appraising

PURPOSE OF THIS CHAPTER

It is the purpose of this chapter to explain how business financial statements are used in the appraisal process, thus providing the reader with the background needed to analyze and understand the financial aspects of the business to be appraised.

Although this chapter includes some discussion of conventional business financial statements and financial statement terminology, this discussion is not intended as a complete introduction to business financial statements for the reader who may not have previous acquaintance with them. Instead, this chapter assumes that the reader already has at least a basic understanding of business financial statements and their more common applications.

For the reader who has little or no previous acquaintance with business financial statements, a list of useful and easy-to-understand books on the subject appears at the end of Chapter 7 under "Suggestions for Further Study."

ROLE OF FINANCIAL STATEMENTS IN APPRAISING

Business financial statements have at least three major functions in an appraisal:

They contribute to the appraiser's total understanding of the business being appraised, by providing a financial picture of the business.

They give the appraiser a starting point for the detailed financial analysis of the business that is a major part of the appraisal process.

They provide the appraiser with historical information to assist in predicting the future performance of the business and thus in estimating its value in accordance with the Principle of Future Benefits.

In theory, a business could be appraised without the use of any existing financial statements. Instead, the appraiser might collect detailed financial information about the business from various sources and then use this information to prepare the various summaries and analyses required for the appraisal process. However, such a process would be exceedingly time-consuming and, as compared to using existing business financial statements as a starting point, would be uneconomic to an extreme degree. Obtaining the required financial information without using existing financial statements would be especially difficult where financial performance during past years is concerned, inasmuch as such historical information is not usually available in any ready form other than the existing financial statements covering the years in question.

Accordingly, rather than attempting to make an appraisal from a mass of detailed information they have collected themselves, all appraisers prefer the simpler and less costly approach of using existing business financial statements as a starting point, supplementing and modifying these existing financial statements as required for appraisal purposes.

KINDS OF FINANCIAL STATEMENTS

Almost all business financial statements include at least a balance sheet and an income/expense statement.

A *balance sheet* is a summary of the financial status of a business at a certain time. A balance sheet always will include as part of its heading a statement of the date as of which the information applies. The balance sheet presents a summary of the financial condition of the business at that date.

An *income/expense statement* (sometimes called a profit/loss statement) presents a summary of the financial operations of the business during an interval of time.

The essential distinction between the balance sheet and the income/expense statement is that the former presents the financial *status* of the business at a *point* in time, while the latter is a summary of the financial *activity* of the business over an *interval* of time. The balance sheet and income/expense statement of a business are almost always issued together as companion documents, each of which supplements the other to provide a fuller understanding of the financial aspects of the business.

In almost all cases, business financial statements are prepared at least once each year, timed to correspond with the end of the calendar year or the fiscal year of the business. In some cases, particularly with larger businesses, financial statements may be prepared more often than once a year, perhaps quarterly or monthly. The usual reason for preparing financial statements more than once a year is to provide the management of the business with more up-to-date information for managerial control purposes than is available on an annual basis.

Financial statements for some businesses, particularly those whose financial statements are professionally prepared, include a third element in addition to the balance sheet and income/expense statement. This third element is the *statement of source and application of funds*. Although frequently useful for managerial control purposes, the statement of source and application of funds is mentioned only briefly here.

Balance sheets and income/expense statements and their uses in appraising are discussed in more detail later in this chapter.

Some businesses, particularly smaller owner-managed ones, do not prepare formal financial statements. When appraising such a business, the appraiser ordinarily will use information from income tax returns in place of the information that otherwise would be obtained from the balance sheet and income/expense statement. The use of income tax returns as a substitute for other financial statements has been discussed in Chapter 5.

Business financial statements, including income tax returns, may be prepared on either cash or an accrual basis.

The essential difference between cash and accrual methods is a difference of timing of certain transactions. In accrual accounting, income and expenses are recognized and are recorded in the financial books of the business, as of the date on which the business first acquires the right to the income or the obligation to pay the expense. With the cash method, on the other hand, income and expenses are recorded on the books only when the money is actually received or paid out.

It is generally conceded that, although cash accounting is somewhat simpler from a purely bookkeeping standpoint, accrual accounting provides a more realistic picture of the financial activities and status of the business and accordingly is more useful for many purposes. For this reason, the great majority of businesses employ accrual accounting and prepare their financial statements on that basis. Cash accounting tends to be limited to very small businesses, especially those that do not use the services of professional accountants.

Further information on the subject of cash versus accrual accounting can be found in some of the references listed at the end of this chapter.

For reasons previously stated, including the fact that the great majority of businesses use the accrual method of accounting, the discussion of financial statements throughout the remainder of this book is in terms of statements reflecting the accrual method. However, the appraiser who may be faced with the necessity of working from financial information prepared on a cash basis will still be able to apply the principles and techniques explained in the book, giving consideration when necessary to those respects in which the cash and accrual methods differ.

It is important to realize that, regardless of how or by whom they are prepared, financial statements are not exact or absolute. Instead, the figures that appear on financial statements are to a considerable extent a matter of viewpoint. This applies equally to business financial statements prepared by an in-house bookkeeper or to certified financial statements prepared by one of the large public accounting firms. At least as far as business financial statements are concerned, truth is a relative matter, depending on the perspective from which the statements were prepared.

The great majority of business financial statements are prepared from a perspective that includes a desire to minimize tax liabilities, and the entries on the statements tend to reflect this perspective. This is not to say that the financial statements are in any way inaccurate or dishonest; rather, they reflect a tax-oriented perspective.

Similarly, the majority of business financial statements reflect a viewpoint that assumes an ongoing business. That is, the financial entries in the statements are considered valid on the basis of the assumption that the business continues in operation; if the business were to be liquidated instead, at least some of the entries on the financial statements would be invalid.

Although financial statements as prepared for different businesses do not all reflect identically the same viewpoint, there are certain perspectives that are shared by the great majority of business financial statements as they are usually prepared, whether by employees of the business itself or by outside accountants. For the purpose of this book, this conventional viewpoint will be referred to as the accountants' viewpoint, and the corresponding financial statements will be referred to as accountants' financial statements.

For reasons that will become apparent later in this book, the appraiser's viewpoint toward financial statements is in some respects significantly different from that of the accountant. In this book, financial statements that reflect or are consistent with the appraiser's viewpoint will be called economic financial statements. This is in contrast to the accountants' financial statements, which typically reflect the accountant's viewpoint and which are the type of statements most readily available to the appraiser as the starting point for financial analysis of the business to be appraised.

Significant differences between the accountants' financial statements and the economic financial statements, and the means of using the former to help arrive at the latter, will become apparent in this chapter.

FINANCIAL STATEMENT TERMINOLOGY

In the interest of a common understanding, a number of key terms used in connection with financial statements will be defined before proceeding further.

Accounts payable: Balance sheet entry reflecting amounts owed by a business to its creditors, usually for goods or services received, and due within the immediate or near future but not yet actually paid. A *current liability*.

Accounts receivable: Balance sheet entry reflecting amounts due to a business, usually for goods sold or services rendered, within the immediate or near future, but not yet actually received. A *current asset*.

Accrued expenses: Balance sheet entry representing costs of various kinds arising out of past events or activities of the business, actual payment for which is not required until some future date. Generally excludes cost of goods and services received from outsiders. (See *accounts payable*.) Examples include cost of labor performed by employees of the business within payroll periods, or pro rata portion of taxes to become due at future date. A liability.

Amortization: Expense item representing provision for retirement or recovery over a period of time of amounts invested or expended for assets or improvements of substantial but finite useful life. Similar to *depreciation* as applied in context of tax-oriented accounting.

Assets: Resources, property, monies, claims, and so on, owned by a business or other financial entity. One of two major categories of items on a balance sheet, the other being *liabilities*.

Book value: The value of an asset or group of assets as stated in the owner's financial statements or accounting records. Book value frequently differs from other kinds of value, such as market value, for reasons including tax considerations.

Contingent liabilities: Potential balance sheet item representing liabilities of such nature that either their existence or their amount is uncertain. Examples include possible lawsuits or tax claims and liabilities under guarantees or warranties. Not always included explicitly in conventional (accountants') financial statements.

Cost of goods sold: Category of expense generally including amount paid for materials incorporated in and labor expended directly on goods delivered or services furnished to customers. Frequently includes cost of subcontract services directly applicable to goods delivered or services furnished to customers of the business. Excludes overhead or indirect expenses. A subtotal item on income/expense statements.

Current assets: Balance sheet category including assets that are in cash, can be converted readily to cash, or will be converted to cash within the relatively near future and during the normal course of business. Assets that are readily available for business purposes. Distinction between current and noncurrent assets applies primarily to conventional business financial analysis and management and is of relatively little importance in appraising.

Current liabilities: Balance sheet category including liabilities that are considered to be payable within one year.

Deferred assets: Assets whose value cannot be realized currently. Not the same as *prepaid expenses*, which are to be written off in future periods.

Depreciation: Loss in value of a fixed asset as a result of wear and tear or obsolescence, which loss cannot be corrected by normal repairs. Loss of value resulting from deterioration in quality rather than quantity. In accountants' financial statements, an expense item the amount of which is determined so as to write off the original cost of the assets, less anticipated salvage value, if any, by charges against operations over the estimated life of the assets. Amount of expense as shown on accountants' income/expense statement usually determined by tax-related considerations.

Diminishing assets: Term referring to assets, such as copyrights, patents, and certain types of contracts (such as limited term franchises), that have income-producing potential over only a limited period of time.

Direct labor: Labor whose results are a direct contribution to production of goods or performance of services furnished to customers. In financial statements, an expense item, part of *cost of goods sold.*

First in–first out (FIFO):   Method of determining the (book) value of inventory, in which withdrawals from inventory are accounted for at a price (value) equal to the cost of the oldest addition to the existing inventory. One of two principal methods of inventory accounting, the other being the *last in–first out* method.

Fixed assets: Assets of such nature as to tend to deteriorate or depreciate in quality rather than quantity. Examples include buildings, machinery, vehicles, and so on.

General and administrative expenses: Expense category generally including all costs of doing business with the exception of (1) costs contributing directly to goods sold or services rendered (direct costs), and (2) indirect costs closely related to manufacturing or service operations (overhead). Distinction between general and administrative costs and overhead costs tends to vary from one business to another but is of relatively little importance in appraising.

Goodwill: Term defined differently by different sources. One definition is that goodwill is represented by those elements of a business that cause customers to return, and that usually enable the business to generate profit in excess of a reasonable return on all other assets of the business. Goodwill may stem from location, personnel, various rights or benefits of a legal nature, or continued public acceptance of and satisfaction with the products or services of the business. Goodwill is an intangible asset, frequently omitted from accountants' balance sheets or, if shown on the balance sheet, shown as having a value that bears little or no relationship to the true value of the goodwill.

Gross profit: Income from operations of a business (income from sales) less cost of goods sold. Profit from operations before provision for overhead and general and administrative expenses.

Hidden assets: Assets that are not directly reflected in the financial statements or accounts of a business or other financial entity, whether by accident or design.

Hidden liabilities: Liabilities that are not directly reflected in the financial statements or accounts of a business or other financial entity, whether by accident or design.

Intangible assets: Broad category of assets, not precisely defined but generally consisting of those assets that are neither physical nor financial in nature. Examples include patents, trademarks, copyrights, franchises, proprietary processes, goodwill, and so on. Accountants' financial statements frequently do not include all intangible assets. Those intangible assets that may be included on accountants' financial statements are not usually identified as being intangible and are frequently shown as having book values determined on a basis bearing little or no relationship to the true value of the corresponding assets.

Inventory: Goods on hand, including materials held for future sale to customers and materials to be consumed during course of business operations. A *current asset.*

Last in–first out (LIFO):   Methods of determining the (book) value of inventory, in which withdrawals from inventory are accounted for at a price (value) equal to the cost of the most recent addition to the inventory. One of two principal methods of inventory accounting, the other being the *first in–first out* method.

Leasehold improvements: Improvements made at the expense of the tenant to property occupied on a lease basis. Such improvements ordinarily become the property of the owner at termination of the lease. For accounting purposes, leasehold improvements are usually treated as fixed assets of the tenant, their cost being amortized by expense entries in the income/expense statement of the business, the amounts of these entries being calculated so as to fully amortize the cost of the improvement over a useful life that does not extend beyond the end of the lease.

Liabilities: Recognized claims against a person or business. Commonly understood as including only claims of creditors and excluding claims of owners as represented by capital stock, surplus, and proprietorship reserve accounts. One of two major categories of items on a balance sheet, the other being *assets*.

Net book value: Difference between total book value of assets and total book value of liabilities as shown on accountants' balance sheet of a business. In accountants' financial statements, net book value is essentially synonymous with *net worth* and *owners' equity*.

Net profit: Difference between total income of a business and its total expenses. Usually the bottom entry on the income/expense statement. May be either net profit before income tax or net profit after income tax.

Net worth: Differences between total assets and total liabilities of a business or other financial entity. In accountants' financial statements, net worth is synonymous with *net book value* and *owners' equity*.

Nonrecurrent items: Income or expense arising from a source or cause not likely to exist in future years, and therefore not ordinarily a factor in predicting or estimating future income or costs.

Original cost: The actual historical or acquisition cost of property. Generally refers to cost to current owner, which is not always the same as cost of the property when new.

Overhead: Broad category of business expenses arising from those activities and operations of the business that do not contribute directly to products manufactured or services rendered. Also sometimes called indirect costs. In some cases, a distinction is made between (1) overhead costs that, although they do not contribute directly to products manufactured or services rendered, correspond with activities in close support of direct activities, and (2) general and administrative costs.

Owner's equity: Difference between total assets and total liabilities of a business or other financial entity. In accountants' financial statements, owners' equity is essentially synonymous with *net book value* and *net worth*.

Perquisites: The special or casual (and sometimes unearned) profits or other benefits received by a person because of his or her position. For example, the owner of a closely held business may sometimes receive perquisites such as company-paid insurance, vacation trips at company expense, personal use of company-owned automobile, or compensation (salary) for services rendered to the business in excess of the amount that would be considered reasonable if he or she were not also the owner of the business. Persons holding important positions in larger businesses may also receive perquisites of various kinds. Although perquisites generally represent expenses to the business and are therefore included in the amounts shown on the income/expense statement of the business, they are not identified as perquisites on the income/expense statement.

Prepaid expenses: Expenses of a business or other financial entity for which payment has been made in advance of the date on which payment is due or the benefits of payment are received. Examples include insurance premiums and certain taxes or tax deposits made in advance of due dates. Similar to but not the same as deposits. An asset item on the balance sheet of the business.

Proprietary income: The total personal income from business operations that the owner of a business receives or that a prospective purchaser of the business could reasonably anticipate, before any personal income taxes. Proprietary income may include officer's salary, bonuses, owner's salary, the value of any perquisites, and the profit of the business.

Redundant assets: Assets owned by a business or other entity that are not required for the normal conduct of the business. Sometimes used in connection with funds on hand or available in excess of normal capital requirements. The concept of redundant assets is especially important when estimating the value of a business by the replacement cost approach.

Reserve for replacements: Financial provision for eventual replacement of assets, especially fixed assets, by making regular additions to a fund, the amount of the addition being determined on a basis such that the total amount of the fund can be expected to be sufficient to meet the full cost of replacement at such time as the corresponding assets have reached the end of their useful lives or otherwise need to be replaced. As an item of business expense, the concept of a reserve for replacements is similar to the charge for depreciation, except that the amount of the former represents a more realistic provision for replacement of the assets at the end of their actual useful life, whereas the latter is usually an amount determined on a more or less artificial basis such as tax considerations, lacking any close relationship with the actual loss of the value of the asset or its actual useful life. In financial statements the term *reserve for renewals and betterments* is sometimes used as a synonym.

Surplus: The excess of net assets over liabilities and paid-in capital of a business or other financial entity.

Tangible assets: Broad category of assets, not precisely defined but generally including all assets of a physical or financial nature, such as cash on hand, accounts receivable, inventory, equipment, land, buildings, and so on. Most of the assets shown on an accountants' balance sheet are tangible assets.

Working capital: The excess of the value of the current assets of a business over its current liabilities. Working capital is generally of liquid nature and is used to finance ongoing operations. The concept of working capital is important in the financial analysis of businesses for purposes such as the granting of credit, but is of only limited importance for appraisal purposes.

ACCOUNTANTS' FINANCIAL STATEMENTS—FUNCTIONS, VIEWPOINTS, AND ATTRIBUTES

As pointed out previously in this chapter, business financial statements are neither exact nor absolute. Rather, the specific figures that appear on business financial statements reflect, to a considerable extent, the viewpoint from which the statements were prepared. This viewpoint is, in turn, closely related to the particular function for which the financial statements are to be used.

Here follows a discussion of the functions and the corresponding viewpoints and attributes of the most common type of business financial statements. These are the financial statements that are most often prepared for businesses by their accountants, and for that reason they are referred to in this book as accountants' financial statements. A second type of business financial statements, the type that is most useful for appraisal purposes, will be referred to as economic financial statements and will be discussed in the following chapter.

The most important single function of accountants' financial statements is to provide a basis for preparation of the income tax returns for the business and to provide information to support such returns after they have been prepared. A second but somewhat less important function of accountants' financial statements is to provide information to the managers of the business to assist them in exercising managerial control of it.

In most businesses, the tax-related function of financial statements takes precedence over the managerial information function.

In most small businesses and in many medium-sized ones, the management of the business is in sufficiently close contact with its operations that there is relatively little need for detailed financial information as an aid to managerial control, and such need as does exist can usually be met by financial statements prepared primarily with tax-related orientation.

In larger businesses, where the size of the business and the scope of its operations are such that upper levels of management may require information for managerial control purposes beyond the information that they can gather personally, management may have special reports prepared to meet its unique control requirements, or it may simply make do with financial reports whose primary purpose and orientation is tax-related. In either case, managerial control needs are seldom allowed to influence the format or content of financial statements at the possible expense of increased tax liability or diminished ability to support and defend tax returns.

Because of their primary purpose, and almost overwhelming importance, of providing the basis for preparation of tax returns and supporting such returns after they have been prepared, it is not at all surprising that accountants' financial statements strongly reflect a tax-oriented viewpoint.

If a business is at all profitable, the usual motivation of its owners is to minimize the amount of tax that must be paid, at least to the extent that this can be done legally. Since the income tax that must be paid is based on the amount of profit the business makes, the desire to minimize taxes leads to a corresponding desire to minimize profits, at least profits as reported on the financial statements that are the basis for the tax returns.

Profits are the difference between income received and expenses incurred, so reported profits can be reduced by reducing reported income, by increasing reported expenses, or by a combination of the two. In practice, increasing reported expenses is the more useful approach.

There are various ways in which the reported expenses of a business can be increased, such as through charges to depreciation and through treating as expenses of the business certain items that otherwise would contribute to profit or to the book value of the assets of the business. These and other ways in which reported expenses can be increased and reported profits can be reduced will be considered further later in this chapter.

The point here, however, is that the tax-related function of accountants' financial statements, together with a viewpoint of minimizing taxes payable insofar as legally and reasonably possible, leads to a major attribute or characteristic of accountants' financial statements.

This attribute is that accountants' financial statements tend to be tax-oriented, specifically in such a way as to reduce the amount of income tax payable such as through increases in reported expenses and other means leading to reduction in reported profits.

A second major attribute of accountants' financial statements arises from the fact that they are prepared by accountants following accepted or conventional accounting practices and procedures.

Although individual accountants have a certain amount of freedom of choice when dealing with individual accounting situations, they are also guided—even to some extent constrained—by various established accounting practices, procedures, and conventions. The total body of established accounting practices and procedures is quite complex and includes many rules and guidelines laid down by the American Institute of Certified Public Accountants, which is the principal professional organization of accountants in the United States.

Although the total body of established accounting practices and procedures is both complex and extensive, it is characterized throughout by a high degree of conservatism. That is, when an accountant is faced with a decision about what approach to follow in a given situation or which of two or more possible numerical values to report, there is a strong tendency to select the procedure or the value that is the most conservative of the available choices. To the nonaccountant, it is almost as though the accountant were saying to himself or herself, "If I am uncertain which procedure to follow or which numerical value to select, I will make the more conservative choice. Since I cannot be completely certain, I would rather have subsequent events show that I was too conservative, instead of too liberal."

This leads to the second major attribute of accountants' financial statements—they have a strong tendency to be conservative.

Finally, since accounting is essentially an historical process (as contrasted to appraising, for example, where the orientation is at least partly toward attempting to anticipate the future), it is not surprising that the third major attribute of accountants' financial statements is that they are essentially historical in nature.

Summarizing, accountants' financial statements exhibit three major attributes that are important to the appraiser of businesses and to his or her efforts to use the information in the accountants' financial statements to assist in estimating the value of the business. These three attributes of accountants' financial statements are:

1. They are tax-oriented, with a specific orientation toward tax minimization through means including maximization of reported expenses to the extent that this is reasonably feasible and legally permissible.
2. They are strongly conservative, particularly with regard to the procedures for determining, and the size of, the various dollar amounts reported in the statements.
3. They are essentially historical in nature.

THE ACCOUNTANTS' BALANCE SHEET

Although no two businesses have balance sheets that are exactly alike, the majority exhibit certain similarities.

Exhibit 3 shows an accountants' balance sheet, which, though prepared for a fictitious company and containing fictitious entries, will serve to illustrate many of the aspects of accountants' balance sheets that are important in appraising.

Accountants' financial statements as actually prepared are accompanied by various explanatory notes that provide further information about some of the entries on the balance sheet. Because they would serve no purpose in the present discussion, notes have been omitted from the fictitious balance sheet in Exhibit 3. However, when reviewing an actual accountants' balance sheet for a business to be appraised, the appraiser will wish to give careful attention to the accompanying financial notes.

For the sake of simplicity, the fictitious accountants' balance sheet for XYZ Corporation also omits some features of actual balance sheets, such as separate subtotals for current assets and current liabilities that, although generally included in accountants' balance sheets as actually prepared, are relatively unimportant from an appraisal standpoint.

There follows an item-by-item discussion of the entries on the accountants' balance sheet for XYZ Corporation.

Exhibit 3
XYZ CORPORATION
BALANCE SHEET AS OF DECEMBER 31, 19X1

ASSETS

Cash		$ 126,845
Accounts receivable:		
Total	$ 482,005	
Less reserve for doubtful accounts	25,000	
Net receivables		457,005
Marketable securities		155,977
Inventory:		
Raw materials	$ 154,136	
Work in process	540,165	
Finished goods	351,971	
Total inventory		1,046,272
Prepaid expenses		4,924
Fixed assets:		
Cost	$1,025,977	
Less accumulated depreciation	595,088	
Net book value of fixed assets		430,889
Other assets:		
Patents and copyrights		45,680
Goodwill		1
Total assets		$2,267,593

LIABILITIES

Accounts payable	$ 446,102
Notes and loans payable	833,436
Mortgages on land, buildings, etc.	610,286
Accrued expenses	26,240
Reserve for taxes	52,000
Other liabilities	45,996
Total liabilities	$2,014,060
NET BOOK VALUE	$ 253,533

Cash: Amount shown is total of cash on hand and on deposit in banks (demand-type deposits only) as of the date of the balance sheet.

Accounts receivable: The amount shown as total accounts receivable is taken directly from the company's detailed records of customer accounts. The "reserve for doubtful accounts" reflects the likelihood that not all of the amounts due from customers actually can be collected. The amount of this reserve is an estimate by the accountant, based on such information as the age of the various receivables and the past payment record of individual customers.

Marketable securities: Reflects any ownership of securities (stocks, bonds, etc.) issued by others and owned by the company to which the balance sheet applies. Until rather recently, accounting conservatism required that marketable securities be shown on the accountants' balance sheet as having a value equal to the lower of (1) their original acquisition cost, or (2) their current market value. Thus, a security whose market value had increased since it was acquired would still be shown at the original acquisition cost, while one whose value had decreased would be shown as having a current value that reflected the decrease in market. Recently, however, there has been a trend toward showing marketable securities on accountants' balance sheets at their current market value, at least in the case of those securities for which there is a relatively ready market. The basis on which securities have been valued usually will be stated in one of the notes accompanying the accountants' balance sheet.

Inventory: Inventory may be shown on the accountants' balance sheet either as a single entry or broken down into a number of entries as shown on the balance sheet for XYZ Corporation. The breakdown as shown would be typical of a manufacturing company. The amount of inventory on hand may be determined from a physical count, from the company's inventory records, or from a combination of the two. The method used to value the inventory, usually either the last in–first out or the first in–first out method, usually will be stated in a note accompanying the accountants' balance sheet.

Inventory—raw materials: Materials acquired for use in production, manufacturing processing of which has not yet begun. On the accountants' balance sheet, raw materials ordinarily will be valued at their original cost (as determined by either the LIFO or FIFO method as applicable), presumably with downward adjustment to reflect any shrinkage or obsolescence that may render some of the raw materials useless for their original intended purpose.

Inventory—work in process: Represents products intended for eventual sale to customers, on which manufacturing has been started but is not yet complete. On the accountants' balance sheet, work in process is shown as having a value equal to its cost as of the date of the balance sheet. This cost includes the original cost of the materials, the cost of manufacturing labor expended on them to date, and in some cases applied overhead as applicable to the material and labor costs. On accountants' balance sheets for companies other than those having very sophisticated cost accounting systems for work in process, the amount shown as the value (cost) of work in process is only an estimate, relying heavily on information provided by various members of company management.

Inventory—finished goods: Products whose manufacture has been completed and that are awaiting sale or delivery to customers. On accountants' balance sheets, finished goods are customarily shown as having a value equal to their total cost, usually including applicable overhead but without any provision for profit. The amount shown on the balance sheet for finished goods usually is based on an actual inventory of the quantity of each product on hand, together with information from the company's cost accounting or standard cost system regarding the manufacturing cost of the various products.

Prepaid expenses: Essentially a miscellaneous item, details of which can be found, if needed, either in the notes accompanying the accountants' financial statements or in the supporting detail which, though not actually part of the financial statements, is usually available to the appraiser.

Fixed assets: May be shown on the accountants' balance sheet either as a single category, as in Exhibit 3, or broken down into individual categories such as buildings, machinery and equipment, furniture and fixtures, vehicles, and so on with separate cost and accumulated depreciation figures for each kind of fixed asset. If the business also owns land, it usually will be shown on the accountants' balance sheet as a separate item, without, of course, any accompanying figure for depreciation.

Fixed assets—cost: Total original acquisition cost, as determined from the company's records, for all fixed assets represented on the accountants' balance sheet. In addition to purchase cost, the cost figure as shown on the accountants' balance sheet also may include other costs, such as tooling or installation costs, directly related to the physical asset in question. The amount shown on the accountants' balance sheet as the cost of fixed assets almost always will include only those fixed assets that are still carried on the company's books as having some value—that is, that have not yet been fully depreciated. In other words, the figures on the accountants' balance sheet will not include any fixed assets that have been fully depreciated, even though they may still be in use. This is a point of obvious importance to the appraiser, since a fixed asset that is still in use obviously has real value, even though it may have been depreciated to zero value for purposes of the accountants' balance sheet.

Fixed assets—accumulated depreciation: The figure on the accountants' balance sheet will be the total of the individual depreciation amounts charged against the various fixed assets, from the date they were originally acquired until the date of the balance sheet. The amount of this depreciation usually will be determined on the basis of current guidelines for depreciation as provided by the Internal Revenue Service. Since depreciation guidelines differ for different categories of fixed assets, the accountants' balance sheet may show fixed assets broken down into a number of categories with separate cost and accumulated depreciation figures for each category. In any case, detailed calculations for depreciation will appear on the accountants' worksheets, which usually will be available to the appraiser. In addition to detailed cost and depreciation data for fixed assets represented on the balance sheet, these worksheets also may include information on other fixed assets that, though fully depreciated, may still be in use.

Patents and copyrights: If the business owns patents or copyrights, they will ordinarily appear as assets on the accountants' balance sheet. This also will be true of any franchises and of certain types of contracts the business may own. However, the figure on the accountants' balance sheet for the value of patents, copyrights, and similar assets almost always will be a figure based on historical costs, which are not necessarily a meaningful measure of the actual value of the asset. In the case of patents, for example, the book value on the accountants' balance sheet frequently will be found to represent the total legal fees and related filing fees that were paid to obtain the patent or copyright, less an allowance for accumulated amortization to reflect the fact that patents and copyrights have a finite life limited by statute. If a patent, copyright, or similar asset was acquired through purchase from a previous owner, the amount shown on the accountants' balance sheet usually will consist of the price paid to acquire the asset, again with an allowance for accumulated amortization based on the remaining statutory life of the asset. Rarely but occasionally, the amount shown on the accountants' balance sheet as the value of patents or copyrights may include some in-house costs, such as salaries paid to scientific or technical personnel for work leading to a patent application, or to employees who prepared material that was subsequently copyrighted. When such in-house costs are included on the accountants' balance sheet as part of the book value of patents or copyrights, it is usually because of company management's desire to reduce reported expenses by capitalizing, as part of assets on the balance sheet, costs that otherwise would appear as current expenses and might result in the company's showing low profit or even a loss for the period in question.

Goodwill: It is relatively rare for an entry for goodwill to appear on the accountants' balance sheet. Even though the business actually may possess a significant amount of goodwill, it is usually omitted from the accountants' balance sheet for at least two reasons: (1) goodwill is very difficult to value, and (2) goodwill is considered to be a nondepreciable asset, and for that reason it cannot contribute to the objective of minimizing taxable profits such as through charges to depreciation. Accordingly, an effort will be made to show, in some other form, transactions that otherwise might appear as goodwill on the accountants' balance sheet. For example, if a business is acquired from a previous owner who enters into a written agreement not to compete with the new owner in the future, a tax-wise buyer usually will attempt to have the noncompete agreement worded so as to be in the form of a contract for services (the cost of which can then be charged as a business expense over the period of the agreement), or at least to cover a finite period of time, so that the amount paid to the previous owner in return for the agreement not to compete can be amortized over the term of the agreement. When an entry for goodwill does appear on an accountants' balance sheet, it is usually shown as having a nominal value, such as the value of one dollar shown on the balance sheet for XYZ Corporation. Thus, even though goodwill may appear as an item on an accountants' balance sheet, the indicated value usually bears little or no relationship to the true value of whatever goodwill exists.

Accounts payable: This liability item on the accountants' balance sheet represents the total, as determined from the company's detailed financial records, of amounts payable to suppliers and other creditors of the business to whom the business is indebted on a short-term basis. In some cases, accounts payable will be broken down into two categories, accounts payable—trade, and accounts payable—other.

Notes and loans payable: Includes amounts due to various creditors of the business in accordance with existing loans for various purposes. Some detail, such as the nature of the various notes and loans payable and possibly the identity of at least the major creditors, usually will be found in the notes accompanying the accountants' financial statements. The appraiser will be especially interested in whether any of the notes and loans payable represents debts on the part of the company to its owner, in which case such debts may require special attention from the appraiser in connection with the estimate of the value of the business.

Mortgages on land, buildings, etc.:   Principal balance remaining, as of the date of the balance sheet, on any existing mortgages. Frequently, the total amount due on such mortgages, and also possibly on notes and loans payable, will be broken into two categories on the accountants' balance sheet: amount due within one year, and amount due later than one year. However, this distinction is relatively unimportant to the appraiser.

Accrued expenses: Total of various expenses accrued but not actually paid as of the date of the balance sheet. Details usually can be found either in the notes accompanying the accountants' balance sheet or in the supporting working papers.

Reserve for taxes: Accountants' estimate of the amount of taxes required to be paid by the business as a result of events and operations up to the date of the balance sheet, but payment of which is not actually required until some future date.

Other liabilities: Miscellaneous item, usually small compared to most of the other entries on the accountants' balance sheet. Details can be found either in the notes accompanying the accountants' financial statement or in the related working papers.

The balance sheet for XYZ Corporation shows one of two common formats for accountants' balance sheets. In this format, there are three major groupings of balance sheet entries: assets, liabilities, and net book value (or net worth or owners' equity), the amount of the third being the difference between the first two.

In the other common format, there are only two major categories on the accountants' balance sheet. One of these categories is assets, while the other combines the figures for liabilities and net book value. This second major category on the balance sheet may be called liabilities and shareholders' equity, or liabilities and net worth. Rather than consisting of a single entry, such as that for net book value on the balance sheet for XYZ Corporation, the portion of the balance sheet in its alternative format that represents the difference between total assets and total liabilities may be broken down into subcategories, such as paid-in capital and retained earnings or surplus.

Regardless of which of the two common formats is used for the accountants' balance sheet, they contain the same information and, except that one is slightly more convenient to use than the other, are equivalent from the viewpoint of the appraiser.

THE ACCOUNTANTS' INCOME/EXPENSE STATEMENT

Accountants' income/expense statements, like accountants' balance sheets, vary in detail from one accountant to another and from one business to another.

However, these differences are primarily in terms of individual detailed entries, and the great majority of accountants' income/expense statements contain essentially the same major categories or groupings of entries. These major categories are shown in Exhibit 4, which is a somewhat simplified version of an accountants' income/expense statement.

Like the accountants' balance sheet for XYZ Corporation, both the business and the entries on the accountants' income/expense statement for ABC Company are fictitious. In order to give added emphasis to the key points about the accountants' income/expense statement, the fictitious statement for ABC Company omits both detailed entries in the various categories and the explanatory notes that would ordinarily accompany an actual accountants' income/expense statement.

Exhibit 4
ABC COMPANY
INCOME/EXPENSE STATEMENT FOR 12 MONTHS
ENDED DECEMBER 31, 19X1
(DETAIL OMITTED)

Income from sales of goods and services	$729,072
Less cost of goods and services sold	267,106
Gross profit	$461,966
Less operating expenses	441,348
Net operating profit	$ 20,618
Other (nonoperating) income/(expenses)	1,216
Net profit before income tax	$ 21,834
Less income tax	4,367
Net profit after income tax	$ 17,467

There follows a discussion of each of the major categories of entries on the accountants' income/expense statement, with emphasis on considerations that are likely to be of special importance in business appraisals.

Income from sales of goods and services: This group of entries on the accountants' balance sheet reflects the company's income (determined on an accrual or cash basis, as applicable) from its sales of products or services during the period to which the income/expense statement applies. On the accountants' income/expense statement, detailed entries in this category might include:

Gross income from sales	$734,396
Less discounts, returns, and allowances	5,324
Net income from sales of goods and services	$729,072

The various dollar amounts are determined from the company's sales or equivalent bookkeeping records and, provided reasonable care has been taken in preparing and interpreting the company's records, usually can be accepted as quite accurate.

Cost of goods and services sold: This group of entries on the accountants' income/expense statement reflects the direct cost of providing the products and services furnished to customers. As most often defined for accounting purposes, these direct costs are considered to include(1) the cost of materials incorporated in the products or consumed during performance of the services, together with (2) the cost of labor expended directly in manufacturing or otherwise obtaining the products or performing the services. In some cases, direct costs also may include incoming transportation charges for direct materials, subcontract or other services performed outside the company and contributing directly to the products or services, and occasionally even certain items of overhead costs that reflect activities (such as manufacturing supervision or factory occupancy costs) in close support of other direct activities. In the simplest case, detailed entries on the accountants' income/expense statement in the cost of goods and services sold category may appear as follows:

Materials	$ 76,979
Direct labor	153,102
Subcontract manufacture or services	37,025
Total cost of goods and services sold	$267,106

Of course, the various cost figures are for costs contributing to the goods and services sold during the period, as contrasted to costs incurred during the period. Thus, the amount shown for direct labor is not simply the total direct labor performed during the period covered by the income/expense statement. Rather, it is the cost of the direct labor performed on the products actually sold, or the services actually furnished, during the period covered by the statement, regardless of whether this labor was performed during the current or previous accounting periods. Depending on the method used by the individual company, the various direct cost amounts may be determined on a direct costing basis, on a standard cost basis, or on a basis that combines both direct and standard costing. The method used to determine the amounts of the various cost entries may be indicated in the notes accompanying the accountants' financial statements. Most often, however, it will be necessary to make inquiries of the cognizant accounting personnel in order to identify the method used to arrive at the entries in the cost of goods and services sold category on the accountants' income/expense statement.

One method of determining direct material costs involves computations that include inventory levels. When this method is used, detailed entries for cost of goods and services sold on the accountants' income/expense statement may typically appear as follows:

Inventory at start of period	$151,150
Purchases of materials during period	184,459
Direct labor	153,102
Subcontract manufacture or services	37,025
	$525,736
Less inventory at end of period	258,630
Net cost of goods and services sold	$267,106

Because of variations in methods used to determine the cost of goods and services sold, and because of opportunities for inaccuracies in some of these methods, the appraiser may wish to pay special attention to the derivation of the figure for cost of goods and services sold as shown on the accountants' income/expense statement.

Gross profit: Gross profit is the mathematical difference between income from sales of goods and services and cost of goods and services sold. The figure for gross profit reflects the profit of the business before provision for those costs of doing business that are not directly connected with providing the products or performing the services that the business furnishes to its customers. Of course, the amount shown on the accountants' income/expense statement for gross profit will reflect whatever errors or inaccuracies may enter into determining the amounts shown as income from sales of goods and services or, particularly, the amount shown for cost of goods and services sold.

Operating expenses: This group of entries on the accountants' income/expense statement includes all costs of the company's normal business activities (operating costs) with the exception of the costs included in the cost of goods and services sold category. Operating costs are sometimes called indirect costs or overhead costs. In most accountants' income/expense statements, the operating expenses category contains the largest number of individual entries of any of the several categories. In some accountants' income/expense statements, particularly those involving larger companies, the operating expense category may be divided into subcategories, such as factory overhead, selling expense, general and administrative expense, and so on. However, this grouping of operating expenses into subcategories is of relatively little importance from an appraisal standpoint. More than any other group of entries on the accountants' income/expense statement, detailed entries within the operating expenses category vary widely from accountant to accountant and from business to business. In most cases, the title of the individual operating expense account will be adequately descriptive of its significance. In the case of some accounts, however, the appraiser will find it appropriate to look further into the meaning of the account title or the means used to determine the related numerical entry on the accountants' income/expense statement.

Exhibit 5 shows a representative breakdown of operating expenses that might be typical of a relatively small closely held business. Those operating expense accounts that are most likely to be of interest to the business appraiser are discussed on the following pages.

Officers' salaries: Officers' salaries (sometimes called owners' salaries) may appear on the accountants' income/expense statement as a separate item of operating expense or may be included along with other salaries and wages paid by the business in a single entry. In either case, officers' salaries are of major interest to the appraiser, especially if the business is closely held. In a closely held business, salaries paid to the owners are a major element of proprietary income and are frequently the source of a significant difference in

Exhibit 5

ABC COMPANY

OPERATING EXPENSE DETAIL FOR 12 MONTHS ENDED

DECEMBER 31, 19X1

Officers' salaries	$ 51,806
Other salaries	116,965
Advertising	17,472
Travel and entertainment	15,527
Other selling expenses	6,815
Rent	20,429
Depreciation and amortization	9,771
Insurance	32,877
Telephone	8,017
Utilities	18,835
Professional fees	12,518
Office expenses	14,849
Vacation pay	13,353
Payroll taxes	32,953
Employee benefits	5,299
Automobile expense	4,519
Interest expense	20,433
Repairs and maintenance	5,974
Factory supplies and small tools	14,215
Miscellaneous	18,721
Total operating expenses	$441,348

dollar amount between the accountants' income/expense statement and the appraiser's economic income/expense statement, preparation of which is discussed in the following chapter. Especially in the case of a closely held business, the appraiser will wish to determine the composition of the total amount of officers' salaries as represented on the accountants' income/expense statement. That is, the appraiser will wish to know the identity of the persons to whom the salaries were paid, the amount paid to each, and what duties are performed for the business by each of these persons. In many cases, a closely held business may pay salaries to its owners that are higher than would ordinarily be justified by the duties they perform. One reason for this is that, if the business is a corporation, the additional amount that is paid as salary to the owners (stockholders) is subject to income tax only as personal income to the stockholders. However, if this same amount were paid as profit from the business, it would be taxed twice, first as income of the corporation, and the balance after corporate income tax would then be taxed again as personal income to the stockholders when paid to them in the form of dividends. In some closely held businesses, the amount paid as owners' salaries may be abnormally low for the duties performed. This may be the case with a business that is only marginally profitable, and that would show a loss if the owners were paid what would otherwise be normal salaries. In a publicly held business, on the other hand, officers' salaries usually will be determined by the board of directors, and can usually be assumed to correspond with market salaries for the position held and the duties performed. Even in such a case, however, the appraiser may wish to obtain details of officers' salaries, especially if the function of the appraisal may involve changes in key executives of the business.

Other salaries: The amount shown on the accountants' income/expense statement for salaries other than those of the owners of the business can usually be accepted at face value by the appraiser. However, if the business is closely held, the appraiser should determine whether the amount shown for other salaries includes any amounts paid to members of the owner's family in addition to the amount shown as owners' (or officers') salaries. If the amount for other salaries does include payments to members of the owner's family, then the appraiser will need to determine to whom the amounts were paid and the duties they perform. This is because, in some cases, amounts paid to members of the owner's family may be excessive in comparison with the duties performed, thus in effect contributing to the proprietary income from the business.

Advertising: The amount shown for advertising on the accountants' income/ expense statement usually can be accepted by the appraiser without question. An exception might exist if the company's advertising business were to be channeled through an advertising agency that was either a subsidiary of the business being appraised or was otherwise owned or controlled by the same owners, in which case the commissions on the advertising actually might be a part of the total proprietary income from the business.

Travel and entertainment: Although travel and entertainment are ordinarily normal and necessary business expenses, in a closely held business the travel and entertainment account frequently includes substantial expenditures by the owners of the business, some of which may benefit the owner personally, rather than the business. In other words, the travel and entertainment expense of a closely held business may include owners' perquisites, which are part of the total proprietary income from the business. Accordingly, the appraiser of a closely held business will wish to determine, of the total amount for travel and entertainment as shown on the accountants' income/expense statement, approximately what portion was expended by the owner and members of his or her family, and of this portion, how much should be considered as being of actual benefit to the business. For example, if members of the owner's family accompanied him or her on a business trip, their expenses may be included in the amount shown on the accountants' income/expense statement as travel and entertainment expense of the business. Unless they actually performed significant duties for the business, however, expenses incurred by members of the owner's family are really personal expenses from the standpoint of the appraiser's economic income/expense statement. Similarly, if the owner attended a business meeting but extended his or her stay beyond the end of the meeting for reasons of a personal nature, the cost of the extended stay should be regarded by the appraiser as a personal, rather than a business, expense.

Other selling expenses: This item in the accountants' income/expense statement may consist of wages or commissions paid to sales personnel, amounts expended for other purposes such as sales materials, or a combination. In the case of a closely held business, the appraiser may wish to determine whether any of the total amount shown for selling expenses was paid to the owner of the business, in which case it may be part of total proprietary income, subject to treatment in the economic balance sheet in the manner described later in this chapter.

Rent: The key question for the appraiser is whether the amount shown as rent on the accountants' income/expense statement was paid to a person or other entity that is independent of the business being appraised, or whether there is a relationship such that part or all of the amount shown as rent may actually benefit, either directly or indirectly, the business being appraised or its owner. In a closely held business, for example, it is not unusual for the premises occupied by the business to be rented from one of the owners of the business or from a corporation owned or controlled by the owner. In larger businesses, title to real estate sometimes may be held by a subsidiary or sister corporation, to whom rent payments are made. If it is determined that there is a relationship between the company being appraised and the landlord to whom rent payments are made, the appraiser then will wish to determine whether the amount of rent is consistent with the market rent for premises of the type and size occupied. If the rent actually paid is consistent with market rents, then the relationship between the company being appraised and the recipient of the rent payments is ordinarily a matter of no further concern to the appraiser. However, if the amount of rent is significantly above (or if it is below) market rents, then the rent account as shown on the accountants' income/expense statement is, in effect, another vehicle for owners' perquisites, and that portion of the rent amount that exceeds market rent is actually an indirect contribution to total proprietary income.

Depreciation and amortization: As previously indicated, the amount shown on the accountants' income/expense statement for depreciation and amortization almost always will reflect the tax-oriented viewpoint from which accountants' financial statements are prepared. Specifically, the amount shown for depreciation and amortization usually will be the maximum amount allowable under the applicable IRS guidelines and will not bear any close relationship to the actual loss of value of the corresponding assets. Accordingly, the entry on the accountants' income/expense statement for depreciation and amortization will not be of direct interest to the appraiser. However, the detailed records of fixed assets, upon which the accountant's charge for depreciation and amortization is based, will contain information of interest to the appraiser. This information relates to the date of acquisition of each of the various fixed assets that, though still in use, may be fully depreciated and therefore may not be represented in the figures on either the accountants' balance sheet or the accountants' income/expense statement.

Insurance: The accountants' income/expense statement may contain either a single entry covering all insurance costs or a number of separate entries for the various kinds of insurance on which the business pays premiums. In either case, the information of interest to the appraiser is whether the total amount shown for insurance costs on the accountants' income/expense statement is for insurance of benefit to the business, or whether some portion of this amount is for insurance of benefit to the owner of the business or his or her family, and resulting from status as owner rather than as an employee of the business. If such insurance arising out of ownership status does exist, then the correponding premium paid by the company is one of the perquisites of ownership and is included as part of proprietary income. Thus, some businesses have life insurance programs for their employees, in which a portion or all of the insurance premium is paid by the business. It is not unusual in such plans for the amount of insurance to be related to the employee's length of service, salary, or a combination of the two. If there is such a program in the company being appraised, and if the amount of insurance on the owner's life is determined according to the same criteria as apply to other employees, then the corresponding premium, even though it is on insurance to benefit the owner or his or her family, is in effect a normal business expense. However, if the amount of insurance on the owner is greater than it would be if he or she were an employee other than the owner, then the amount of the additional premium is in effect a perquisite of ownership. Similarly, if the business is paying for other insurance of benefit to the owner, such as medical insurance or automobile insurance, and if any portion of this insurance coverage is based upon status as owner rather than as an employee of the business, then the insurance premium is a perquisite of ownership rather than being part of normal business operating expense. Of course, if there is insurance, such as so-called key man insurance on the life of the owner, but for which the business rather than a member of the owner's family is the beneficiary, then the corresponding premium usually is regarded as a normal business expense. Essentially the same reasoning applies to insurance plans under some so-called partnership buy-out agreements. In such situations, the lives of the owners of a closely held business are insured under policies naming the other owners of the business as beneficiaries. Such policies are ordinarily part of an agreement under which, in the event of the death of one of the owners, the proceeds from the insurance policy on his or her life will be used by the other owners to buy the deceased owner's interest in the business from his or her estate or heirs. Even though the policies in question name individuals rather than the company as beneficiaries, the premiums for such cross-insurance policies usually are considered to be a normal business expense, not a perquisite.

Telephone: Usually the only question in connection with the expense amount for telephone costs is what, if any, portion of the total charge reflects use by the owner for personal, rather than business, purposes.

Utilities: Unless the business is paying personal utility charges for the owner, the amount shown on the accountants' income/expense statement can be accepted at face value by the appraiser.

Professional fees: Although the appraiser may wish to determine the composition of the amount shown for professional fees if it is substantial, this is not otherwise an expense with which the appraiser needs to be particularly concerned.

Office expenses: This entry on the accountants' income/expense statement usually represents costs for office supplies and related costs, such as for postage, incurred in connection with the office functions of the business. Unless the amount of the charges shown is unusually large or there is some other reason to suspect that the account may contain charges of a personal rather than business nature, the appraiser usually can accept the amount shown on the accountants' income/expense statement at face value.

Vacation pay: This item reflects pay to employees of the business for time when they are on vacation rather than actually at work. In many businesses, the amount of paid vacation to which an employee is entitled is based on considerations such as length of service. Even though the amount shown for vacation pay may include payment to the owner of the business, such payments should be considered part of normal business expense so long as the amount of paid vacation taken by the owner is determined from the same formula as applies to other employees. However, if the owner is paid for vacation in addition to the amount to which he or she would be entitled as an employee, then the additional vacation pay is a perquisite of ownership and part of proprietary income. Similar reasoning applies to paid leave, which is shown as a separate expense item on income/expense statements for some businesses.

Payroll taxes: This item represents taxes paid by the business on the basis of payroll, such as the employer's share of social security tax and unemployment insurance tax. If salaries paid to the owners of the business or to members of the owners' families are excessive for the duties performed, then the corresponding portion of payroll taxes on these salaries, though not actually paid to the owners or members of their families, reflect owners' perquisites rather than normal business expense.

Employee benefits: This item may include any of a number of different kinds of employee benefits whose cost is paid by the business. Investigation of the source of the amount shown for employee benefits on the accountants' income/expense statement should serve to determine what portion, if any, of the total represents owners' perquisites.

Automobile expense: In a closely held business, it is not at all unusual for the automobile expense account to include expenses arising out of the owners' personal use of automobiles, in addition to use for business purposes. Of course, any personal use of automobiles whose cost is paid by the business is part of owners' perquisites and contributes to total proprietary income. An interview with the owner of the business, or with the accountant, usually will provide the appraiser with information needed to estimate how much of the total automobile expense shown on the accountants' income/expense statement is for personal use.

Interest expense: This item reflects interest paid on money borrowed by the business. It will not usually include any interest on money that may have been borrowed by the owner of the business for personal reasons, since interest is an allowable deduction for personal income tax purposes, and there would therefore be no advantage in showing the owners' personal interest expense as business expense. Among business appraisers, there are two schools of thought about how to deal with interest expense. One school holds, in effect, that interest expense is a normal cost of doing business, and accordingly, only abnormal interest expenses require special attention when appraising a business. If he or she is a member of this school of thought, the appraiser will wish to investigate the source of the interest expense charges shown on the accountants' income/expense statement, to determine whether there are any unusual circumstances, such as loans to the business from its owners at interest rates that are either substantially above or substantially below rates that would be charged on loans under arm's-length conditions. The other school of thought holds that interest expense is a cost of obtaining capital rather than an operating expense. According to this school, interest expense has no place on the economic income/expense statement, but instead is taken into account, at least indirectly, in the way the economic income/expense statement and related information are used to arrive at an estimate of the value of the business. This second school of thought is followed in this book.

Repairs and maintenance: Unless there is reason to believe that it includes expenditures to benefit the owner personally, the amount shown on the accountants' income/expense statement usually can be taken at face value by the appraiser.

Factory supplies and small tools: This is another account that the appraiser can take at face value.

Miscellaneous: Unless the total shown on the accountants' income/expense statement is so small as to be insignificant, the appraiser will wish to investigate the makeup of the miscellaneous expense category, to determine what, if any, portion of the total shown represents owner's perquisites rather than normal business expenses.

Other operating expense considerations: In reviewing the various operating expense categories on the accountants' income/expense statement, the appraiser should be alert for the possible existence of circumstances or situations that may involve charges to operating expenses for what are, in fact, contributions to long-term assets of the business. For example, purchases charged against current operations on the accountants' income/expense statement may include items that, although possibly nominal in cost, actually make a long-term contribution to the business rather than having an effect that is limited to operations during the period covered by the income/expense statement. This might include, for example, tools having a relatively low unit cost or inexpensive items of office equipment. If the total of such purchases included in the accountants' income/expense statement is typical in comparison with similar purchases during other years, then it should be of no further concern to the appraiser. However, if there is an abnormal total of such purchases included in the figures on the accountants' income/expense statement, then the matter may be of special interest. Similarly, many businesses that incur what might be called research and development expense find it desirable (particularly from a tax standpoint) to consider such costs as an expense of current operations, even though the research and development activities may be of benefit primarily in future years, with little or no benefit to the current year's operations. If the total amount of such research and development expenses charged against current operations is significant, then the appraiser may wish to consider excluding the amount in question when preparing the economic income/expense statement of the business.

Net operating profit: Net operating profit, which is one of the major categories on the accountants' income/expense statement, is the mathematical difference between gross profit and total operating expenses. As its name suggests, net operating profit is the profit that results from the normal operations of the business, as distinct from the income or expenses arising from nonoperating sources (see below).

Other (nonoperating) income/(expense):   This category on the accountants' income/expense statement includes income received from and expenses incurred in connection with activities of the business that are outside the scope of its normal business operations. Depending, of course, on the relative amounts of nonoperating income and nonoperating expenses, this category may result in either a net addition to or a net deduction from net operating profit. Items included as part of nonoperating income and expenses may include interest income received by the business on investments or on loans for which the business is the lender, profit or loss on sales of assets of the business, and various items of an essentially accounting nature such as adjustments to figures already reported in previous years.

Net profit before income tax: This is the mathematical sum of net operating profit and other (nonoperating) income, or the mathematical difference between net operating profit and other (nonoperating) expense.

Income tax: This is the tax on the amount shown as net profit before income tax, computed in accordance with the applicable tax tables.

Net profit after income tax: This is the mathematical difference between the net profit before income tax and the applicable income tax. It is frequently referred to as the bottom line on the accountants' income/expense statement.

7

Preparing the Economic Financial Statements

7

Preparing the Economic Financial Statements

ECONOMIC FINANCIAL STATEMENTS—FUNCTIONS AND VIEWPOINTS

The term *economic financial statements* refers to financial statements whose nature and content reflect the appraiser's viewpoint toward a business that is being appraised. This is in contrast to the accountants' financial statements, which are customarily prepared by accountants and are the most readily available financial statements for a business.

In the preceding chapter, covering accountants' financial statements, it was brought out that, as a result of the functions they are intended to serve, the financial statements customarily prepared for a business by its accountants reflect certain viewpoints and possess certain attributes. These include (1) tax-related orientation, specifically with a view toward minimizing taxes payable, (2) a high degree of conservatism, and (3) a basically historical orientation.

In contrast, economic financial statements have the principal purpose of providing the appraiser or other user with an understanding of the financial aspects of the business to aid in estimating its value. In most cases, the type of value to be estimated is market value. This is in contrast to book value, which is the type of value most often associated with accountants' financial statements.

Since a large portion of the process of determining the estimated value of a business involves comparisons (this is evident from the Principle of Substitution), a principal requirement of economic financial statements is that they be useful for comparison purposes.

Further, as is evident from the Principle of Future Benefits, economic financial statements frequently will be used, either directly or indirectly, as an aid in predicting the future of the business to which they apply.

The requirements imposed on economic financial statements include the following:

The information in the statements should, insofar as reasonably feasible, reflect or represent market values.

The statements and the information they contain should be useful for various kinds of comparisons.

The economic financial statements should, insofar as possible, be useful for forecasting purposes—that is, as a basis for predicting the future of the business being appraised.

CONSTRUCTING THE ECONOMIC BALANCE SHEET

The economic balance sheet is constructed item by item, line by line, following a format similar to that of the accountants' balance sheet.

Since the purpose of the economic balance sheet is to assist the appraiser in arriving at an estimate of the value of the business or other property being appraised, the specific assets and liabilities that are represented on the economic balance sheet will depend on the definition of the property to be appraised. Thus, if a complete going business is to be appraised, then the economic balance sheet will include all assets and all liabilities of the business, essentially the same items that are included on the accountants' balance sheet.

On the other hand, if a business is to be appraised for possible sale, and the contemplated sale is to be a sale of assets rather than of a complete going business, the economic balance sheet ordinarily will omit cash and frequently other asset items such as accounts receivable. Again depending on the exact definition of the property to be appraised, an economic balance sheet may omit some or all liabilities of the business, thus differing substantially from the accountants' balance sheet.

As for the amounts shown on the economic balance sheet for the values of the various assets and liabilities, it most often will be the case that these values should be chosen to reflect current market values as of the effective date of the appraisal. This will be the case when the economic balance sheet is to be used by the appraiser in estimating value according to the replacement cost approach, which is the purpose for which the economic balance sheet is used most often.

In some situations, however, the values on the economic balance sheet will be determined on a basis other than current market value. This will be the case, for example, when the economic balance sheet is to be used for an estimate of the liquidation value of a business, or when it is to be used to estimate certain other types of value, such as insurable value or loan value.

As previously suggested, it is at least theoretically possible to construct an economic balance sheet without any use of existing financial statements such as the accountants' balance sheet. In practice, however, it almost always will be easier, less time-consuming, and more accurate to prepare the economic balance sheet in a manner that makes maximum use of pertinent information found in the accountants' balance sheet and associated backup material.

Exhibit 6 illustrates a typical economic balance sheet as it might be prepared for the business whose accountants' balance sheet was illustrated in Exhibit 3 in Chapter 6. It is assumed that the economic balance sheet for XYZ Corporation as shown in Exhibit 6 is to be used in estimating the fair market value of the business according to the replacement cost approach. Accordingly, the various dollar amounts in the economic balance sheet are intended to represent current market values of the various assets and liabilities.

Using the economic balance sheet for the fictitious XYZ Corporation as an example, the following is a discussion of how the various dollar amounts are determined, using information as appropriate.

Cash: If the definition of the property to be appraised is such that the balance sheet includes an item for cash, the dollar amount ordinarily will be the same as for the cash item on the accountants' balance sheet for the same date.

Exhibit 6

XYZ CORPORATION

ECONOMIC BALANCE SHEET AS OF DECEMBER 31, 19X1
(CURRENT MARKET VALUES)

ASSETS

Cash		$ 126,845
Accounts receivable		457,005
Marketable securities		216,631
Inventory:		
Raw materials	$154,136	
Work in process	604,985	
Finished goods	394,208	
Total inventory		1,153,329
Prepaid expenses		4,924
Fixed assets		515,744
Patents and copyrights		96,280
Goodwill		15,400
Total assets		$2,586,158

LIABILITIES

Accounts payable	$ 446,102
Notes and loans payable	783,436
Mortgages on land, buildings, etc.	610,286
Accrued expenses	26,240
Reserve for taxes	52,000
Other liabilities	45,996
Total liabilities	$1,964,060

TOTAL ASSETS LESS TOTAL LIABILITIES	$ 622,098

Accounts receivable: The amount of accounts receivable on the economic
balance sheet usually will be at least approximately the same as the net
amount, after the reserve for doubtful accounts, as shown on the accountants'
balance sheet. This assumes, of course, that the analysis of receivables leading
to the figures on the accountants' balance sheet is considered reasonable by
the appraiser. Accounts receivable is another item that, depending on the
definition of property to be appraised, may be omitted entirely from the
economic balance sheet.

Marketable securities: As previously stated, marketable securities may be shown on the accountants' balance sheet as having a value corresponding to either their actual market value as of the date of the balance sheet, or their original cost or current market value, whichever is lower. If the appraiser determines that marketable securities have been shown on the accountants' balance sheet at current market value, then this ordinarily will be the value at which they are shown on the economic balance sheet. Otherwise, the appraiser will need to determine the current market value of the securities in question. In the case of securities for which there is a reasonably active market, information on current market prices should be available from sources such as stockbrokers or one of several published listings of stock transactions. Of course, the security price information of interest is that for transactions occurring on or as close as possible to the effective date of the economic balance sheet. In the case of securities that are not regularly traded on a market, the appraiser may find it necessary to arrive at value estimates by other means, such as the market data approach described in Chapter 8 or by capitalizing income from the securities according to the investment value approach described in Chapter 10.

Inventory: As previously stated, the values for inventory as shown on the accountants' balance sheet usually will reflect the cost of the inventory, as contrasted to the market value orientation of the economic balance sheet. If the amount of inventory is substantial in comparison with total assets, as is frequently the case when appraising a manufacturing or distribution business, the appraiser may wish to give special attention to inventory values to be shown on the economic balance sheet.

Inventory—raw materials: Because it is still in the form in which it was originally acquired, raw material inventory usually is considered to have a current value equal to its acquisition cost. Accordingly, the figure shown on the economic balance sheet for the value of raw material usually will be the same as that shown on the accountants' balance sheet. (This assumes, of course, that the business is being valued on an ongoing basis. Otherwise, raw material may have a current value that is actually less than its original cost, at least to the extent of the supplier's restocking charge.) In some cases, if the amount of raw material inventory is substantial and if there has been significant price inflation since it was acquired, the economic balance sheet may show raw material inventory at a current market value that includes the effect of price inflation.

Inventory—work in process: This is inventory on which some production work has been done, but which is not yet in finished product form. The term usually applies to manufacturing businesses, not to other types of businesses. On the accountants' balance sheet, work in process will be shown as having a book value equal to its estimated cost—including material cost, cost of labor expended to date, and frequently applied overhead as well—as of the date of the balance sheet. The amount of this cost as shown on the accountants' balance sheet may be determined in any of several ways, principal among which are actual cost records if the business has a sufficiently detailed cost accounting system, or estimates made by appropriate members of company management. Because of the wide variety of different situations that may be encountered, the valuation of work in process for purposes of the economic balance sheet is a matter on which the appraiser will need to exercise judgment. Thus, if the amount of work in process is relatively small in comparison with other items on the economic balance sheet, it may be sufficient for purposes of the economic balance sheet to use the same figure for value of work in process as appears on the accountants' balance sheet. On the other hand, because it represents partially completed end products, work in process may be thought of as having acquired a value that exceeds costs expended to date to the extent of a pro rata portion of the profit that is anticipated at such time as the finished products are sold. If this viewpoint is chosen by the appraiser, the cost of work in process (as typically shown on the accountants' balance sheet) can be multiplied by a figure reflecting the company's average ratio of product selling price to product cost, thereby obtaining a value figure for work in process that includes pro rata provision for expected profit on the work in question. In making such a calculation, the appraiser will need to distinguish between work in process costs determined on a basis that (1) includes applied overhead, in which case a net profit multiplier should be used, and one that (2) includes only material and labor cost without overhead, in which case a gross profit multiplier should be used.

Inventory—finished goods: On the accountants' balance sheet, finished goods almost always will be shown as having a book value equal to their total cost but excluding any provision for profit. (An exception will exist if the cost of finished goods exceeds its anticipated selling price, in which case the "lower of cost or market rule" will require that finished goods be shown on the accountants' balance sheet as having a value equal to the lower of the two figures.) So long as their cost is lower than their anticipated selling price, finished goods usually are shown on the economic balance sheet at their market value. One common method for determining the value of finished goods for purposes of the economic balance sheet is to use the figure for cost of finished goods as shown on the accountants' balance sheet, multiplying this figure by the company's established or average ratio of product selling price to total product cost. If product sales or marketing costs are substantial, as for example when sales are made through commission representatives, that portion of total product price that represents sales or marketing costs may be omitted from the figure for market value of finished goods as shown on the economic balance sheet. (This exclusion of sales and marketing costs from value as shown on the economic balance sheet also applies to the figure for work in process.)

Prepaid expenses: Because of the basis on which they are determined for purposes of the accountants' balance sheet, and also because the total amount is generally small in comparison with other balance sheet items, prepaid expenses almost always are shown on the economic balance sheet as having the same value as on the accountants' balance sheet.

Fixed assets: The fixed assets category almost always will be of major importance when preparing the economic balance sheet. This is because, for many businesses, the value of fixed assets is a substantial portion of the total value of the business, and because the book values of fixed assets as shown on the accountants' balance sheet are so affected by tax considerations as not to be a good indication of actual market values. In determining fixed asset values for purposes of the economic balance sheet, the appraiser usually will employ one or a combination of the various approaches to estimating value as covered in Chapters 8, 9, and 10 of this book. Some of the techniques for estimating fixed asset values for the economic balance sheet are suggested by the following discussions of individual kinds of fixed assets.

Fixed assets—land and buildings: The value of land and buildings as shown on the economic balance sheet usually will be determined by one or a combination of the standard methods applicable to appraisal of real property, namely the market data approach, the replacement cost approach, and the investment value approach.

Fixed assets—machinery and equipment: When feasible, the current market value of machinery and equipment preferably should be determined by direct comparison, that is, through use of the market data approach. For machinery of relatively common types, current market values frequently can be determined from information regarding the used equipment market. Such information may be available either from dealers in used equipment of the type in question, or in some cases from publications offering used machinery for sale. Another method used in estimating the market value of used machinery and equipment is to start with a base figure representing the cost of a new machine of the type in question, and then deduct an allowance representing the estimated effect on value of observed depreciation of the actual machinery being appraised. The base figure, representing the cost of a new but otherwise equivalent machine, may be either the present price of a new machine of the same type or the original acquisition cost (determined from the company's records) of the actual machine in question, possibly with some upward adjustment for the effect of price inflation between the date of acquisition and the effective date of the appraisal. The amount of the deduction for observed depreciation is essentially a judgment on the part of the appraiser, taking into consideration such factors as the estimated total useful life of a machine of the type in question, the actual age of the specific machine being appraised, and its condition as determined from visual inspection or other means. Because of the judgmental considerations involved, this "cost less observed depreciation" method of estimating the market value of machinery is less accurate and therefore less desirable than the direct market comparison method. If the appraisal is one in which the value of machinery and equipment will have an important effect on the total value estimate, and if the appraiser is not acquainted with machinery and equipment of the type in question, it is helpful to enlist the help of someone with more knowledge, either a used machinery dealer or an appraiser who specializes in machinery and equipment appraisals.

Fixed assets—furniture, fixtures, office equipment: The amount of attention and effort devoted to estimating the market value of fixed assets falling into the classification of furniture, fixtures, and office equipment will depend, as a practical matter, on the value they represent as compared to other kinds of fixed assets and as compared to the value of the business as a whole. In a manufacturing business, for example, furniture, fixtures, and office equipment usually will have a total value that is relatively small compared to the value of the business as a whole. In a distribution or service business, on the other hand, furniture, fixtures, and office equipment may represent the largest category, in terms of value, of any fixed asset category. Market values for furniture, fixtures, and office equipment are determined in a manner similar to that used for machinery and equipment. Direct market comparison may be used in the case of those individual assets whose value is significant and for which the necessary market data are available. Otherwise, the replacement cost less observed depreciation method is frequently used.

Fixed assets—vehicles: The market value of vehicles, particularly automobiles and trucks owned by the business, usually can be estimated by the market data approach, using comparative price information that is relatively readily available. Current price information on automobiles and on many kinds of trucks can be found in various published guides, which almost any automobile dealer will have a copy of, and which sometimes can be found in public libraries. In the alternative, the cost less observed depreciation approach can be used to estimate market values of vehicles.

Patents and copyrights: The book value of patents and copyrights as shown on the accountants' balance sheet is ordinarily determined on the basis of cost, less an allowance for depreciation determined on the basis of the statutory life of the patent or copyright. On the economic balance sheet, on the other hand, patents, copyrights, and similar assets (such as franchise agreements) should be shown at estimated market value insofar as this can be determined. The market value of patents, copyrights, and similar assets is essentially intangible, and like all intangible asset values is difficult to determine with a high degree of confidence. A further complication arises from the fact that the value of patents, copyrights, and related assets is frequently different, from the standpoint of the going business of which they may be a part, from the value they would have if offered for sale independently of either a going business or other related assets. Thus, determination of the value of patents, copyrights, and so on, for the purpose of the economic balance sheet is a matter requiring considerable thought on the part of the appraiser. In the simplest, but unfortunately rare, case in which the patent or copyright has been acquired through purchase, it can be shown on the economic balance sheet as having a current market value equal to its purchase cost reduced pro rata over the estimated useful economic life of the patent or copyright (which in any event should not exceed the statutory life). In the case of franchise agreements, the current market value may be estimated either from the going price for similar franchises or, if there is no such market information available, from the initial cost of the agreement reduced to reflect the portion of its estimated useful life which has expired from the original acquisition date to the date of the appraisal. In the most common case in which patents or copyrights were obtained on work performed by employees of the business rather than through purchase of an existing patent or copyright, there are two principal methods for estimating the value of the patent or copyright. One of these methods involves the investment value approach, in which the income attributable to the patent or copyright is determined and is then capitalized at an appropriate capitalization rate to arrive at an estimate of value. The second method is to estimate the amount of labor and other costs that would be required to produce a patent or copyright of comparable value and to use this estimated cost as an estimate of the value of the patent or copyright that is being appraised. The valuation of patents, copyrights, franchise agreements, and similar intangibles is a difficult matter at best. Fortunately, such assets usually represent only a small fraction of the total value of a complete business enterprise, with the result that any errors in estimating their values will have relatively little effect on the accuracy of the estimated value of the complete business. However, in those situations in which the values of patents, copyrights, and similar assets may be crucial to the outcome of the appraisal assignment, appraisal of these assets should be left to an appraiser who specializes in such matters.

Goodwill: Determining an appropriate value for goodwill is possibly the most difficult problem faced when constructing an economic balance sheet. As an intangible asset, goodwill presents all of the valuation problems that apply to intangible assets, in addition to which there are considerable differences of opinion in various quarters regarding the correct definition of *goodwill*. The most common method for estimating the value of goodwill involves application of the investment value approach. In applying this method, the income attributable to goodwill is determined, such as through the excess earnings method, and this income is then capitalized at what is considered to be an appropriate rate to arrive at an estimate of the total value of goodwill. Further information on this subject will be found in Chapter 10. An alternative method for estimating the value of goodwill, but one that is employed less often, is the cost to create method, in which those historical costs believed to have contributed to existing goodwill are used as an indication of its value. This approach to valuing goodwill is described in Chapter 11.

Other assets: In addition to the assets represented on the accountants' balance sheet, there sometimes may be other assets that should be shown on the economic balance sheet. These may include, for example, (1) fixed assets that have been fully depreciated for tax purposes and thus were omitted from the figures leading to the book values on the accountants' balance sheet, (2) assets that were charged as current operating expense when they were acquired rather than being capitalized as fixed assets, and (3) various kinds of intangible assets. The third category may include proprietary processes, customer lists, and goodwill, which is not always shown on the accountants' balance sheet and, if shown, is usually shown as having a book value that is artificially low compared to its actual contribution to the market value of the business. The major problem in connection with these other assets that do not appear on the accountants' balance sheet is identifying their existence. Once they have been identified, they can be valued by one or more of the methods applicable to the specific kind of asset in question.

Liabilities: As already mentioned, some appraisals involve a definition of property to be appraised such that it consists of assets only, without provision for liabilities. Thus, the economic balance sheet is sometimes not a balance sheet in the strict sense of that term, but rather a listing of assets with their estimated values. If the appraisal assignment is such that liabilities are shown on the economic balance sheet, they will be shown in most cases as having values identical to the book values on the accountants' balance sheet. Of course, there may be exceptions in individual situations, in which one or more liabilities will be shown on the economic balance sheet at values that differ from the book values of the corresponding liabilities as shown on the accountants' balance sheet. In the case of closely held businesses in particular, one situation sometimes occurs and results in a difference between the amount of liabilities as shown on the accountants' balance sheet and the amount as shown on the economic balance sheet. This concerns loan transactions between the business and its owner. An owner may sometimes make a loan to his or her business under circumstances such that, although it may be convenient or expedient—for reasons including possible tax considerations— to show the transaction as a loan, repayment from the business to the owner is not actually contemplated. In such a case, the amount of the so-called loan usually will be excluded from the figure for notes and loans payable on the economic balance sheet. Of course, there are also converse situations, in which case the accountants' balance sheet of a business may show an amount receivable from the owner of the business, when in fact there is no real intent that the amount in question will ever be repaid.

RELATIONSHIP BETWEEN ACCOUNTANTS' BALANCE SHEET AND ECONOMIC BALANCE SHEET—SUMMARY

Recapitulating the preceding discussion of individual balance sheet items, Exhibit 7 summarizes the typical relationships between dollar amounts as shown on the accountants' balance sheet and those for the corresponding balance sheet items as shown on the economic balance sheet.

Exhibit 7

TYPICAL RELATIONSHIP BETWEEN ACCOUNTANTS' BALANCE SHEET AND ECONOMIC BALANCE SHEET

	Usual basis for dollar amount shown on:	
	Accountants' Balance Sheet	Economic Balance Sheet
ASSETS		
Cash	Actual amount	Actual amount
Accounts receivable	Actual amount after reserve for doubtful accounts	Actual amount, collectible portion only
Marketable securities	(1) Lower of cost or ket value, or (2) market value	Market value
Inventory:		
Raw materials	Cost	Cost
Work in process	Cost	(1) Cost, or (2) cost plus pro rata profit
Finished goods	Cost	Market value
Prepaid expenses	Actual amount	Actual amount
Fixed assets	Cost less accumulated depreciation at maximum rate allowable for tax purposes	(1) Market value, or (2) estimated cost to replace
Patents and copyrights	Cost, narrowly interpreted	(1) Market value, or (2) estimated contribution to total value of business
Goodwill and other intangibles	(1) Omitted entirely, or (2) shown at nominal value	Estimated actual value
LIABILITIES	Actual amounts	Actual amounts, adjusted for unusual items such as transactions with owner

CONSTRUCTING THE ECONOMIC INCOME/EXPENSE STATEMENT

Like the economic balance sheet, the economic income/expense statement is constructed by the appraiser item by item, line by line. Much of the information for the economic income/expense statement is taken from the accountants' income/expense statement and its supporting detail or, if an accountants' income/expense statement is not available, from the federal income tax return.

As previously explained, a principal function of the economic income/expense statement is to provide the appraiser with information as a basis for various kinds of comparisons. A major requirement of the economic income/expense statement is that it present standardized information, in the sense that the information derived from the economic income/expense statement can be compared meaningfully with similar information on other businesses or other types of investments. The accountants' financial statements for a business frequently will reflect circumstances and situations that may be unique to the individual business, such as the accounting treatment of owners' perquisites and proprietary income. The economic income/expense statement, on the other hand, should be constructed so that, while it reflects the same business transactions as the accountants' income/expense statement, the information in the economic income/expense statement leads to valid comparisons with similar information for other businesses or other investments.

The specific information on the economic income/expense statement that is of greatest interest to the appraiser for comparison purposes is information relating to net operating profit before taxes and, to a lesser extent, income from sales of goods and services. The importance of these two kinds of information will be further evident in the discussion that follows and in succeeding chapters in this book.

In constructing the economic income/expense statement from the accountants' income/expense statement and supporting detail, the appraiser faces somewhat different situations depending on whether the business being studied is a small, closely held one, or whether it is a larger, possibly publicly owned business.

In either case, the objective in constructing the economic income/expense statement is to present the income and expense information for the business in a manner that will be useful for comparison purposes. This applies particularly to information on the net operating profit and also to information on income from sales of goods and services.

In preparing the accountants' income/expense statement for a closely held business, the accountant or other person responsible for preparation of the statement has considerable latitude in the accounting treatment given to certain kinds of expenses. Depending on the nature and circumstances of the company's business, the inclinations of the accountant, and particularly the desires of the owner, certain items of expense may be treated in one way or another, with corresponding effect on the various profit figures as shown on the accountants' income/expense statement. From the standpoint of the economic income/expense statement, these variations in treatment of expenses on the accountants' income/expense statement are especially important as they relate to owners' perquisites and to proprietary income.

In a large publicly held company, on the other hand, although there still may be variations in accounting treatment from one company to another, these variations are less likely to affect the critical figures on the accountants' income/expense statement, namely the figures for the various types of profit and for income from sales of goods and services. Accordingly, preparation of an economic income/expense statement for a large publicly held business is usually less of a problem for the appraiser than preparation of such a statement for a closely held business.

With the foregoing as background, Exhibit 8 shows an economic income/expense statement for a small closely held business, the fictitious ABC Company, whose accountants' income/expense information appeared in Exhibits 4 and 5 in Chapter 6.

The following is an item-by-item discussion of the basis for the various entries on the economic income/expense statement.

Exhibit 8
ABC COMPANY
ECONOMIC INCOME/EXPENSE STATEMENT FOR 12 MONTHS ENDED DECEMBER 31, 19X1

Net income from sales of goods and services		$729,072
Less cost of goods and services sold		267,106
Gross profit		$461,966
Less operating expenses:		
Officer's salary	$ 30,000	
Other salaries	116,965	
Advertising	17,472	
Travel and entertainment	10,527	
Other selling expenses	6,815	
Rent	20,429	
Reserve for replacements	3,500	
Insurance	32,877	
Telephone	8,017	
Utilities	18,835	

(Continued)

Exhibit 8 (*Continued*)

Professional fees	12,518	
Office expenses	14,849	
Vacation pay	12,514	
Payroll taxes	28,695	
Employee benefits	5,299	
Automobile expense	2,260	
Repairs and maintenance	5,974	
Factory supplies and small tools	14,215	
Miscellaneous	18,721	
Total operating expenses		$380,482
Net operating profit		$ 81,484

Net income from sales of goods and services: In constructing the economic income/expense statement, the appraiser's principal concern with income from sales of goods and services is whether the figure as shown on the accountants' income/expense statement includes all operating income. In many cases this will be true, and the appraiser then can use the figure from the accountants' income/expense statement for income from sales of goods and services on the economic income/expense statement. In some cases, however, it may be necessary to make adjustments to the figure on the accountants' income/expense statement. If the figure for net income on the accountants' income/expense statement includes income from nonoperating sources, such as interest income or income from sales of assets, this will have an effect on the overall income/expense statement that will tend to distort comparisons with figures for other businesses. Accordingly, the appraiser should exclude any such nonoperating income from the figure for net income from sales of goods and services as shown on the economic income/expense statement.

Cost of goods and services: If the accountants' income/expense statement has been prepared by a professional accountant, and especially if the statement is certified, the appraiser usually can accept at face value the figure for cost of goods and services sold as shown on the accountants' income/expense statement. Otherwise, however, the appraiser may wish to determine how the figure on the accountants' income/expense statement was determined before accepting it. As was explained in the discussion of the accountants' income/expense statement earlier in this chapter, there are a number of different ways of computing the cost of goods and services sold. The most straightforward method is the one in which the cost of materials, direct labor, and subcontract manufacture or services entering into the goods are entered directly on the income/expense statement. If this method has been used to arrive at the figure for cost of goods and services sold on the accountants' income/expense statement, and if the individual figures (especially those for cost of materials and direct labor) were obtained from an appropriately detailed cost accounting system, then the figure as shown on the accountants' income/expense statement almost always can be used directly on the economic income/expense statement. However, if some of the individual figures, such as those for cost of materials or direct labor entering into the goods and services sold, are the result of unfounded guesses or estimates, then the figure for total cost of goods and services sold is correspondingly suspect. In such a case, the appraiser may wish either to use a figure derived by some other method for the cost of goods and services sold as shown on the economic income/expense statement or, at minimum, he or she should qualify the value conclusions with a statement to the effect that they are based in part on data that the appraiser has not been able to substantiate. A second method of calculating cost of goods and services sold has been described in Chapter 6. In this method, the net cost of goods and services sold is determined in a manner that takes into account the change in inventory during the period covered by the income/expense statement. If the detailed data are from reliable sources, and especially if the figures for inventory at start of period and inventory at end of period are accurate, cost of goods and services sold as calculated by this method can be accepted at face value by the appraiser. However, because the method involves the difference between two inventory figures that are of similar order of magnitude, any error in either or both of these figures is, in effect, magnified in the final figure for net cost of goods and services sold. The appraiser needs to be especially cautious in accepting a figure for cost of goods and services sold that is based on inventory estimates, rather than on detailed inventory records or an actual physical count. A third method that is sometimes used for calculating cost of goods and services sold involves standard cost figures for various products, or sometimes even a single such figure for average ratio of cost of goods to income from sales. This third method, using so-called standard cost figures, is potentially the least accurate of the several methods for determining cost of goods and services sold. Because the determination of cost of goods and services sold involves information that is to a substantial extent past history at the time of the appraisal, it is usually impossible for the appraiser to make his or her own determination of an appropriate figure for cost of goods and services sold, other than by investigating the source of the corresponding figure as shown on the accountants' income/expense statement, forming judgments about the likely accuracy of this figure, and proceeding accordingly.

Gross profit: As with the accountants' income/expense statement, the figure for gross profit on the economic income/expense statement is the mathematical difference between net income from sales of goods and services and cost of goods and services sold. The figure for gross profit on the economic income/expense statement will differ, of course, from that on the accountants' income/expense statement to the extent of any difference in the respective component figures.

Officer's salary: Particularly in the case of a closely held company, the expense item for officers' salaries is of primary concern to the appraiser. The amount of officer's salary as shown on the accountants' income/expense statement will frequently reflect circumstances unique to the particular business and to the desires of its owner. Accordingly, the salary actually paid to the owner or officer of a closely held company is not necessarily consistent with market salaries for the type of position and the duties performed. To contribute to valid comparisons between the business being appraised and other businesses, officers' salaries as shown on the economic income/expense statement should reflect at least approximate market salaries, even though this may be substantially different from the salary actually paid to the owner or officer. There are various means by which the appraiser may arrive at an estimate of an appropriate market salary. This includes information that may be available from personnel managers of similar companies or from local organizations of personnel managers, from trade associations, from various other published sources, and, if necessary, from an informal survey conducted by the appraiser. In the case of publicly held companies, unlike closely held ones, officers' salaries usually are set by the board of directors and tend to reflect actual market salaries for the type of position and duties performed, at least in the opinion of the board of directors. When appraising a publicly held company, therefore, the appraiser usually can use, on the economic income/expense statement, the same figure for officer's salary as appears on the accountants' income/expense statement.

Other salaries: In a closely held company, the expense item for other salaries sometimes may include relatives or friends of the owner who are being paid salaries that are more or less out of line with the market salary for the position held and duties performed. Except for adjustments to reflect any such situation that may exist, the appraiser usually can take at face value the figure for other salaries as shown on the accountants' income/expense statement.

Advertising: Advertising is another expense item that, unless there are unusual circumstances such as common or interlocking ownership between the business being appraised and its advertising agency, usually can be taken at face value as shown on the accountants' income/expense statement.

Travel and entertainment: In a closely held company, the item for travel and entertainment expense as shown on the accountants' income/expense statement sometimes will include the cost of personal travel or entertainment for the owner or members of his or her family, of such nature that it does not directly benefit the business. As a part of the effort to eliminate owners' perquisites from the figures on the economic income/expense statement, the appraiser should adjust the amount for travel and entertainment as shown on the accountants' income/expense statement as necessary to eliminate any personal expense. Ordinarily, the best way to determine the appropriate amount of any such personal expense is through discussion with the owner of the business or its accountant.

Other selling expenses: An investigation of the content of the figure for other selling expenses as shown on the accountants' income/expense statement should provide the appraiser with information from which he or she can determine whether it includes any expenses, such as possibly additional income to the owner or owners' perquisites, that should be eliminated from the figure as used for the economic income/expense statement.

Rent: If the property being rented by the business is owned by the business itself, or if they are under common ownership, the amount of rent as shown on the accountants' income/expense statement needs to be compared with actual market rents, so that it can be determined whether any adjustment in the rent amount is required on the economic income/expense statement. If there is no such common ownership, the figure on the accountants' income/expense statement for rent usually can be accepted by the appraiser at face value.

Reserve for replacements: This is an item on the economic income/expense statement that, in a sense, is a substitute for the depreciation and amortization item that appears on the accountants' income/expense statement. The intent of the amount for reserve for replacements as shown on the economic income/expense statement is to reflect the actual loss of value, during the period covered by the income/expense statement, of the fixed assets of the business. This loss in value may be in terms of market value of the various fixed assets, or in terms of an annual contribution to a fund (which frequently exists only in concept) whose purpose is to provide financial means to replace the various assets at such time as they have reached the end of their useful lives. Probably the most common method for calculating the amount of the reserve for replacements is to (1) identify the individual assets (including any that may have been fully depreciated for tax purposes but are still in use), usually with the aid of the backup detail for the accountants' calculation of depreciation and amortization, (2) estimate the actual useful life of each asset, and (3) calculate a corresponding figure for the reserve for replacements for the year in question.

Insurance: If the amount on the accountants' income/expense statement includes any cost for insurance of benefit to the owner or his or her family, and that is available to him or her as owner but not as an employee of the business, then this amount should be excluded on the economic income/expense statement from the amount for insurance as shown on the accountants' income/expense statement.

Telephone: The amount for telephone expense ordinarily may be accepted at face value as shown on the accountants' income/expense statement.

Utilities: This is almost always a straightforward item and can be accepted by the appraiser at face value as shown on the accountants' income/expense statement.

Professional fees: If the amount shown for professional fees on the accountants' income/expense statement seems large in comparison with other expense items, the appraiser may wish to investigate the source of the charges for professional fees. Otherwise, this item usually can be accepted at face value as shown on the accountants' income/expense statement.

Office expenses: Unless the amount shown for office expenses on the accountants' income/expense statement includes owners' perquisites in addition to normal office expenses of the business, the amount shown on the accountants' income/expense statement can be accepted at face value.

Vacation pay: In a closely held business, if officers' or owners' salaries have been adjusted (usually downward, occasionally upward) to reflect estimated market salaries instead of salaries as actually paid, a corresponding adjustment should be made in the amount of vacation pay as shown on the accountants' income/expense statement. An adjustment to vacation pay also may be in order if the owner of the business receives a longer period of paid vacation than he or she would as an employee but not the owner.

Payroll taxes: Any adjustments in owner's salary (and possibly also in vacation pay) from the amounts shown on the accountants' income/expense statement should be accompanied by a corresponding adjustment in the amount of payroll taxes associated with the salary in question.

Employee benefits: If the amount of employee benefits as shown on the accountants' income/expense statement includes any owners' perquisites, the corresponding costs should be omitted from the amount for employee benefits as shown on the economic income/expense statement.

Automobile expense: Any use of automobiles for personal purposes, but charged as a business expense, should be eliminated from the amount for automobile expense as shown on the economic income/expense statement. An estimate of the amount of any such personal use of automobiles usually can be obtained through conversation with the owner of the business or with its accountant.

Repairs and maintenance: This item usually can be accepted at face value as shown on the accountants' income/expense statement.

Factory supplies and small tools: This is another item that usually can be accepted at face value.

Miscellaneous: If the miscellaneous expense item as shown on the accountants' income/expense statement is of significant size, the appraiser should investigate the source of the amount shown and act accordingly when reflecting this item on the economic income/expense statement.

Net operating profit: As with the accountants' income/expense statement, net operating profit as shown on the economic income/expense statement will be the mathematical difference between gross profit and total operating expense. Of course, the figure for net operating profit on the economic income/expense statement will differ from the corresponding figure on the accountants' income/expense statement to the extent of differences in the component figures, especially the various items of operating expense.

Other income or expenses: Comparing the economic income/expense statement as illustrated in Exhibit 8 with the accountants' income/expense statement as shown in Exhibits 4 and 5, it will be noted that the figure for net operating profit is the final entry on the economic income/expense statement, whereas the accountants' income/expense statement continues with the entries for other (nonoperating) income/(expenses), net profit before income tax, income tax, and net profit after income tax. These differences, of course, reflect differences in the purposes of the two kinds of income/expense statements. When the economic income/expense statement is being used as a basis for comparing the business being appraised with other businesses or investments, these comparisons should be made on the basis of net operating profit (that is, before provision for nonoperating income or expense and before provision for income tax). This is because, of the various figures, net operating profit is the best single indicator of the financial performance of a business. In some cases, however, information on the comparable businesses or investments may not include a figure for net operating profit nor other information from which net operating profit can be determined. This may be the case, for example, when using published figures that include information on profit after taxes but which lack sufficient detail to permit the appraiser to determine the corresponding figure for net operating profit. In such a case, because valid comparisons require a comparison between like things, it will be necessary to estimate the corresponding amount of income tax and thus the net profit after income tax for the business being appraised. This ordinarily will be done by continuing the economic income/expense statement beyond the figure for net operating profit, to a new bottom-line figure, net profit after income tax.

RELATIONSHIP BETWEEN ACCOUNTANTS' INCOME/EXPENSE STATEMENT AND ECONOMIC INCOME/EXPENSE STATEMENT—SUMMARY

For the fictitious ABC Company, Exhibit 9 summarizes the differences in amount (which in the case in question are limited to items of operating expense) between the accountants' income/expense statement, as shown in Exhibits 4 and 5, and the economic income/expense statement as shown in Exhibit 8.

Even though the data are fictitious, the situation with ABC Company is not unlike what appraisers frequently encounter in practice.

As shown in the summary, the differences between the economic income/ expense statement and the accountants' income/expense statement (sometimes referred to as adjustments to the accountants' income/expense statement) total roughly $60,000. This total difference in operating expenses

Exhibit 9

ABC COMPANY

COMPARISON OF ACCOUNTANTS' INCOME/EXPENSE STATEMENT AND ECONOMIC INCOME/EXPENSE STATEMENT

	Amount per:			
	Accountants' I/E Statement	Economic I/E Statement	Difference	Reason for Difference
Net operating income	$729,072	$729,072	$ 0	
Less cost of sales	267,106	267,106	0	
Gross profit	$461,966	$461,966	$ 0	
Less operating expenses:				
Officer's salary	$ 51,806	$ 30,000	$ 21,806	Actual salary exceeds market
Travel and entertainment	15,527	10,527	5,000	Owner's personal travel and entertainment
Depreciation and amortization	9,771	—	9,771	Omitted from Economic I/E Statement
Reserve for replacements	—	3,500	(3,500)	Appears on Economic I/E Statement only
Vacation pay	13,353	12,514	839 ⎫	Reflects adjustment to officer's salary
Payroll taxes	32,953	28,695	4,258 ⎬	
Automobile expense	4,519	2,260	2,259	Owner's personal use of auto
Interest expense	20,433	—	20,433	Interest not considered an operating expense
All other operating expenses	292,986	292,986	0	
Total operating expenses	$441,348	$380,482	$ 60,866	_Decrease_ in operating expenses
	$ 20,618	$ 81,484	($ 60,866)	_Increase_ in operating profit

between the two income/expense statements amounts to somewhat less than 15% of total operating expenses as shown on the accountants' income/expense statement. For ABC Company, these differences between the two statements are entirely the result of owners' perquisites, including the fact that the owner's actual salary is significantly above market. Had the situation been one calling for other adjustments, such as in other categories of operating expense and also in the figures on the accountants' income/expense statement for income or cost of sales, the difference between the two income/expense statements would have been, of course, correspondingly greater.

In spite of the relatively modest adjustments in the case of ABC Company, however, net operating profit as shown on the economic income/expense statement is almost four times that shown on the accountants' income/expense statement. Of course, this is because differences in operating expenses as shown in the two statements translate, dollar for dollar, into differences in net operating profit. Net operating profit is in any event a relatively small difference between two relatively large numbers, so any change in either of the component numbers is magnified in terms of the percentage change in the difference.

Much of the significance of the economic income/expense statement, and of the differences between it and the accountants' statement, is apparent from the comparison in Exhibit 9. It is obvious that, if the profit produced by a business is to be used as a primary consideration in determining its value, the value estimate resulting from use of figures as shown on the economic income/expense statement will be very different from the case if figures from the accountants' income/expense statement had been used.

USING FINANCIAL STATEMENTS TO DETERMINE TRENDS—FORECASTING

A discussion on using financial statements in appraising would not be complete without some mention of the use of such statements in forecasting future business performance. The importance of forecasting future performance is evident from the Principle of Future Benefits, and some of its specific applications to estimating value will be covered in succeeding chapters of this book.

Historical financial statements for the business being appraised offer the appraiser the best available source for predicting future performance to the extent that it reflects internal factors—that is, factors that are intrinsic to the business itself, rather than external influences such as competition, market conditions, general economic inflation, and so on.

To provide the basis for forecasting the future performance of a business, the appraiser should gather financial statements, especially income/expense statements, for the past several years. He or she will use the information in these statements to identify trends that, if they are found, can be extremely helpful in predicting future performance of the business.

There is no absolute rule for the number of past years for which financial statements should be studied in an effort to identify trends. In many cases, statements for as few as the past five years will be sufficient. In some cases, particularly if trends are difficult to identify (or nonexistent), the appraiser may wish to obtain financial statements covering a period substantially longer than five years. In a few cases, such as when the business has been in existence for less than five years, it may be necessary to work with financial statements covering a shorter period.

In studying the financial statements of the business over a period of time, the appraiser will be primarily concerned with the figures for profit (preferably net operating profit) and to a lesser extent with total sales volume. Other detailed information in the financial statements will be of interest primarily to the extent that it may help to explain unusual circumstances that are evident in the figures for profit in the various years.

Although economic income/expense statements are somewhat better for trend analysis purposes than accountants' income/expense statements, the latter can be used if they are prepared on a basis that is consistent from year to year.

As for the actual identification of trends and use of information on these trends to predict future performance, there are a number of mathematical techniques, some of which are quite sophisticated, which are available to the appraiser who is inclined to use them. Unfortunately, many of these techniques for forecasting on the basis of historical data are quite complex, frequently more so than can be justified in view of the uncertainties in the raw data and the frequently questionable assumptions on which the forecasting techniques are based.

In the majority of cases, the appraiser may find it sufficient merely to compare financial data on the business for several successive years and from this comparison to identify whatever trends may exist.

By way of example, Exhibit 10 shows hypothetical sales, cost of sales, operating expense, and net operating profit data for the fictitious DEF

Corporation. In this table, the data are presented as they might be arranged by an appraiser to assist in searching for trends.

From the five-year comparison of financial data for DEF Corporation as shown in Exhibit 10, an appraiser might reach conclusions including the following:

Net income from sales shows a constantly increasing trend. Year-to-year changes in sales volume range between 11.5% and 18.0%, with an average annual sales increase of 13.5%. This trend of income from sales is indicative of a business that, although certainly not showing phenomenal sales growth, is at least holding its own in its market.

Cost of sales figures are reasonably stable as a percentage of net sales. Cost of sales as a percentage of net sales range between 33.7% and 36.6% for the five-year period. The five-year average ratio of cost of sales to net sales is 35.4%, and there is at least a suggestion in the data that the relationship between cost of sales and net sales may be on a slightly decreasing trend.

Operating expenses are also reasonably stable in comparison with net sales, ranging between 52.1% and 54.3% of sales, with a five-year average of 53.5% of sales.

Net operating profit as a percentage of net sales, although modest, is also reasonably stable, ranging between 9.9% and 12.0% of sales for the five-year period, with a five-year average operating profit of 11.1% of sales.

Overall, the five-year comparison of sales, cost of sales, operating expenses, and net operating profit indicates that DEF Corporation is a reasonably stable business, with no particularly unusual fluctuations in sales volume, costs, or profits. One phenomenon that is apparent in the data and might be worth further investigation is the unusually large increase in income from sales between 19X8 and 19X9, along with the simultaneous decrease in net operating profit as a percentage of sales. However, this is not necessarily unusual, and there is probably a reasonable explanation for it.

With information such as that shown in Exhibit 10 for DEF Corporation, and assuming the investigation of the business has not disclosed any other significant factors that are not apparent in the historical data, an appraiser might reasonably conclude that DEF Corporation can be expected to show, at least for the next few years, continued sales growth in the vicinity of perhaps 12% per year, with more or less corresponding growth in net operating profit.

Although five-year data as shown in Exhibit 10 for DEF Corporation would not be particularly unusual, there are also situations in which comparison of

Exhibit 10

DEF CORPORATION

FIVE-YEAR COMPARISON OF SALES, COST OF SALES, OPERATING EXPENSES, AND NET OPERATING PROFIT

	12 mos. 19X7	12 mos. 19X8	12 mos. 19X9	12 mos. 19X0	12 mos. 19X1	Five-year average
Net income from sales	$126,553	$141,056	$166,457	$186,626	$209,406	$166,020
Less cost of sales	46,294	51,062	59,758	62,812	73,767	58,739
Gross profit	$ 80,259	$ 89,994	$106,699	$123,814	$135,639	$107,281
Less operating expenses	67,304	73,550	90,219	101,313	111,455	88,768
Net operating profit	$ 12,955	$ 16,444	$ 16,480	$ 22,501	$ 24,184	$ 18,513
Percentages:						
Cost of sales to net sales	36.6%	36.2%	35.9%	33.7%	35.2%	35.4%
Gross profit to net sales	63.4%	63.8%	64.1%	66.3%	64.8%	64.6%
Operating expenses to net sales	53.2%	52.1%	54.2%	54.3%	53.2%	53.5%
Net operating profit to net sales	10.2%	11.7%	9.9%	12.0%	11.5%	11.1%
Change from previous year:						
Net income from sales	—	11.5%	18.0%	12.1%	12.2%	13.5%
Net operating profit	—	26.9%	0.2%	36.5%	7.5%	17.8%

historical data will show one or more anomalous years—years in which, for example, sales volume may have increased (or decreased) sharply, possibly with related sharp changes in net operating profit. If the anomalous situation is apparent in only one year of perhaps five years for which data are compared, the appraiser will wish to seek an explanation for the anomaly, presumably through discussion with key management personnel of the business being studied. Usually, such a discussion will produce information seemingly sufficient to explain the anomaly, and the appraiser can give this information appropriate consideration in a prediction of the future financial performance of the business.

If the historical data for a business show an anomalous year that is also the most recent year for which information is available, then the appraiser must be especially careful in interpreting the data in search of trends. While the apparently anomalous year may in fact be just that—an anomaly—it also could signal the beginning of a new trend that is a departure from the trend of previous years. If the appraiser decides, on the basis of the available information, that the latter is the case, it will have a profound effect on predictions of the financial future of the business.

There are also some businesses for which data from past years' financial operations will fail to disclose any significant trends. When faced with such a situation, the appraiser first will wish to seek information on additional past years in the hope that a trend may develop. If it does not, and if discussions with key management personnel fail to provide a resolution to the forecasting problem, then the appraiser should proceed with extreme caution in any forecast of the future financial performance of the business.

SUGGESTIONS FOR FURTHER STUDY

The following publications will be of interest to readers who wish to learn more about the subjects covered in this chapter, including business financial statements and their uses.

The Analysis of Financial Statements, by Leopold A. Bernstein. Dow Jones–Irwin, 1818 Ridge Rd., Homewood, IL 60430. 1978.

Beyond the Balance Sheet: Evaluating Profit Potential, by J. Lines. John Wiley and Sons, Inc., 605 Third Ave., New York, NY 10016. 1974. 166 pages.

The Dictionary of Accounting, by Ralph Estes. MIT Press, 28 Carleton St., Cambridge, MA 02142. 1981. 176 pages.

Handbook of Modern Accounting, edited by Sidney Davidson and Roman L. Weil. McGraw-Hill Book Company, 1221 Avenue of the Americas, New York, NY 10020. 1977. 1363 pages.

How to Keep Score in Business, by Robert Follett. New American Library, P.O. Box 999, Bergenfield, NJ 07621. 1980. 167 pages.

How to Price a Business, by Raymond C. Miles. Institute for Business Planning, Inc., IBP Plaza, Englewood Cliffs, NJ 07632. 1982. 133 pages.

How to Read a Financial Report: Wringing Cash Flow and Other Vital Signs out of the Numbers, by John A. Tracy. John Wiley and Sons, Inc., 605 Third Ave., New York, NY 10016. 1979. 160 pages.

Operation Financial Analysis: A Practical Handbook with Forms, by Ronald A. Feiner. Prentice-Hall, Inc., Englewood Cliffs, NJ 07632. 1977. 288 pages.

Reading and Evaluating Financial Reports. Xerox Learning Systems, One Pickwick Plaza, Greenwich, CT 06830. 1977. 120 pages.

Understanding Financial Statements, by John M. Myers. New American Library, 1633 Broadway, New York, NY 10019. 1964. 206 pages.

8

Analyzing the Facts— The Market Data Approach

8

Analyzing the Facts—
The Market Data
Approach

THE MARKET DATA APPROACH

The *market data approach* to estimating value is sometimes called the market comparison approach or the sales comparison approach.

The market data approach is one of the three most widely recognized approaches to estimating value. The other two are the replacement cost approach and the investment value approach, which are the subjects of Chapters 9 and 10, respectively. Certain other approaches, not as widely known but nevertheless useful in some appraisal situations, are covered in Chapter 11.

SUMMARY OF MARKET DATA APPROACH

The market data approach has its theoretical basis in the Principle of Substitution, which states that "the value of a thing tends to be determined by the cost of acquiring an equally desirable substitute."

In estimating the value of any kind of property by the market data approach, the appraiser attempts to identify other properties, generally similar to the one being appraised, that actually have been sold. The appraiser then uses information about the selling prices of these other properties as a basis for estimating the value of the property being appraised.

Because it is based on actual selling prices of similar properties, the market data approach is certainly the most direct application of the Principle of Substitution to estimating the market value of any kind of property. Indeed, the market data approach is the most powerful and the most often used method for estimating the market value of residential real estate.

With some other kinds of property, however, application of the market data approach is sometimes hindered by lack of sufficient reliable information on actual sales of property similar to that being appraised. This is particularly true of appraisals of complete businesses and of certain kinds of business assets. This matter is further discussed later in this chapter.

In attempting to use information on actual sales to estimate the value of property by the market data approach, the appraiser frequently will find that none of the comparable properties is identical in all respects to the property being appraised. The appraiser then employs a technique called adjusting, to account for differences between each of the comparable properties and the property being appraised, as these differences affect value.

There are two different ways in which this process of adjusting can be accomplished.

In one method, the actual total selling price of each of the comparable properties is adjusted by a dollar amount that the appraiser determines is appropriate to account for differences in value arising out of differences between the comparable sale and the property being appraised. These adjustments to the actual selling price of the comparable property may be either positive or negative, depending on whether the property being appraised is considered to be superior or inferior in value to the comparable sale.

The second technique of adjusting is to normalize all prices to a common unit basis and then to make comparisons on this unit basis rather than on the basis of the total property. In appraising real property, for example, prices actually paid for tracts of land can be converted to equivalent prices per acre, and these per acre prices then can be used as a basis for estimating the market value of land that is being appraised. Similarly, selling prices for certain types of buildings may be reduced to an equivalent price per square foot, prices paid for securities consisting of blocks of capital stock can be compared on the basis of price per share, and so on.

In appraising complete businesses, the most common bases of comparison are (1) profits earned by the business, and (2) sales volume of the business. Other units of comparison sometimes are used for specific kinds of businesses.

More detailed information on the criteria for what constitutes adequate comparability, and on adjustments to compensate for lack of complete comparability, will be found later in this chapter.

In general, successful application of the market data approach depends on availability of information on a statistically significant number of sales of other property, of such nature and under such circumstances as to be meaningful in terms of the market value of the property being appraised. Preferably, these comparable sales of other property should not require extensive adjustments to the actual selling prices, thereby tending to cast doubt on the validity of the resulting conclusion.

APPLICATION OF MARKET DATA APPROACH IN BUSINESS APPRAISING

As previously indicated, the market data approach is extremely important in the appraisal of real property. It is almost certainly the most powerful single approach to estimating the value of residential real estate, and it also has important applications in the valuation of commercial and industrial real property.

In business appraising, however, the situation is somewhat different. Although the concepts underlying the market data approach are certainly applicable to appraisal of businesses, their practical application is severely limited. This is because of (1) the relative scarcity of sales of businesses that could be regarded as comparable to a given business to be appraised, and (2) the difficulty of obtaining reliable information on the pertinent aspects of such comparable sales as actually do exist. Thus, although the appraiser certainly should attempt to apply the market data approach to each business that he or she appraises (if for no other reason than that readers of the appraisal report will tend to expect it), he or she will find in many cases that the market data approach sheds relatively little light on the question about the value of the specific business being appraised.

However, the market data approach does have important applications in business appraising, though not always in estimating the value of a complete business enterprise.

Instead, the market data approach is applicable to estimating values of many kinds of business assets, thus providing information on asset values for use in connection with the replacement cost approach, which is described in detail in Chapter 9.

In a somewhat different sense, by providing information on market yields, the market data approach also contributes to estimating business values by the investment value approach, which is discussed in Chapter 10.

The remainder of this chapter is devoted to discussion of the market data approach with specific applications to business appraising.

REQUIREMENTS FOR COMPARABILITY

Because the validity of the market data approach as a means to estimating the value of property being appraised is based on the Principle of Substitution, it is apparent that, in order for an actual sale of property to qualify as a comparable sale, it must meet two general requirements:

The property sold must be of such nature as to represent an equally desirable substitute for the property being appraised.

The circumstances of the sale must be such that the price paid for the comparable property is truly meaningful in terms of the market value of the property being appraised.

From the standpoint of the appraiser attempting to apply the market data approach, the above two general requirements involve four specific areas of concern:

The availability of information on comparable sales

Similarity of each of the comparable properties to the property being appraised

The circumstances of each comparable sale

The terms of each comparable sale

REQUIREMENTS FOR COMPARABILITY— AVAILABILITY OF INFORMATION

Any attempt to apply the market data approach obviously depends on the availability of information on a significant number of pertinent comparable sales.

It must be emphasized that this information must concern actual sales. Value estimates, appraisals, assessed values, asking prices, and offers that did not result in consummation of an actual sale should not be used with the market data approach, since they do not reflect the actual market action on which the market data approach is based.

The one possible exception concerns an offer that may have been made for purchase of the property being appraised. If such an offer otherwise satisfies the requirements for comparability as explained in this chapter, and if the reason it did not result in an actual sale does not affect the validity of the offer as an indication of market value, then such an offer can provide a valid indication of the market value of the property. Otherwise, however, offers not resulting in sales should be excluded from the market data approach.

As for the number of comparable sales needed for valid application of the market data approach, there is no hard and fast rule. Obviously, the more sales that meet the comparability requirements and for which information is available, the more reliable will be the information on market values that these sales provide. As a practical matter, however, the number of comparable sales that the appraiser is able to identify and for which he or she can obtain the necessary information almost always will be quite limited. Information on only one or two comparable sales is better than no information at all, even though the confidence that can be placed in only one or two sales as an indication of market viewpoint is very limited.

As a practical matter, if the appraiser can identify as many as four to six truly comparable sales, and if the value indications provided by the individual sales form a pattern of reasonable consistency, then the appraiser should be able to apply the market data approach with some degree of confidence in the validity of the results.

Otherwise, if the appraiser is not able to locate more than two or three comparable sales, or if the value indications provided by the comparable sales do not appear to fit any clear pattern, he or she still may wish to attempt application of the market data approach, but the results should be viewed with a degree of skepticism. In such a case, the appraiser probably will wish to give greater weight to estimated values as reached by one or more of the other approaches when he or she arrives at a final value conclusion.

Whatever number of comparable sales the appraiser is able to identify, the information that is available regarding these sales must meet the requirements of (1) reliability and (2) reasonable completeness.

Available information regarding the comparable sales must be reliable in the sense that it is free from significant distortions, deliberate or otherwise. And it must be complete to the extent of providing the appraiser with all information about the sale that is pertinent from the standpoint of application of the market data approach.

As an example of the latter, businesses are sometimes sold under circumstances that include the buyer's giving an employment contract to the seller. For various reasons, frequently relating to tax benefits for one or both parties, the dollar amount associated with such employment contracts is frequently greater than would customarily apply to a contract for personal services if the buyer–seller relationship did not exist. In such a situation, a substantial portion of the financial consideration that is nominally related to the employment contract is, in fact, part of the purchase price of the business. It is evident that, if such an employment contract existed and if the appraiser did not know of it, conclusions regarding market values could be adversely affected.

REQUIREMENTS FOR COMPARABILITY— SIMILARITY OF PROPERTIES

The importance of a high degree of similarity between the property being appraised and comparable properties used in connection with the market data approach is apparent from the Principle of Substitution.

Ideally, each comparable property should be identical in all respects to the property being appraised. Since this rarely happens in practice, the question of similarity between properties becomes one of degree. The greater the similarity between a comparable property and the property being appraised, the more meaningful is information about sale of the comparable property in terms of the market value of the property being appraised. Likewise, the greater the dissimilarities between the properties, the less valuable is information on sale of the comparable in terms of the market value of the property being appraised.

To some extent, dissimilarities between a comparable property and the property being appraised can be accounted for by means of adjustments. However, there is a limit to the number and degree of dissimilarities that can be overcome adequately by the adjustment process. If the dissimilarities between the comparable property and the property being appraised are too great in either number or degree, then the adjustments needed to overcome these dissimilarities themselves can become the source of errors and uncertainties, thereby tending to destroy the validity of the comparison process as a means of estimating the market value of the property being appraised.

One requirement that must always be met by a comparable property is that it have the same highest and best use as the property being appraised. Because of the importance of highest and best use in determining the economic value of property, there is no adjustment or similar means that can be used to validate comparisons between properties of different highest and best use, even though the properties might be identical in all other respects.

The selling price of a tract of land whose highest and best use is for high-density residential development does not provide a valid indication of the market value of another tract of land—even though it may be of identical size, topography, and character—that is situated so that its highest and best use is agricultural.

In the case of businesses, the fact that the economic purpose of most businesses is to provide their owners with a return on investment does not necessarily mean that all businesses have the same highest and best use in the sense that affects market value. A closely held business that provides employment for its owners may well have a greater value, in terms of the price a buyer would pay for it, than an otherwise identical business that is the property of an absentee owner. Specifically, a potential owner–manager of the business may be willing to pay a higher price for it than a buyer who regarded the business solely as an investment.

Likewise, a manufacturing entity whose function is that of a captive subcontractor, supplying its output for use by its parent company, may have a different market value from that of a similar manufacturing entity producing the same products but for sale on the open market.

Further discussion of requirements for similarity of comparable properties appears in the following two sections of this chapter, the first dealing with complete operating businesses and the second dealing with individual business assets that are to be appraised by means of the market data approach.

REQUIREMENTS FOR COMPARABILITY— OPERATING BUSINESSES

When using the market data approach in connection with appraisal of a complete operating business, there are at least nine points of comparison between the business being appraised and each of the comparable businesses whose selling price is to be used as an indication of market value. These nine points of comparison are:

Type of business activity in which engaged

Size of business

Form of ownership of business—closely held or publicly held

Capital structure

Degree of profitability

Competitive position within industry

Historical growth rate

Physical facilities

Type of sale—capital stock or sale of assets and, if the latter, which specific assets

It is evident that, if two businesses are to be compared in the sense that the selling price of one is to provide an indication of the value of the other, then the two businesses should be engaged in the same line of activity. Distribution businesses should be compared only with other distribution businesses, manufacturing businesses only with other manufacturing businesses, and businesses that provide a service to their customers only with other service businesses.

It is also desirable that, insofar as possible, distribution businesses handling a certain kind of products be compared only with other distribution businesses handling the same kind of product, and similarly with manufacturing businesses and service businesses. As a practical matter, however, relatively few distribution or manufacturing businesses handle only a single product, and it frequently will be impossible to find other comparable businesses with the identical product or product mix. It may be necessary when comparing businesses to make comparisons between businesses whose products or product mixes are not exactly alike. So long as the differences in product or product mix do not significantly affect the market value of the business, comparisons involving businesses with nonidentical products or services should not affect the validity of the market data approach.

To be comparable for purposes of the market data approach, businesses should be at least roughly similar in size. This is not to say that they need to be exactly the same size as measured by sales volume, for example, since size differences can be taken into account by such means as normalizing various indices of business performance on the basis of sales volume or other measure of business size. However, businesses of vastly different size are likely to differ in other respects that will affect value, such as their relative stability, the market to which they will appeal, and so on. Accordingly, relatively little confidence can be placed in value indications based on comparisons of businesses of vastly different size.

Also significant but less widely recognized when comparing businesses under the market data approach is the matter of form of ownership of the businesses being compared. A publicly owned business is not as directly comparable with a closely held business as would be the case with two businesses that were both under the same form of ownership, other things being equal.

Publicly owned and closely held businesses differ in a number of respects that are significant from the standpoint of the market values of the respective businesses. One of these respects concerns the buyer market to which the businesses are likely to appeal. Thus, a closely held business might be of interest to one group of buyers, while a publicly owned business would be of interest to a somewhat different set of potential buyers.

Another significant difference between publicly owned and closely held businesses concerns their relative stability. The stability of a closely held business, particularly if it is owner-managed as most closely held businesses are, tends to be closely related to the continuity of ownership. If ownership of the business changes, the stability of the business may be affected accordingly. Publicly owned businesses, on the other hand, are better able to withstand changes in ownership. And, of course, differences in stability between businesses directly affect the degree of business risk, which in turn affects the market value of the business.

Still another difference between publicly owned and closely held businesses concerns their respective degree of individuality. Although all businesses tend to some extent to reflect the personality of the chief executive, this is especially true of closely held businesses, where the chief executive—who is usually also the owner—exerts more direct control over the business than would usually be the case with the chief executive of a publicly held company.

Capital structure is another consideration influencing the comparability of businesses for purposes of the market data approach. A business with little or no funded debt will have a different market value from that of a business with a substantial amount of such debt, everything else being equal. Similarly, a corporation with one or more classes of preferred stock outstanding will have a different value from that of one with only a single class of common stock, especially when value is measured on a basis such as dividend-paying capacity.

Profitability is, of course, an important basis for comparing businesses according to the market data approach. To account for differences in sizes of businesses, profitability ordinarily will be normalized on a basis such as profit as a percentage of sales or, more to the point, profit in relation to the value (selling price in the case of a comparable business) of the business. In making comparisons on the basis of profit, the appraiser must take care that all comparisons are made on the basis of like quantities. That is, if information is available about the pretax operating profits of the comparable businesses, then all comparisons should be made on this basis. On the other hand, if, as often happens, only after-tax profit information is available for the comparable businesses, then this is the basis on which the comparable businesses must be compared with the business being appraised.

Competitive position within the industry is another point of comparison, since a business with a relative competitive advantage, other things being equal, will have a greater value than a business without such an advantage. Competitive position frequently involves factors such as size of the business, reputation, and quality of management.

Historical growth rate, measured in such terms as rate of growth of net income or possibly of total sales, is another consideration affecting the value of a business. Other things being equal, a business showing a relatively high growth rate will have a greater value than one showing a lower growth rate.

Physical facilities are another characteristic of a business that affects its value. When comparing businesses according to the market data approach, it is desirable to give at least some consideration to the relative extent and condition of the physical facilities of each of the comparable businesses as compared to the business being appraised. Even though two businesses may exhibit essentially the same performance as measured according to the usual criteria, the one with the better (more valuable) physical facilities will have a somewhat greater value in the market.

Finally, the type of sale —that is, whether a sale of capital stock or a sale of assets—must be given consideration when using the actual selling price of a comparable business as an aid in determining the value of a business being appraised. Of the two types of sales, the sale of capital stock is frequently less advantageous to the buyer than a sale of assets. This is because, in a sale of capital stock, the buyer usually assumes all of the liabilities of the corporation, including possible contingent liabilities whose magnitude may be undeterminable at the time of sale, or even unknown liabilities whose very existence may not be apparent at the time of sale. Also, the buyer who buys a business through a purchase of capital stock inherits existing fixed asset values and depreciation schedules. On a purchase of assets, on the other hand, the buyer is usually able to restate the values of various fixed assets to their current market values, thus giving himself or herself the benefit of greater depreciation deductions in the future. (Of course, it is possible for a buyer who acquires a business through purchase of capital stock to liquidate the corporation or otherwise transfer the assets to a new legal owner, and thereby to establish a new depreciation base.)

If a comparable sale involved a sale of assets, it is important, in interpreting the selling price in terms of the value of the business being appraised, to know precisely which assets were included in the sale and also which, if any, liabilities were assumed by the buyer. In particular, cash on hand may be included as part of a business in a sale of assets, even though this is not usually the case. Likewise, accounts receivable may or may not be included among the assets purchased by the buyer. The same is also true of real estate owned by the business or by its seller personally. With respect to liabilities, some asset sales do not include any liabilities, while others may include certain selected liabilities of the business, or even all of its liabilities. These matters are, for obvious reasons, important for the appraiser to determine when applying the market data approach.

Obviously, if it were required that comparable businesses selected for application of the market data approach be limited to those businesses that were identical to the business being appraised in all of the foregoing respects, it would be virtually impossible to find a comparable sale. As previously indicated, complete conformity is not essential, since some differences can be compensated for by means of appropriate adjustments, and other differences, if sufficiently minor in effect, can be tolerated without having a significant adverse effect on the validity of the market data approach.

These matters are dealt with further later in this chapter.

REQUIREMENTS FOR COMPARABILITY— INDIVIDUAL BUSINESS ASSETS

As explained earlier in this chapter, the market data approach can be applied either to estimating the value of a complete business or to estimating the value of individual business assets, as in connection with the replacement cost approach or one of the other approaches to estimating the total value of a business.

In applying the market data approach to estimate the value of individual business assets, points of comparison between comparable sales and the asset being appraised include the following:

Type or kind of the asset

Age (applies to limited life assets)

Physical condition or utility

Possible amenities or features of the asset in question

It is obvious that, when using the market data approach as a basis for estimating the value of a particular kind of asset, information on sales of other assets should be limited to assets of the same general type. That is, a machine tool should be compared only with other machine tools, an aircraft only with other aircraft, and so on. Further, milling machines should be compared only with other milling machines, twin-engine piston aircraft only with other twin-engine aircraft, and so on. Whenever possible, in fact, comparisons should be limited not only to items of the same kind but preferably also to products of the same manufacturer and, if possible, of the same type or model number.

Age is another consideration affecting the value of individual business assets. The only possible exception consists of assets, mostly of an intangible nature, that have no definitely determinable life, such as proprietary processes, trade secrets, and the like. As for the majority of assets whose useful life is limited, it is not necessary for individual assets to be of the same age in order for comparisons to be valid. Instead, differences in age usually can be taken into account by means of appropriate adjustments to actual selling prices. However, it is important that the appraiser have at least approximate information about the age of the assets involved in comparable sales, in order to make the necessary adjustments.

Physical condition, especially as it relates to the utility of an item for its intended purpose, is another important factor in determining the value of individual assets. Differences in physical condition can, of course, be taken into account to some extent by means of adjustments.

Obsolescence resulting from factors other than age and physical condition, such as recent technological developments or changes in industry practices, are another consideration affecting the validity of comparisons of assets under the market data approach.

Finally, various amenities or features, such as the speed of operation of office equipment or of production machinery, tooling, or accessories, can affect value, and, accordingly, the presence or absence of such amenities or features should be taken into account by the appraiser when arriving at value estimates through application of the market data approach.

REQUIREMENTS FOR COMPARABILITY— CIRCUMSTANCES OF COMPARABLE SALES

After the availability of information on comparable sales and the requirements for similarity of comparable properties to the property being appraised, the third area of concern in applying the market data approach involves the circumstances of each individual sale, that is, the conditions under which the sale took place as distinct from the nature of the property sold and the terms of the sale itself.

For valid application of the market data approach, it is important for each comparable sale to satisfy the following requirements:

The sale must have been a true open market transaction, in which the property was exposed for sale on the open market for a reasonable period of time, with ample opportunity for a substantial number of potential buyers to come forward, consider the property being offered, and make whatever offer to purchase it they deem appropriate.

Sales resulting solely from negotiations with a single potential buyer, with other potential buyers having little or no opportunity to come forward with possible offers, do not necessarily provide a true indication of market value and should be excluded from comparable sales when applying the market data approach.

The sale must have been an arm's-length transaction. Transactions between members of the same family, or between businesses under common ownership or control, are frequently not arm's-length transactions and in many cases are at prices other than market value. The key here is that there should have been no preferential treatment accorded to either party.

The sale should have been free from compulsion or pressure affecting either party. Sales at times when the seller is under financial pressure, possibly facing bankruptcy or foreclosure, are frequently at prices significantly below market value. The same is true with sales under other circumstances involving pressure on either buyer or seller, such as imminent loss of the property sold through process of eminent domain.

The date of each comparable sale should be reasonably close to the valuation date. Although it is possible to adjust for differences in time of sale, the greater the time difference involved, the greater the difficulty of arriving at an appropriate adjustment, and therefore the greater the likelihood that the adjustment itself will introduce distortions into the comparison process.

Each comparable sale must have taken place in essentially the same market as the market for the property being appraised. Specifically, the market for the comparable sale should involve essentially the same group of potential buyers that make up the (potential) market for the property being appraised. Depending on the kind of business or other property being appraised, this requirement for similarity of market may involve geographical or other considerations related to the nature of the business itself.

Also important is the state of the market at the time of each comparable sale. Depending on a number of influences, the market in which a comparable sale took place may have been abnormally depressed or possibly abnormally stimulated at the time of the actual sale. Obviously, any abnormal state of the market is likely to affect the price paid for the comparable property and is a consideration that must be taken into account by the appraiser in arriving at an estimate of the value of the property being studied.

REQUIREMENTS FOR COMPARABILITY—
TERMS OF SALE

The fourth area of concern to the appraiser in attempting to apply the market data approach involves the terms of each comparable sale.

Broadly speaking, terms of sale include both the terms of payment as agreed upon between seller and buyer and the form of payment. Also important in interpreting comparable sales information is whether the sale involved full ownership of the property sold or only a part interest in it.

Terms of payment for a business or business asset may be either all cash at time of sale or a combination of cash and promissory notes. The price may very well be different depending on the terms of payment, and, accordingly, the appraiser needs to know the terms of payment for each comparable sale.

Similarly, some sales involving promissory notes are at interest rates substantially below market interest, in which case the low interest rate frequently influences the agreed selling price and needs to be taken into account by the appraiser when using information on the comparable sale.

Instead of being for a consideration in the form of cash or a combination of cash and promissory notes, some sales of businesses are for some other form of consideration, typically stock of the buyer corporation. In the case of such a stock sale, if the buyers's stock is regularly traded on a market such that it can be converted quickly into cash, and if the terms of sale do not involve any restrictions on the seller's disposition of the stock received for the business, then the transaction is essentially not different from one for cash. In many instances, however, sales in which the seller receives stock from the buyer involve either stock for which there is no ready market or so-called restricted stock, which carries with it various limitations or constraints whose effect is such that it cannot be converted immediately into cash.

Otherwise comparable sales involving stock that is either restricted or for which there is no ready market may involve a selling price that was affected by the terms of the sale, and the appraiser should be extremely cautious in interpreting the nominal selling price of the comparable business for purposes of the market data approach.

Also important to the appraiser is the question of whether each comparable sale involved a sale of full ownership of the business or business asset or whether it involved a partial interest. Obviously, if only a partial ownership interest was involved, the price paid must be factored upward accordingly in order to provide a basis for estimating the value of the complete business being appraised.

In many circumstances the sale of a part ownership interest in a business may be at a price that, pro rata, differs significantly from the value of the complete business. A buyer may be willing to pay a higher price per share for a controlling interest in a business than he or she would be willing to pay for a noncontrolling interest. On the other hand, when the principal stockholder of a closely held business sells a minority ownership interest in the business, such as to one or more employees of the business, the sale may be at a below-market price so as to give the employee an ownership interest in the business with the expectation that the business will benefit accordingly from the employee's increased interest in its success.

For the foregoing and other reasons, sales of partial ownership interests must be considered carefully by the appraiser before they are accepted as comparable sales for the purposes of the market data approach.

STEPS IN APPLYING THE MARKET DATA APPROACH

The market data approach is applied in three steps:

1. The appraiser identifies a number of recent sales that meet the comparability requirements as explained earlier in this chapter.
2. The appraiser then compares each comparable sale with the property being appraised, adjusting the actual selling price of each comparable property to compensate for significant differences between the property being appraised and the comparable sale.
3. The appraiser then uses the adjusted selling prices of the comparable properties as the basis for a conclusion regarding the market value of the property being appraised.

SOURCES OF COMPARABLE SALES INFORMATION

The first step in applying the market data approach is to gather information on comparable sales.

Leads to the existence of sales of property similar to that being appraised may come from any of a variety of sources, depending to some extent on the nature of the property being appraised.

Thus, if a complete business is to be appraised by means of the market data approach, information on actual sales of businesses may be obtained from the sources described in Chapter 5, particularly the section on "Information on Actual Sales of Companies," and the corresponding portion of the bibliography of sources that appears at the end of that chapter.

Other possible sources of information on sales of complete businesses include trade associations and business brokers. Trade association executives are often aware of sales of businesses within their industry, and they may be able to provide the appraiser with important leads to such sales. In many communities, there are one or more business brokers who specialize in the sale of businesses of one or more of the most common types, such as bars, restaurants, coin-operated laundries, and so on.

Brokers who specialize in specific kinds of businesses usually can be identified either from listings in the local yellow pages, or from advertising in the business opportunities section of local newspapers.

There are also some brokers who operate nationally, specializing in certain types of businesses, such as marinas, banks, and insurance companies. One way to identify such brokers is by inquiring at the appropriate trade association. Another way is through ads that the brokers themselves place from time to time in national periodicals, particularly *The Wall Street Journal.*

If the property to be appraised by means of the market data approach consists of securities (such as stocks and bonds), information on comparable sales can be obtained from sources such as stock brokerage firms or, if the security is either listed on one of the national exchanges or traded frequently on the over-the-counter market, selling price information can be found in listings of securities transactions that appear in publications such as *The Wall Street Journal* or the business sections of local newspapers. Of course, it is necessary for information on selling prices of securities to be current as of the effective date of the appraisal. This may require searching back issues of periodicals for the needed information.

If real property is to be appraised by means of the market data approach, there are a number of sources to which the appraiser can turn for information on comparable sales. These sources include local tax assessors, the local register of deeds, title companies, local real estate brokers, and the local real estate multiple listing service. In using sources from within the real estate industry, such as real estate brokers and the multiple listing service, the appraiser must take care that the information obtained is information on actual sales, not merely information on listings for sale, or unsupported opinions about the value of property.

Information on sales of various kinds of fixed assets, such as machinery and equipment, furniture and fixtures, motor vehicles, and so on, usually can be obtained from dealers in the kind of equipment involved. Other possible sources of leads include advertisements in local newspapers and, in the case of some kinds of property, ads in periodicals that circulate nationally and are devoted to a specific industry, such as aircraft, production machinery, or data processing equipment. If the appraiser is faced with the need to obtain comparable sales information on a type of equipment or other asset with which he or she is not familiar, and if local or national dealers are not of sufficient help, the appraiser would do well to consult someone who specializes in appraisals of the type of equipment in question.

In addition to the various kinds of tangible assets, the market data approach is also applicable, in theory, to various intangible assets such as patents, copyrights, proprietary processes, and even business goodwill. However, it is extremely difficult to find comparable sales of such intangible assets, and it will be only through a rare stroke of good luck that the appraiser will be able to locate such information.

Largely because of the lack of information on comparable sales, the appraiser should find it desirable to estimate the value of intangible assets by means of one of the other approaches, such as the replacement cost approach or, more frequently, the investment value approach.

One possible exception to the foregoing consists of franchise agreements. If the franchise agreement to be appraised by means of the market data approach is one of a number of such agreements in existence, it may be possible to identify sales of other franchises that can provide information for application of the market data approach. Of course, these other sales may require adjustments to account for differences in date of sale, size of franchised territory, and so on. Preferably, comparable sales of franchises should consist of franchises issued by the same company as the franchise being appraised. Otherwise, it may be necessary to use information on franchises of other issuers but within the same industry (fast foods, quick printing, etc.).

In the search for comparable sales, the appraiser should not overlook the actual property being appraised as a source of such information. In many cases, the property being appraised has changed ownership in the relatively recent past. Provided that the circumstances of the sale meet the requirements for comparability, including having been an arm's-length transaction on the open market, recent sales of the property being appraised can be a valuable source of comparable sales information. One important advantage, of course, is that detailed information on a past sale of the property being appraised is almost certain to be more readily available than in the case of many comparable sales of other property.

Once the appraiser has succeeded in identifying the existence of what appear to be comparable sales, he or she then must proceed to gather information to establish that each such sale meets the requirements for comparability as previously discussed in this chapter and to provide the basis for any necessary adjustments to the selling prices of the comparable properties.

Preferably, the required information on the circumstances and details of each comparable sale should be determined, or at least verified, by contact with someone who was a participant in the actual sale. This may be the buyer, the seller, an attorney who represented one of the parties, or a broker who helped to bring about the sale. In some cases, it may be necessary to rely on information from published reports. However, published information may omit facts that are important from an appraisal standpoint and may distort or misstate other information. Accordingly, information from unverified published reports should be used only when the appraiser has essentially no alternative.

ADJUSTING FOR LACK OF COMPARABILITY

After identifying a number of sales of property comparable to the property being appraised, the appraiser's next step in applying the market data approach is to compare each of these comparable sales with the property being appraised and to adjust the selling price of each comparable property to compensate for significant differences disclosed by the comparison with the property being appraised.

Of course, if it were possible to find comparable sales of property identical to the property being appraised, and under circumstances corresponding to the definition of value and other conditions on which the appraisal is based, then such comparable sales could be compared directly with the property being appraised, and value conclusions could be reached without any adjustments. In practice, however, it is almost always impossible to find such identical sales; hence the necessity for adjustments.

There are a number of possible differences between the property being appraised and a sale of another property that cannot effectively be compensated for by adjustments. When one or more of these differences exists, the sale exhibiting the difference is not actually a comparable sale and must be discarded.

These differences for which it is essentially impossible to adjust, and that therefore require that the noncomparable sale be discarded entirely, include:

Sales for which the available information is not sufficient to establish comparability or to provide the basis for the appropriate quantitative adjustments

Sales that were not on an arm's-length basis

Sales that did not take place in an open market

Sales in which one or both parties were under compulsion or pressure

Sales in which the type of business or asset sold was not the same as the type of business or asset being appraised

Sales occurring in a market different from the market for the property being appraised

Sales of businesses in which the form of ownership (publicly held or closely held) differs from the form of ownership of the business being appraised

Aside from the foregoing, most other differences between comparable sales and the property being appraised can be taken into account, at least in theory, by means of adjustments. As a practical matter, the amount of the adjustment that should be made to compensate for a difference between a comparable sale and the property being appraised is frequently difficult to determine and in many cases may amount to little more than a subjective judgment on the part of the appraiser. This is particularly true when the property to be appraised is a complete business being compared with sales of other businesses.

The general rule when adjusting comparable sales in order to apply the market data approach is that all adjustments are made to the selling price of the comparable property. Thus, if the comparable property is in some respect inferior in value to the property being appraised, the actual selling price of the comparable property should be adjusted *upward* by the amount that the appraiser determines to be appropriate. Likewise, if the comparable property is superior to the property being appraised in some respect, then the selling price of the comparable property should be adjusted *downward*. It will be apparent that this process of adjusting to the property being appraised leads to an adjusted selling price for each of the comparable properties that can be compared directly with adjusted selling prices for the other comparable properties, thus leading to an estimated market value for the property being appraised.

In all cases, the amount of the adjustment to the selling price of a comparable property should reflect what the appraiser determines to be the difference in the value to the market as a result of the difference between the comparable property and the property being appraised.

Depending primarily on the nature of the difference between the comparable property and the property being appraised, adjustments to actual selling prices may be on either a percentage or a dollar basis. Thus, differences in time of sale will ordinarily result in adjustments on a percentage basis, according to the appraiser's estimate of the difference in the general state of the market between the date of actual sale of the comparable property and the effective date of the appraisal. Differences, such as in accessory features of various kinds of equipment, on the other hand, usually will be accounted for by means of dollar adjustments reflecting the appraiser's estimate of the impact on market value of the equipment of the accessories in question.

Regardless of the kind of property being appraised, whether a complete business or individual assets, adjustments for time differences between the date of each comparable sale and the effective date of the appraisal are almost always made by means a percentage adjustment to the selling price of the comparable property. The amount and direction (that is, whether positive or negative) of this percentage adjustment will reflect the appraiser's judgment regarding the effect on market prices of changes in the market between the date of the actual sale of the comparable property and the effective date of the appraisal. Thus, if the appraiser concludes that changes in the market are such that the comparable property would sell for 10% more if it were to be offered for sale at the effective date of the appraisal, he or she will adjust the actual selling price of the comparable property upward by 10%. On the other hand, if the appraiser concludes that the general market level has declined since the date on which the comparable property was sold, then the selling price of the comparable property will be adjusted downward accordingly.

Lacking other information on market trends, appraisers sometimes base the amount of adjustments for differences in time of sale on the cost of living index as computed and published by the U.S. government. Although this is a fairly common practice, it is not necessarily an accurate one, as markets for many kinds of property are strongly influenced by factors other than changes in the overall cost of living. Accordingly, adjustments for differences in time of sale should be based, whenever possible, on information about actual changes in price levels in the market for the particular kind of property being appraised.

Because of inherent uncertainty about the appropriate percentage adjustment to reflect differences in time of sale, the adjustment process becomes less accurate as the time difference requiring adjustment becomes greater. For this reason, choice of comparable sales, whenever possible, should be limited to sales occurring during a relatively short period prior to the effective date of appraisal, say during the previous two or three years, or in any event during a time period such that the required adjustment for time of sale does not exceed perhaps 10% or 20%.

Aside from differences in time of sale, the technique of adjusting for other kinds of differences between comparable sales and the property being appraised depends to at least some extent on the kind of property involved. This is evident from the following discussion of application of the market data approach to specific kinds of property.

APPLICATION OF MARKET DATA APPROACH TO APPRAISAL OF COMPLETE BUSINESSES

The appraisal of complete operating businesses represents one of the most difficult, and in a sense least rewarding, applications of the market data approach. This is because of (1) difficulties in identifying sales of businesses reasonably similar to the business being appraised, (2) problems in obtaining sufficient information regarding some or all of the comparable sales that are identified, and (3) limitations of the adjustment process as a means of compensating or correcting for differences between the property being appraised and the comparable sales, including circumstances and terms of sale in addition to differences between the properties themselves.

Typically, the appraiser who is attempting to apply the market data approach to appraisal of a complete operating business will find that, even after identifying a number of what appear to be comparable sales and gathering information on as many of these sales as possible, he or she is still faced with differences between the comparable sales and the property being appraised in such areas as time of sale, size of business, profitability, competitive position, and probably a host of other differences, such as in capital structure, historical growth rate, type of sale (stock or assets), terms of sale, and so on.

As previously indicated, differences in time of sale can ordinarily be taken into account by means of a percentage adjustment to reflect the appraiser's conclusion regarding changes in the overall market between the date of each comparable sale and the effective date of the appraisal.

Differences in size between each comparable sale and the business being appraised can be taken into account, within limits, by normalizing information to a common unit of measurement. This is also true of differences in profitability. The manner in which this is done will be apparent from the example that follows.

As for other likely differences between each comparable sale and the business being appraised, however, it is frequently impossible to arrive at meaningful adjustments on the basis of available information. Ordinarily, the best that can be done in attempting to adjust for differences such as competitive position, growth rate, type and terms of sale, capital structure, and so on, is for the appraiser to attempt to reach some overall judgment regarding each comparable sale, and to reflect this judgment, not necessarily in terms of an actual numerical adjustment, but in terms of the emphasis placed on each of the comparable sales when arriving at an estimate, according to the market data approach, of the market value of the property being appraised.

EXAMPLE OF APPRAISAL OF COMPLETE OPERATING BUSINESS BY MARKET DATA APPROACH

As an example of application of the market data approach to appraisal of a complete business, consider the following. Except for the names of the companies, the data used in the following example reflect actual sales of businesses. Accordingly, the example may be taken as being more or less typical of what the appraiser may encounter when attempting to apply the market data approach in appraising a complete business.

We have been asked to appraise a business, which we shall call Company X, that manufactures low-priced sheet metal products for sale to home accessory stores serving the consumer market. Our study of Company X has led us to conclude that it is a relatively stable business, with a steady but moderate rate of historical growth in both sales and earnings. From this study, we have concluded that the financial performance of Company X during the years immediately preceding the date of appraisal is representative of the company's long-term financial performance and is an appropriate basis on which to compare Company X with other companies in the same business.

Company X's financial performance during the year immediately prior to the date of appraisal included total sales of $5.0 million, with a net operating profit (pretax) of approximately $1.0 million and an after-tax profit of $0.5 million.

From a search of published sources, we have identified five other companies, each of which also manufactures sheet metal products for a market similar to that of Company X, which have actually been sold within the relatively recent past. Although the amount of detailed information that is available on each of these five comparable sales is limited, we have concluded that the five companies are indeed comparable to Company X and that available information on the five sales does provide an appropriate basis for estimating the market value of Company X.

Designating the five comparable companies as Companies A through E, and putting the available information in tabular form, along with similar information for Company X, we arrive at the following:

	Annual Sales (in millions)	Annual Profit (in millions)	Selling Price (in millions)	Date of Sale
Company A	$ 7.6	$0.5	$3.3	March 19X1
Company B	$ 3.1	$0.2	$2.1	February 19X2
Company C	$21.2	$0.9	$5.0	December 19X0
Company D	$ 7.8	$0.3	$3.5	October 19X1
Company E	$11.6	$0.2	$6.3	June 19X2
Company X	$ 5.0	$0.5	?	December 19X2

Before proceeding further, there are two observations that may be made with respect to the above table.

The first is that the figures for annual profit for the various companies are not identified as being either before-tax or after-tax figures. In almost all cases, however, published information on profits will be in terms of profit after taxes, and, accordingly, this may be assumed to be the case with the published information on Companies A through E. Thus, even though comparisons on the basis of net operating profit before taxes are considered somewhat more meaningful from an appraisal standpoint than comparisons based on after-tax profits, in the present situation (and in many other practical applications of the market data approach to appraisal of businesses) we have no choice but to compare profit on an after-tax basis. For this reason, the profit as shown in the above table for the company being appraised is also the after-tax profit.

The second observation regarding the table is that all of the dollar figures have been rounded to the nearest $0.1 million. Such rounding is common with published figures but in the present instance does no particular harm, as the accuracy of the appraisal process itself is such that carrying out results to more than two or three significant figures would not be justified.

Reviewing the information on the sales of Companies A through E and comparing this information with the information on Company X, it is by no means immediately apparent what conclusions should be drawn, from the information on the five comparable sales, about the market value of Company X. The five comparable companies vary over a range of roughly 7 to 1 in annual sales, 5 to 1 in annual profit, and 3 to 1 in selling price.

To compensate for these differences in the size of the various companies, the information can be normalized to a common basis by using ratios in place of actual dollar figures. In the present instance, the appropriate ratios are the ratio of (1) selling price to annual sales and (2) selling price to annual net of the individual companies.

First, however, the selling prices of the five companies should be adjusted to account for differences in time of sale. We decided that, on the basis of the available information, an appropriate adjustment to reflect changes in market conditions during the period covered by the five sales would be an adjustment of 10% per year, compounded.

The resulting adjustments for time of sale, along with the respective ratios of selling price to annual sales volume, and selling price to annual profit, are shown in Exhibit 11.

Scanning the figures for ratios of adjusted selling price to annual sales as shown in the exhibit, it will be seen that, for the five comparable companies, selling prices covered a range from 0.29 times annual sales to 0.74 times annual sales, a range of roughly 2.5 to 1. Certainly such a range of values does not suggest a high degree of accuracy in terms of using the selling prices of the comparable companies to determine the market value of Company X.

Scanning the ratios of adjusted price to annual profit as shown in the table, we find that the situation is even worse. Ratios of adjusted selling price to

Exhibit 11
SUMMARY OF COMPARABLE SALES

	Annual Sales (in millions)	Annual Profit (in millions)	Selling Price (in millions) Actual	Selling Price (in millions) Adjusted to Dec. 19X2	Adjusted Selling Price Annual Sales	Adjusted Selling Price Annual Profit
Company A	$ 7.6	$0.5	$3.3	$3.9	0.51	7.8
Company B	$ 3.1	$0.2	$2.1	$2.3	0.74	11.5
Company C	$21.2	$0.9	$5.0	$6.1	0.29	6.8
Company D	$ 7.8	$0.3	$3.5	$3.9	0.50	13.0
Company E	$11.6	$0.2	$6.3	$6.6	0.57	33.0

annual profit range from a maximum of 33.0 to a minimum of 6.8, a range of almost 5 to 1.

However, it is also apparent from the table that there must have been something very unusual about Company E or about the circumstances of its sale. Specifically, Company E had an annual profit of only $0.2 million on sales of $11.6 million. This is the worst profit performance of any of the five comparable companies, and yet Company E sold for the highest price of any of the five companies.

Without knowing the reason for this unusual situation involving Company E, it is apparent that there must have been something about the situation—such as a sale that did not take place in the open market or was not on an arm's-length basis—such that the information on Company E is almost certainly not valid as a basis for estimating the market value of the company being appraised. That is, it is concluded from the available information on Company E that it is not a comparable situation. Accordingly, the data regarding the sale of Company E will be discarded. (In addition to being logical under the circumstances, the discarding of Company E from the assemblage of data is consistent with mathematical principles, which allow exclusion of sports from a statistical population before attempting to draw conclusions from the data.)

Having determined that the sale of Company E is not in fact a comparable situation, the next logical stop in attempting to arrive at an estimate of the value of Company X is to compute the arithmetic mean (average) of the two ratios for the remaining four companies, Companies A through D.

This leads to the following:

	$\dfrac{\text{Adjusted Selling Price}}{\text{Annual Sales}}$	$\dfrac{\text{Adjusted Selling Price}}{\text{Annual Profit}}$
Company A	0.51	7.8
Company B	0.74	11.5
Company C	0.29	6.8
Company D	0.50	13.0
Arithmetic mean	0.51	9.8

The remaining step in using the information on sales of the four comparable companies to estimate the market value of Company X is to apply the average ratios for the four comparable sales to the applicable information on the annual sales and annual profit, respectively, of Company X.

Thus, application of the average ratio of adjusted selling price to annual sales leads to an estimated market value for Company X of

indicated value of Company X = 0.51 × $5.0 million = $2.55 million

Similarly, application to Company X of the average ratio of adjusted selling price to annual profit leads to

indicated value of Company X = 9.8 × $0.5 million = $4.90 million

Thus, depending on which of the two average ratios is used, Company X has an estimated market value of either $2.55 million or $4.90 million. Further, the variation in the individual ratios making up each of the two average ratios is such that it is not reasonable to place a high degree of confidence in results obtained by either method.

Considering that profits are more important to most buyers of businesses than sales volume, it is reasonable to place greater confidence in value estimates arrived at by considering profits than in estimates based on sales volume. In the present instance, this means that the appraiser can have somewhat more confidence in the value estimate of $4.90 million for Company X, as based on the average profit ratio of the four comparable companies, than in the value estimate of $2.55 million reached on the basis of the average sales volume ratio. It must be pointed out again, however, that neither of these estimates deserves a high degree of confidence on the part of the appraiser.

As previously stated, the example just given is more or less typical of what the appraiser is likely to encounter when attempting to use the market data approach to estimate the value of a complete business. Had the company being appraised been a smaller business than Company X, the appraiser would have found it even more difficult to identify and obtain information on comparable sales, since sales of small businesses are seldom reported in publications.

It should be evident from the foregoing example why the market data approach is much less valuable and is less often applied in appraising businesses than it is in appraising real property.

APPLICATION OF MARKET DATA APPROACH TO APPRAISAL OF SECURITIES

The market data approach may be used to estimate the value of securities, either as a step in applying the replacement cost approach (see Chapter 9) to appraise a business whose assets include securities, or when the securities are themselves the property the appraiser has been asked to appraise.

If the securities in question are traded on a sufficiently wide market and with sufficient frequency as to be included in securities price information as available in various financial periodicals, then the appraiser's best source of information on comparable sales is to consult issues of the appropriate financial periodicals for the effective date of the appraisal, or as close thereto as possible. Prices as reported in such periodicals usually can be used directly by the appraiser as the estimated market value of the securities in question.

In some cases, abnormal conditions, such as short-term market fluctuations or unusually large blocks of securities traded, can introduce perturbations into an otherwise reasonably stable market price. The possible existence of such short-term phenomena can be determined by reviewing information on prices at which the securities in question traded over a period of time prior to and, if feasible, a period of time subsequent to the effective date of the appraisal.

If the securities whose value is to be determined by the market data approach are not among those for which price information is available from published sources, the appraiser may be able to obtain useful information on market prices by contacting the issuer of the securities, especially if the issuer is also active in the market for the securities.

Otherwise, application of the market data approach to estimating the value of securities for which there appears to be no active market may require that the appraiser base the estimate of the value of the securities being appraised on market information for other securities that are similar to the securities being appraised in such respects as yield (interest rate, dividends paid, etc.), relative safety of principal, and so on. In making such comparisons, yield normally will be expressed as a percentage of selling price, and at least in the case of some securities, comparisons of relative degree of risk can be made with the aid of information such as Moody's ratings of bonds.

Should the appraiser fail to locate the information needed to estimate the market value of securities by means of the market data approach, he or she will then ordinarily make the value estimate by some other method, such as by estimating the value of underlying assets.

APPLICATION OF MARKET DATA APPROACH TO APPRAISAL OF REAL PROPERTY

Use of the market data approach to estimate the value of real property has been well developed and is described in considerable detail in books and other literature dealing with the appraisal of real estate.

In appraising land, information on prices of comparable sales will ordinarily be normalized to a per acre, per square foot, or equivalent basis, and thus used in conjunction with appropriate adjustments for time of sale to estimate the value of the land that is being appraised.

Although not often involved in a business appraisal, individual residences are perhaps the easiest kind of real property to appraise by means of the market data approach. Because of their relatively large number, it is ordinarily easy for the appraiser to identify sales of property comparable to the property being appraised and, having done so, to obtain the necessary information regarding each comparable sale and apply to the appropriate adjustments.

APPLICATION OF MARKET DATA APPROACH TO APPRAISAL OF OTHER TANGIBLE FIXED ASSETS

The market data approach is commonly used to estimate the value of various business assets such as machinery, office equipment, furniture, motor vehicles, and so on. This may occur either as a means of estimating the value of individual assets when using the replacement cost approach to arrive at the estimated value of a complete business or when assets of the type mentioned are themselves the property being appraised.

Sales of items similar to the property to be appraised are identified from the appropriate sources, such as through contact with used equipment dealers, and information on actual selling prices is then adjusted as applicable to account for differences such as in time of sale (ordinarily a percentage adjustment), condition of equipment (either a percentage or a dollar adjustment), special features and accessories (usually a dollar adjustment), and so on.

Automobiles and some of the more common types of trucks represent a special case from the standpoint of application of the market data approach, in that what amounts to information on comparable sales is available in the form of various published guides that are utilized by dealers to assist them in setting prices. The price information in these guides is, in effect, a distillation of market data for a large number of different makes, models, and ages of motor vehicles. In making an appraisal that includes motor vehicles listed in one of these guides, the appraiser ordinarily can use price information contained in the guide as a direct indication of the value of property being appraised. Most of the guides even provide a range of prices to account for differences in physical condition of the vehicles, various accessories with which they may be equipped, and other factors.

In appraising various kinds of fixed assets, one of the best sources of price information for comparison purposes consists of information on the actual asset being appraised. The price paid for the asset when it was acquired can be adjusted to account for various factors such as age and condition of the asset and market trends (inflation) since it was acquired, the resulting adjusted figure being taken as indicative of the market value of the asset in question at the date of appraisal. Like all adjustments for time differences, adjustments to acquisition prices of the actual asset being appraised are most reliable when they cover only a relatively short period of time. If the asset in question was acquired five, ten, or more years ago, a preferable means for arriving at an estimate of its present value would be through information on actual recent sales of similar items.

APPLICATION OF MARKET DATA APPROACH TO APPRAISAL OF INTANGIBLES

As previously explained, it is seldom possible to obtain the information that would be needed to apply the market data approach to estimate the value of intangibles such as patents, copyrights, proprietary processes, customer lists, and so on. Instead, the values of these assets ordinarily must be estimated by one of the other approaches, usually the investment value approach.

However, there is one type of intangible asset whose market value can be estimated by means of the market data approach. Franchise agreements and similar contracts granting rights can be appraised by means of the market data approach if information is available on actual sales of other franchises, either identical to the one being appraised or sufficiently similar to make it feasible to apply the appropriate adjustments.

Sales of franchises can be identified through contact with the issuer of the franchise to be appraised or with holders of similar franchises. Once sales of comparable franchises have been identified and the necessary information on the details and circumstances of each sale has been obtained, appropriate adjustments for differences, such as in time of sale, size of territory covered by each franchise, and relative profitability (especially in the case of franchises for similar but not identical services or products), can be applied to give the appraiser a basis for estimating the value of the franchise being appraised.

P/E RATIOS OF PUBLICLY TRADED STOCKS

A widely used method of estimating the value of businesses that is in effect an application of the market data approach involves the use of so-called P/E ratios (price-to-earnings ratios) of publicly traded stocks, especially those listed on major exchanges such as the New York Stock Exchange.

The theory underlying this method is that the relationship between the earnings of a publicly traded company and the market price of its common stock is a good indication of the value of the company as a whole, and that this relationship as it exists for publicly traded companies can be applied directly to determine the value of a company whose stock may be closely held and may not be traded at all. If there are a number of companies engaged in a given line of business whose stock is traded on the New York Stock Exchange, and if the ratio of the stock selling price to the company's annual earnings averages, say, 7, then the theory holds that another company engaged in the same line of business should have a value equal to about 7 times its annual earnings.

Notwithstanding the relative popularity of this means of estimating the value of companies whose stock is not publicly traded, the basic theory is unsound in a number of respects.

In the first place, the P/E ratio method of pricing violates the requirements of the Principle of Substitution, to the effect that a comparable property should represent an equally desirable substitute for the property being appraised. The fact is that a block of shares of common stock in a publicly owned company is seldom a substitute in any sense for a complete smaller business, even though they may be involved in the same industry. Rather, the buyer of a block of shares in a publicly owned company almost always regards his or her purchase as an investment in securities, more than acquisition of an ownership interest in a business. Thus, the P/E ratio approach to estimating the value of a closely held business is contrary to the Principle of Substitution.

A second fallacy in the P/E ratio approach is that, even if the buyer of a block of shares in a publicly held company makes the purchase with the viewpoint of acquiring an ownership interest in the business, the value of a small fractional ownership interest is seldom a reliable indication of the value of the entire company. This is evident, if in no other way, from the wide discrepancy between prices actually paid by corporate buyers when acquiring complete companies as compared to the per share prices at which the acquired company's stock was traded on the open market immediately before information on the pending acquisition became available.

For the foregoing and other reasons, the use of P/E ratios of the stock of publicly held companies is generally not a valid means for estimating the market value of a complete business, even though engaged in the same industry or line of activity.

The best that can be said for the P/E ratio method is that fluctuations in the P/E ratios of stocks in a given industry, to the extent that these fluctuations can be distinguished and separated from fluctuations in the stock market as a whole, may provide an indication of the relative economic health, at least in the view of the investing public, of the industry in question. However, prices of publicly traded stocks are influenced by so many other factors, not directly pertinent to the economic health of a given industry or to the total value of the complete company, as to make the P/E ratio method almost useless as a means of appraising closely held businesses.

RULES OF THUMB

There is one other rather popular method of estimating the value of a business that should be mentioned in any discussion of the market data approach. This is the use of so-called rules of thumb.

A rule of thumb is a mathematical relationship between or among variables, based on experience, observation, empirical evidence, hearsay, or a combination of these. In its simplest form, a rule of thumb as applied to determining the value of a business might express, for example, a purported relationship between the annual sales volume of a business and the market value of the entire business.

The P/E ratio method of estimating the value of a business as just discussed is, in effect, a rule of thumb. The so-called gross rents multiplier, often used in estimating the value of certain types of commercial real estate, is another example of a rule of thumb.

The entire subject of rules of thumb as applied in appraising businesses is a troublesome one. This is because, although some rules of thumb may be valid when applied under the proper circumstances, most rules of thumb are at best oversimplifications and, at worst, may be based on totally fallacious information or no information at all.

That most rules of thumb are at least oversimplifications is evident from considering the contrast between the typical rule of thumb, which expresses a supposed value relationship based on a single parameter of a business (such as the number of customers served daily in a restaurant), and the very large number of variables that, as is evident from this book, actually contribute to determining the market value of a business.

Also, almost all rules of thumb are based on circumstances and assumptions that, although contributing to the rule of thumb, are not explicitly included in the rule as stated. Should one or more of these (frequently unstated) conditions not be present or assumptions not apply in a given situation, then the rule will be invalid to that extent. Thus, even though use of a gross rents multiplier may be an appropriate means for estimating the market value of a rental apartment building in most circumstances, the existence of abnormally depressed rents, for example, caused by excessive competition or governmental rent control, can almost totally destroy the validity of the resulting value estimate.

Notwithstanding their numerous and more or less serious limitations, rules of thumb nevertheless do have at least some place in the appraisal of businesses. In particular, a rule of thumb may be useful as a rough check on a value estimate reached by other more accurate means or, less desirably, as the sole means for arriving at a rough estimate of the value of a business in instances in which no other information is available.

A discussion of rules of thumb as applied to estimating the value of each of several dozen different kinds of more or less common businesses appears in the book *Guide to Buying or Selling a Business* by James M. Hansen (Grenadier Press, Mercer Island, Washington, 1979).

SUMMARY OF ADVANTAGES AND DISADVANTAGES OF MARKET DATA APPROACH

The greatest single advantage of the market data approach to estimating the value of property is that it uses information taken directly from the market. Thus, it provides the most direct approach to estimating the market value of property which, of course, is the purpose of the great majority of appraisals.

Another advantage of the market data approach is that it is easily understood and its significance is readily grasped by persons who are not otherwise acquainted with appraisal theory. For this reason alone, many appraisers prefer to make some mention in their appraisal reports of the market data approach, even though they may have found that it actually contributes little or nothing to their final estimate of the value of the property being appraised.

As applied to appraisal of certain types of assets, such as some kinds of real property, automobiles, and some kinds of machinery, furniture, and the like, the market data approach has the further advantage that information on comparable sales may be available rather readily. Thus, the market data approach is often used to estimate the value of individual assets, as when a complete business is being appraised by one of the other approaches, such as the replacement cost approach.

Probably the greatest single disadvantage of the market data approach is that it requires a reasonably active market for the type of property being appraised.

This requirement for an active market is most serious when the property being appraised is a complete business. In such a case, it is almost always very difficult, and sometimes totally impossible, to identify sales of businesses that could be considered to be comparable to the business being appraised, and to obtain the necessary information regarding the circumstances and terms of sale of these comparable businesses.

Another disadvantage of the market data approach arises from the necessity for making adjustments to selling prices in an effort to compensate for differences between the comparable property and the property being appraised. The more extensive the differences involved, and therefore the more extensive the adjustments needed to compensate for their effect on value, the greater the error that is likely to be introduced in the resulting value conclusion.

Finally, the market data approach is almost never applicable, for reasons related primarily to the nonexistence of information on comparable sales, to estimating the value of most kinds of intangibles. Instead, when the value of an intangible is to be estimated, either separately or as part of an estimate of the value of a complete business, it is almost always necessary to resort to one of the other approaches, most often the investment value approach.

9
Analyzing the Facts— The Replacement Cost Approach

9

Analyzing the Facts— The Replacement Cost Approach

THE REPLACEMENT COST APPROACH

The *replacement cost approach* is the second of the three most widely recognized approaches to estimating economic value. The replacement cost approach yields a figure for estimated value of property that is sometimes referred to as its replacement value.

Whereas the market data approach discussed in Chapter 8 is a market-oriented method of estimating value, the replacement cost approach is an asset-oriented method. Another unique aspect of the replacement cost approach is that it is the only one of the three principal approaches that reaches the estimate of total value by a process of summation; the result of each of the other two principal approaches is a single figure for the total value of the business or other property being appraised, not broken down into component parts as it is with the replacement cost approach.

SUMMARY OF REPLACEMENT COST APPROACH

Like the other two major approaches to estimating value, the replacement cost approach has its theoretical basis in the Principle of Substitution.

With the replacement cost approach, the assumption is made that one form of equally desirable substitute for the property being appraised would be an exact duplicate of the property itself. Accordingly, the replacement cost approach attempts to estimate the cost of duplicating the business or other property being appraised, item by item, asset by asset, liability by liability.

Because of the reasonable assumption that no potential buyer of a business would pay more for the business than the cost of duplicating it, the value estimate as determined by the replacement cost approach is sometimes said to represent the upper limit on the actual value of the business. While valid as applied to residential real estate, for example, the upper limit viewpoint overlooks an important aspect of the replacement cost approach as applied to valuation of businesses and many other kinds of income-producing property.

In practical application, the replacement cost approach is essentially limited to providing the appraiser with an estimate of the cost of replacing, or duplicating, the tangible assets (and liabilities) of the business or other property. This is because there is usually no reasonable way of arriving at an estimate of the cost of replacing such intangibles as patents, copyrights, customer lists, proprietary processes, business goodwill, and so on. Accordingly, the total estimated value as reached by the replacement cost approach either omits the value of whatever intangibles exist or provides for them by means of values estimated by one of the other approaches.

Because a substantial part of the total value of most businesses consists of intangibles (especially goodwill), the value of a business as estimated according to the replacement cost approach does not necessarily represent the upper limit on its actual value. Rather, if the value estimate reached by the replacement cost approach includes tangible items only, then it can be assumed to represent the upper limit of the value of the tangible assets and liabilities of the business. On the other hand, if the estimated value does include provision for the value of intangibles (presumably as a result of intangible value estimates made by one of the other approaches), then the value of the business as estimated by the replacement cost approach reflects the value of the total business according to one estimating approach. It is not necessarily either an upper or a lower limit on the true value of the business.

In brief, application of the replacement cost approach in appraising businesses involves an item-by-item, or in some cases category-by-category, estimate of the cost of replacing each of the various contributing elements of the property being appraised with other items of like kind and in similar condition (of similar utility). The estimated replacement costs of the individual items are then totaled to determine the estimated replacement cost of all elements of the property in aggregate. If the definition of the property to be appraised is such that liabilities are to be taken into account, the estimated value of each existing liability is determined, and the total value of all liabilities is then subtracted from the total estimated cost of replacing assets, to arrive at a net estimated value for the business according to the replacement cost approach.

In practical application of the replacement cost approach, there are a number of precautions that must be observed by the appraiser, as explained in the following portions of this chapter.

APPLICATION OF REPLACEMENT COST APPROACH IN BUSINESS APPRAISING

The replacement cost approach can be applied to estimate the value of complete businesses and of various business assets and asset groupings.

The replacement cost approach is also applicable, of course, to estimating the value of individual business assets. When so applied, however, it frequently becomes almost indistinguishable from the market data approach.

As applied to estimating the value of complete businesses, the replacement cost approach is especially powerful in estimating the value of businesses of a nonoperating nature. The replacement cost approach can provide the best available indication of the value of a business whose principal function is to manage income-producing assets, so-called holding companies. Since such businesses usually involve little or no goodwill as such, with essentially all of their earning power residing directly in the various assets they own, the previously mentioned limitation of the replacement cost approach regarding intangible asset values is of little or no importance. Since the assets owned by many such holding companies are such that the cost of replacing them can be estimated with a relatively high degree of accuracy, the replacement cost approach frequently offers the best method for estimating the market value of such companies.

The replacement cost approach is especially powerful when making value estimates for insurance-related purposes. This is because the majority of definitions of value as used for insurance purposes reflect what is, in effect, replacement cost of tangible assets rather than actual market value or one of the other kinds of value.

Notwithstanding the previously mentioned limitations of the replacement cost approach relative to the value of intangibles, the approach is still useful in appraising conventional operating businesses.

Under normal circumstances, application of the replacement cost approach will provide the appraiser with a reasonably reliable figure for the cost of replacing the tangible assets of the business being appraised. Use of the replacement cost approach to estimate the value of tangible assets essentially limits the appraiser's uncertainty about the total value of the business to that portion of the total value represented by intangibles. Depending on the particular business being appraised, the value of intangibles may make up a relatively small (or, on the other hand, sometimes a relatively large) portion of the total value.

The value of a business as estimated by the replacement cost approach is also useful to the appraiser when making comparisons between businesses, as when applying the market data approach or when attempting to select an appropriate capitalization rate for use with the investment value approach. That is, as between two businesses that are otherwise similar, the one having the greater tangible asset value will generally involve less downside risk, will be better able to withstand periods of business adversity, and otherwise will tend to be superior, from a value standpoint in particular, to an otherwise similar business but one with lower tangible asset values.

For the foregoing and other reasons, most appraisers include the replacement cost approach among the approaches they use when appraising complete operating businesses.

STEPS IN APPLYING THE REPLACEMENT COST APPROACH

In estimating the value of a business or other property by means of the replacement cost approach, the appraiser proceeds as follows:

1. The appraiser prepares a list of all assets, either individually or by category, that are to be included in the business or other property as

appraised. If the appraisal is one that is also to take liabilities into account, these are listed as well.

2. The appraiser then eliminates from the list any assets that, although they may actually be part of the business or other property, do not contribute to its economic performance.

3. Next, an estimate is made of the current cost to replace each asset, or the assets in each asset category, with a functionally equivalent substitute. If existing liabilities are to be taken into account, an estimate is also made of the current value of each such liability.

4. Finally, the estimated costs to replace individual assets or asset categories are added to determine the total estimated replacement cost of all assets in aggregate. If liabilities are part of the property as it is to be appraised, the current values of such liabilities are also totaled, and this total is subtracted from the total replacement cost of the assets. The result is the estimated value of the business or other property according to the replacement cost approach.

PREPARING THE LIST OF ASSETS

The first step in estimating the value of a business according to the replacement cost approach is to prepare a list of all the assets of the business or other property to be appraised. If some or all of the liabilities of the business are to be included in the appraisal, these liabilities also should be listed.

The best starting point for preparing the list of assets (and of liabilities, if applicable) is a current balance sheet for the business. This should be the economic balance sheet for the business, if one has been prepared as described in Chapter 7. Otherwise, the current accountants' balance sheet can be used, although it will require somewhat more work from the appraiser.

If the business does not have a balance sheet, as may sometimes be the case with very small businesses, then the appraiser should prepare the list of assets (and liabilities, if applicable) from information obtained from such sources as interviews with the owners and key employees of the business, physical inspection of the business premises, and examination of income tax returns for the business. The appraiser will find it convenient, when preparing such a list of assets and liabilities for a business that does not have any form of balance sheet, to follow the typical balance sheet format as illustrated in Chapters 6 and 7. Although preparing the list of assets and liabilities from scratch involves more work for the appraiser than if a balance sheet were already available, it usually will be necessary only in the case of very small businesses, which typically have only a limited number of individual assets and liabilities.

Whatever starting point the appraiser uses when preparing the list of assets in connection with the replacement cost approach, he or she should take care to ensure that the final list actually includes all contributing assets of the business. In particular, the appraiser must take care that the final list includes assets that, for one reason or another, do not appear either on the balance sheet of the business or in the related detailed records such as fixed asset depreciation schedules.

In searching for assets that may not be represented on the balance sheet of the business but that nevertheless should be taken into account in estimating the value of the business by the replacement cost approach, the appraiser should pay particular attention to the following:

Assets that, because they are of an intangible nature, do not appear on the accountants' balance sheet. Examples include patents, copyrights, various types of contracts, customer lists, proprietary processes, formulas, and, of course, goodwill.

Machinery, equipment, furniture, vehicles, and other so-called fixed assets that, having been fully depreciated for tax purposes, are no longer reflected in the asset values as shown on the accountants' balance sheet for the business. Such fully depreciated assets may or may not still be listed in the inventory of fixed assets that is part of the working papers the accountant uses to calculate fixed asset depreciation. In any event, such fully depreciated assets should be included in the list of assets prepared as a basis for application of the replacement cost approach, so long as the assets in question are still actually in use and are still contributing to the overall economic performance of the business.

Assets that, although contributing to the performance of the business on a long-term basis, were treated as a current operating expense when they were purchased or otherwise acquired, and that therefore have never been reflected in the balance sheet of the business. Possible examples include research and development expense, cost of installing various items of machinery or equipment, tooling or accessories for items of equipment that do appear on the balance sheet, computer programs, mailing lists and similar information compiled with in-house labor, hand tools, various minor items of office equipment, and so on.

ELIMINATION OF NONCONTRIBUTING ASSETS AND LIABILITIES

After the list of assets and liabilities of the business or other property to be appraised has been completed, care having been taken to ensure that the list includes all assets even though they may not be reflected in the balance sheet of the business, the next step in applying the replacement cost approach is to go over the list to eliminate any assets that are not currently contributing to the economic performance of the business. This includes elimination of any liabilities of such nature that they do not affect the replacement cost of the total business.

In identifying any existing assets that do not actually contribute to the performance of the business, the appraiser's principal clue will be whether the asset is actually in use by the business.

Identification of any noncontributing assets involves application of the appraiser's understanding of the operation of the business, including knowledge of the internal facts as covered in Chapter 5, supplemented by a combination of the appraiser's personal observation and interviews with the owners and key employees of the business.

Although noncontributing assets can be found in any asset category, special attention should be paid to the following:

Accounts receivable: Are all of the receivables actually collectible, or does some portion of the total amount of receivables as shown on the balance sheet of the business reflect receivables that are not likely ever to be collected? If the balance sheet entry for accounts receivable includes a reserve for uncollectible accounts or equivalent, knowledge of the basis on which this amount was determined can help the appraiser to decide whether it represents adequate allowance for uncollectibles. Otherwise, the appraiser may find it desirable to review the actual list of receivables, or at least the larger ones, and to reach a judgment based on the circumstances in each instance of whether or not the amount shown as being receivable is likely to be collectible.

Securities: If the list of assets includes securities of another issuer, do they actually contribute to the value of the business? Is there a market for the securities such that, if desired, they could be sold without undue delay? If not, do they provide income, such as in the form of dividends or interest, sufficient to justify their inclusion among the assets of the business being appraised? Especially suspect as noncontributing assets are securities of closely held businesses, including subsidiaries of affiliates of the business being appraised, for which there is no ready market.

Inventory: Many businesses have obsolete inventory for which there is no market or other economically sound application, even though the inventory may be included among the inventory shown on the balance sheet of the business. Such noncontributing inventory may consist of raw material, work in process, finished goods, or a combination. Although the existence of obsolete inventory frequently can be determined through discussion with key executives of the business, the appraiser sometimes may find it desirable to resort to additional sources of information. These may include, for example, the inventory records of the business showing when the various items of inventory were acquired or completed, conversations with stockroom personnel (who will generally know which inventory is not moving, even though no one else in the company may be aware of that fact), and physical inspection of inventory by the appraiser to locate items that, through accumulation of dust or other clues, give evidence of long periods of inactivity.

Machinery, equipment, and so on: Within the broad category of fixed assets, there may be items that, although still contributing to the figures for fixed asset values as shown on the balance sheet of the business, are actually no longer in use. Such items usually can be identified either through discussions with key personnel of the business or from a physical inspection of the business premises.

Intangible assets: If intangible assets are included in the list of assets for purposes of the replacement cost approach, each such asset should be reviewed to verify that it is actually in use and contributing to the economic performance of the business. This applies to such assets as patents, copyrights, customer lists, and the like. Goodwill is a special case, requiring special consideration as explained later in this chapter and in Chapter 10.

If liabilities are to be taken into account in arriving at the final value estimate, then each liability on the list prepared for application of the replacement cost approach must be reviewed to determine whether it actually contributes (in a negative sense, in the case of liabilities) to the economic value of the business. Particularly suspect are liabilities arising out of debts to the owners of the business, or to subsidiary, parent, or otherwise affiliated business entities. The key test is whether each such liability represents a debt that is actually intended to be paid, or whether it represents only a bookkeeping entry for convenience or other reasons.

ESTIMATING REPLACEMENT COSTS

After a list of assets (and possibly liabilities) has been prepared and non-contributing assets (and liabilities) have been eliminated from the list, the next step is to arrive at an estimate of the replacement cost of each asset remaining on the list.

If an economic balance sheet has been prepared for the business, many of the required estimates will already be available. However, the estimated values as shown on the economic balance sheet still will need to be checked against the appropriate criteria, to ensure that the definition of value as used in preparing the economic balance sheet is the same one that applies for purposes of the replacement cost approach.

If there is no economic balance sheet for the business, then the replacement costs of the various assets can be estimated with the help of the suggestions given in Chapters 6 and 7 and in this chapter.

The process of estimating the replacement cost of individual assets of a business and then adding the individual figures to arrive at the estimated value of the complete business according to the replacement cost approach is an application of what is sometimes called the Principle of Contribution. According to the Principle of Contribution, *the value of an individual item as part of a complete enterprise is measured by the contribution of the item to the net return of the enterprise.* (It will be noted that this is similar to the familiar principle that the whole is equal to the sum of its parts.)

The elimination of noncontributing assets from the total list of assets, which was the second step in application of the replacement cost approach, is a reflection of this Principle of Contribution. An item that is not contributing to the results produced by an enterprise has no value to the enterprise.

In the replacement cost approach, the value of each individual item as a part of the total business is expressed in terms of the estimated cost of replacing that item. To satisfy the Principle of Contribution, these estimated replacement costs should meet a number of requirements, in addition to the requirement that noncontributing items be eliminated entirely. These requirements include:

The values of individual assets, as reflected by their estimated replacement costs, should be in terms of value to an ongoing business. That is, the figures should not reflect so-called liquidation values, which are almost always significantly lower than value to an ongoing business.

The replacement cost of an item as estimated for purposes of the replacement cost approach should represent the cost of replacing the existing item with one of like utility, which, depending on circumstances, may or may not consist of a physically identical item.

In the case of an item, such as machinery or equipment, that must be installed, modified, or improved (such as by the addition of tooling) before it can be put to use, the estimated replacement cost of the item should include all costs necessary to put the item to use.

In the case of items that, although contributing to some extent to the overall result of the enterprise, are significantly underutilized in comparison with the total capability of the item, there are two possibilities relative to the amount of the replacement cost to be used for purposes of the replacement cost approach. The appraiser should attempt to identify a substitute item or technique, presumably less costly than the actual item in use, capable of producing the desired result but without being significantly underutilized. The cost of this substitute item should then be used in the replacement cost approach in place of the actual (underutilized) item. However, if the appraiser is unsuccessful in finding a substitute item capable of the desired result, then the full cost of the existing underutilized item should be used as its replacement cost for purposes of the replacement cost approach.

Exhibit 12 summarizes the principal sources of replacement cost estimates for the various categories of assets and liabilities of a business.

ADVANTAGES AND DISADVANTAGES OF REPLACEMENT COST APPROACH

Although it requires a significant amount of effort to arrive at the estimated values for the individual assets (and liabilities) of a business, the replacement

Exhibit 12
SOURCES OF REPLACEMENT COST ESTIMATES FOR USE WITH THE REPLACEMENT COST APPROACH

Source of Replacement Cost Estimate

	Preferred Source	Alternative Source(s)
ASSETS		
Cash	Actual amount	
Accounts receivable	Economic balance sheet	Actual amount less provision for uncollectible portion
Securities	Market data approach	Investment value approach
Inventory	Current cost to replace less provision for obsolete inventory	Economic balance sheet Accountants' balance sheet
Prepaid expenses	Actual amount	
Fixed assets	Market data approach	Current cost to replace new, less provision for observed depreciation
Intangible assets (if included)	Investment value approach	Cost to create approach
LIABILITIES (if included)	Actual amount less any liabilities whose repayment is not actually contemplated	

cost approach is potentially the most accurate of the three principal approaches to estimating economic value. This is particularly true as far as tangible asset values are concerned.

Another advantage of the replacement cost approach is that it is more likely to reflect the actual economic value of a business than does book value as shown on an accountants' balance sheet.

The replacement cost approach is frequently the best method for estimating the value of nonoperating businesses, such as so-called holding companies, as well as certain other asset-heavy businesses, such as hotels and motels, and some types of natural resource businesses, such as mining.

Also, the replacement cost approach offers a method for valuing unique property, such as special-purpose buildings, nonprofit organizations, and so on, where other valuation approaches do not apply and cannot be used.

In the case of appraisals for insurance-related purposes, the replacement cost approach has the further advantage that it can lead directly to an estimate of value that is consistent with the definition of value customarily used for insurance purposes.

Against the foregoing advantages, the replacement cost approach also has certain disadvantages.

From the standpoint of appraising ongoing businesses, the most serious disadvantage of the replacement cost approach is that the value indication it provides is ordinarily limited to tangible asset values and fails to take account of the earning power of the business, which is usually an important part of its total value. Intangible values cannot ordinarily be estimated by means of the replacement cost approach, and if they are included at all in the total value estimate as reached by this approach, they must be determined by another method, such as the investment value approach.

Another disadvantage of the replacement cost approach is that, while it represents one possible application of the Principle of Substitution, the process of duplicating a business as assumed by the replacement cost approach is not always the best way of finding a substitute for the business in an economic sense.

Still another disadvantage of the replacement cost approach is that it is frequently more time-consuming for the appraiser than either the market data approach or the investment value approach.

10

Analyzing the Facts—
The Investment Value
Approach

10

Analyzing the Facts— The Investment Value Approach

THE INVESTMENT VALUE APPROACH

The *investment value approach* is the third widely recognized approach to estimating economic value. It is sometimes called the income approach.

Whereas the market data approach is a market-oriented method and the replacement cost approach is an asset-oriented method, the investment value approach is an income-oriented method of estimating economic value. The investment value approach considers a business or other income-producing property more or less as though it were a money machine, a mechanism whose purpose is to produce money for its owner.

Essentially, the investment value approach involves estimating the amount of future income that will be produced by a business or other investment, determining the applicable relationship between income and value, and then converting the estimated income into an estimate of value.

SUMMARY OF INVESTMENT VALUE APPROACH

Like the other approaches to estimating economic value, the investment value approach is based on the Principle of Substitution. As compared to the other approaches, however, the investment value approach reflects the broadest possible interpretation of the principle.

Under the investment value approach, the universe of equally desirable substitutes for the business or other property being appraised is considered to encompass a wide variety of different possible investments, each producing an amount of income comparable to that produced by the business being appraised and having certain other characteristics in common with it, but not limited to businesses or other investments of the same or similar type as that being appraised. This is the money machine concept previously mentioned.

Mathematically, the investment value approach expresses a relationship among (1) the amount of income produced by an investment, (2) the principal amount invested, and (3) the rate of return on the amount invested. In its most familiar form, this relationship is used to determine the amount of income (interest) on a known amount of principal, invested at a specific rate of return (interest rate). Thus,

$$\text{amount of income} = \text{amount invested} \times \text{rate of return}$$

If a principal amount of $100,000 is invested for one year at a rate of return of 12% per year, the amount of return, or interest, on the investment is

$$\$100,000 \times 0.12 = \$12,000$$

This same relationship can be rearranged to calculate the amount of principal invested when the amount of return and rate of return are known. Thus,

$$\text{amount invested} = \frac{\text{amount of income}}{\text{rate of return}}$$

Using this form of the relationship, if the amount of income and rate of return in the preceding example were known, the principal amount invested could have been calculated as

$$\text{amount invested} = \frac{\$12,000}{0.12} = \$100,000$$

The investment value approach, then, is a method for determining the value of an actual or contemplated investment from a known or estimated amount of income, together with a known or assumed rate of return on investment. Specifically, the investment value approach says that

$$\text{investment value} = \frac{\text{amount of return}}{\text{rate of return}}$$

The process of dividing an amount of return by a rate of return in order to determine the value of an investment is called capitalization.

THE CAPITALIZATION PROCESS

The term *capitalization* refers to the process of dividing a known or assumed amount of return on an investment by a known or assumed rate of return to determine the corresponding principal amount invested.

Thus, a $12,000 annual return on investment can be capitalized at 12% to determine the corresponding principal amount:

$$\text{principal amount} = \frac{\text{amount of return}}{\text{rate of return}} = \frac{\$12,000}{0.12} = \$100,000$$

This is the essence of the investment value approach to estimating the economic value of a business or other income-producing investment. The known or estimated amount of income from the business or other investment is capitalized at what is considered to be an appropriate rate of return on investment, the result being the investment value. Thus, as previously stated,

$$\text{investment value} = \frac{\text{amount of return}}{\text{rate of return}}$$

While the mathematics of capitalization are quite simple, it will be apparent from the remainder of this chapter that, in applying the investment value approach to estimate the economic value of a business the appraiser encounters difficulties of considerable magnitude, first in determining the applicable figure for income and, second, in arriving at an appropriate rate of return, or capitalization rate.

The rate of return, or capitalization rate, is expressed as a decimal figure divided into the amount of return in order to determine amount of investment, or investment value. However, it should be mentioned that the reciprocal of the capitalization rate can be used as a multiplier to calculate investment value from the amount of return on investment. Thus, a rate of return of 0.20 (20%) corresponds to a multiplier of 5.00, a rate of return of 0.12 (12%) corresponds to a multiplier of 8.33, and so on.

Although multiplication is, from a purely mathematical standpoint, somewhat more convenient than division, the nature of the process used to select an appropriate rate of return leads to a decimal figure rather than a multiplier. Accordingly, the capitalization approach, requiring amount of income to be divided by rate of return, will be followed in this chapter.

At first thought, it might be assumed that the multiplier that is the reciprocal of the capitalization rate is somehow related to the price-to-earnings (or P/E ratio) terminology frequently used in referring to yields on corporate stocks, particularly stocks of publicly traded companies. However, this apparent relationship between P/E ratio and the reciprocal of capitalization rate is to a considerable extent illusory, for reasons already mentioned in Chapter 8 and to be discussed further in this chapter. Accordingly, the appraiser should be wary of using P/E ratios of publicly traded companies in estimating the value of a business being appraised, regardless of how similar a publicly owned company may appear to be to the business being appraised.

APPLICATION OF INVESTMENT VALUE APPROACH IN BUSINESS APPRAISING

The investment value approach is applicable to estimating the economic value of any kind of property whose purpose is to produce income for its owner. This includes almost all businesses, as well as so-called commercial, industrial, or other income-producing real property.

However, the investment value approach is not applicable to certain kinds of property whose principal function is not that of producing income for the owner. This includes various kinds of not-for-profit organizations and establishments, as well as owner-occupied residential real estate.

In addition to valuing complete businesses, the investment value approach is sometimes employed to estimate the value of individual business assets.

This is especially true in the case of some kinds of intangible assets, valuation of which is difficult or impossible by means of other approaches. Examples of intangible assets that are sometimes valued by means of the investment value approach include patents, copyrights, and business goodwill.

The investment value approach is also an appropriate means for estimating the value of some kinds of securities, such as bonds that are commonly bought and sold at prices other than their face value. This includes so-called zero coupon bonds, which are redeemable at face value at a stated future date but which do not include any explicit provision for payment of interest and are therefore bought and sold before their maturity date at various discounts from face value.

As applied to businesses, the investment value approach is theoretically applicable to any business (or other investment) whose intended purpose is to provide a return to its owner. As a practical matter, however, the investment value approach provides useful information only in the case of businesses or other investments that actually provide a positive return to the owner, or at least can be expected to do so in the future. If the investment value approach were to be used to estimate the value of an unprofitable business, it would lead to a figure for investment value that would be either zero (in the case of a break-even business) or negative (in the case of a money-losing business).

In the case of unprofitable businesses, one or more of the other approaches to estimating value will yield results that will be more useful from an appraisal standpoint than the result that would follow from application of the investment value approach.

STEPS IN APPLYING THE INVESTMENT VALUE APPROACH

Use of the investment value approach to estimate the economic value of a business or other income-producing property involves the following steps:

1. The appraiser selects the type of income to be capitalized.
2. The appraiser then determines or estimates the corresponding amount of income to be capitalized. Ordinarily, this amount of income will reflect anticipated future income from the business or other investment.

3. Next, the appraiser selects an appropriate capitalization rate, or rate of return on investment, to be applied to the amount of income determined in the preceding step.

4. Finally, the appraiser calculates the investment value by dividing the amount of income determined in the second step by the capitalization rate selected in the third step.

CHOOSING THE TYPE OF INCOME TO BE CAPITALIZED

The appraiser's first step in applying the investment value approach is to determine the type of income to be capitalized in order to determine the investment value of the business or other property being appraised.

There are a number of possible choices for type of income to be capitalized, including:

Net operating income

Dividend income (or, in the case of most closely held businesses, dividend-paying capacity)

Less frequently, other types of income, such as:

Gross income before expenses

Gross profit

Cash flow

In applications of the investment value approach to estimate the value of individual assets, such as goodwill, it will be the income that is attributed to the specific asset to be valued that will be used by the appraiser.

Whatever the type of income selected as a basis for applying the investment value approach, it will be evident from the Principle of Future Benefits that it will be the anticipated future amount of such income that will be of interest.

Also, it will be normal income, exclusive of any extraordinary income or expenses, that will be used as a basis for predicting the amount of future income of the selected type.

Another question, of course, concerns whether the income to be used for determining value according to the investment value approach is to be pretax or after-tax income. For reasons related to differences in applicable tax rates between businesses and owners in different circumstances, it is generally preferable to use pretax profits in estimating the value of a business from information on the income it produces. In some instances, however, circumstances may dictate the use of after-tax figures. In either case, the choice of capitalization rate, of course, must be consistent with the type of profit, whether pretax or after-tax, used as a basis for estimating investment value.

Of course, the investment value approach may be applied in a given appraisal situation using two or more different types of income, each of which is converted into an indication of investment value by use of an appropriate capitalization rate. Thus, appraisal of rental real estate may include one value estimate obtained by capitalizing estimated effective gross income and another obtained by capitalizing estimated net income, in each case using a capitalization rate appropriate to the type of income being capitalized.

In appraisals of businesses by means of the investment value approach, the most common choice for type of income is anticipated net operating income. That is, historical financial data and other information about the business and the environment in which it operates are used to estimate an amount of annual income, after provision for all normal operating expenses, considered to represent the anticipated future net operating income of the business. Techniques for determining the amount of such expected future income and for selecting an appropriate and related capitalization rate are dealt with in following sections of this chapter.

Another type of income that is sometimes used to estimate the value of businesses by means of the investment value approach is dividend income. An estimate of value on the basis of dividend income, which may be used either by itself or in combination with an estimate based on net operating income, is especially appropriate in circumstances, such as absentee owner situations, in which dividends are an important benefit of ownership.

Closely held businesses, especially the majority of such businesses that are also owner-managed, usually do not pay dividends as such. However, it is still possible to use dividend income as a basis for estimating the value of such a business, by resorting to the concept of dividend-paying capacity. An estimate of investment value based on dividend-paying capacity may be in order, for example, when the appraisal is likely to be subjected to the provisions of the Internal Revenue Service's Revenue Ruling 59–60, which includes an explicit requirement that dividends or dividend-paying capacity be included among the considerations leading to an estimate of the value of closely held stock.

As previously indicated, cash flow is another type of income sometimes used as a basis for estimating the value of a business or other investment.

Although it can be used in other circumstances, the choice of anticipated future cash flow as an indicator of the value of an investment is especially appropriate in circumstances in which anticipated future income from a business or investment can be expected to vary in a known or predictable manner from year to year in the future. This is in contrast to the assumption of a constant, or at least steadily changing, amount of future income that is implicit in the valuation method based on choice of net operating income as the type of income to be capitalized.

The techniques for converting anticipated future cash flow into an estimate of value, although similar in concept to the capitalization technique, actually involve a process of discounting. This is also true of a related method, the discounted future earnings method of arriving at a value estimate.

Valuation techniques based on anticipated cash flow, and also the related discounted future earnings technique, are treated separately in Chapter 11.

As previously indicated, other possible choices for type of income to be capitalized in using the investment value approach include gross income and even gross profit. In practice, however, gross income and gross profit are seldom used in estimating the value of a business by means of the investment value approach.

In rare cases, gross income may be capitalized at an appropriate capitalization rate to provide an indication of the value of a business. This is most likely to be done with certain types of service businesses, such as insurance agencies, in which gross income provides a reasonably reliable indication of the net income to be expected from the business in the future. When this is done, the implicit assumption is that essentially all businesses of the type in question are sufficiently standardized that the relationship between gross income and market value that exists in one or several businesses also will exist in essentially all other businesses of the same type. Applied in this manner, the investment value approach amounts to little more than appraisal by rule of thumb, as previously discussed in Chapter 8.

DETERMINING AMOUNT OF INCOME

After the type of income to be capitalized has been determined, the next step in applying the investment value approach is to determine the applicable amount of such income.

Whatever type of income is chosen for the capitalization process, the following considerations apply in determining its amount:

It is the anticipated future amount of income, rather than the past historical amount, that is of interest. This is evident from the Principle of Future Benefits as explained in Chapter 2.

The amount of income to be capitalized should represent normal income exclusive of any extraordinary income or losses.

Efforts to predict the amount of future income of a business, whether for purposes of the investment value approach or otherwise, must be based in large part on information about actual historical income. In interpreting historical data, however, the appraiser must constantly bear in mind that it is actually anticipated future income that he or she is attempting to determine.

The future income of a business may be said to be characterized by its amount, its future time pattern (that is, anticipated change in amount of future income as a function of time), its expected duration, and its relative certainty.

In predicting future income of a business for purposes of the investment value approach, the appraiser attempts to arrive at a single figure for amount of anticipated future income that he or she believes is typical of the likely future performance of the business. Although the figure selected will be expressed in terms of amount of income per year, it should represent the appraiser's judgment of the amount of income that will be typical of a number of future years, rather than of a single year.

Methods for using historical financial information on a business to forecast future trends were discussed briefly in Chapter 7. Desirably, the appraiser's analysis of historical information about the income of the business, together with other information bearing on probable future income, will lead to a figure for anticipated future income that represents either (1) an amount of future income that is expected to remain more or less constant from year to year for at least several years in the future, or (2) a base figure for income in an immediate future year (such as the year immediately following the date of appraisal) and that is part of what the appraiser believes to be a constantly increasing (or even in some cases constantly decreasing) trend of future income.

In either case, the appraiser should find it possible to select a corresponding capitalization rate that can be applied to the estimated annual amount of future income to yield the investment value of the business. It is important to note, however, that the capitalization rate will not necessarily be the same in the two cases. This point is further discussed in the next section of this chapter.

If the anticipated time pattern of future income is substantially irregular—that is, if it consists of other than a constant or steadily increasing (or decreasing) amount—then the capitalization process is generally not applicable, and the investment value approach to estimating the value of the business or other investment should not be used.

If the time pattern of anticipated future income, though irregular, is reasonably predictable, then discounted future income techniques, as discussed in Chapter 11, may apply. If the anticipated future income of the business is neither regular nor predictable (as may happen, for example, with a business that exhibits no consistent pattern of historical income), then income-based appraisal methods are generally inapplicable altogether, and some other method of estimating the value of the business must be used.

As for the duration of anticipated future income, the capitalization process as applied in most business appraisals incorporates an assumption (frequently implicit rather than explicitly stated) that the anticipated future income is of indefinite but substantial duration. That is, although it is not necessarily assumed that the anticipated level of future income will exist forever, the assumption is that it will exist for at least a substantial number of years into the future, rather than being limited to only a few years. If it is known, or can be anticipated on the basis of available information, that the expected future income will last for only a relatively short time, such as less than five years, then a discounted future income approach is preferable to the investment value approach as a means of estimating the value of a business or other income-producing property on the basis of the amount of income it produces.

There are some cases, particularly in real estate appraising, in which value attributable to a future income stream of relatively short duration nevertheless can be estimated by means of the investment value approach. The key is in the choice of capitalization rate to be used; that is, the rate chosen must reflect, among other considerations, the relatively short duration of the anticipated future income. Further discussion of this point appears in the next section of this chapter.

Related to the assumption that the predicted level of future income from a business will be of substantial time duration is the assumption, which applies to most but not all business appraisals, that the business or other income-producing property will retain its value, which in the present instance is to say its income-producing capability, for the foreseeable future. This is true of most businesses and many other kinds of income-producing investments, and is part of the basis for choosing the capitalization rate to be applied to the predicted level of future income.

However, there are some types of income-producing investments that naturally tend to lose their income-producing capacity over a period of time. This is the case, for example, with businesses based on natural resources that are depleted with use and with income-producing real estate investments that include improvements subject to depreciation, part or all of which is not readily correctable. The investment value approach still can be applied to estimate the value of such investments, provided the capitalization rate is chosen in such a manner as to reflect, among other considerations, the loss of value of the business or investment with use or through the passage of time. This matter is further discussed in the next section of this chapter.

The fourth characteristic of the future income of a business or other investment, namely its relative certainty, is one of the considerations that enter into the determination of capitalization rate as discussed in the next section. Concerning the appraiser's estimate of the amount of expected future income, it is usually the most probable amount that he or she is seeking to estimate. As for the question of how probable this most probable amount is, that matter is considered when choosing the capitalization rate.

As indicated in the preceding section of this chapter, the type of income that is selected most often as a basis for estimating the value of a business by means of the investment value approach is net operating income, either after income tax or, preferably and when circumstances permit, before provision for income tax.

When it is future net operating income that the appraiser is attempting to estimate, the principal source of historical financial information will be income/expense statements of the business for the past several years. These may be either accountants' income/expense statements or economic income/expense statements.

The nature of accountants' income/expense statements and economic income/expense statements, including the differences between the two types of statements, has been discussed at length in Chapters 6 and 7, and no purpose would be served in repeating the discussion at this point. Instead, the reader may wish to review the applicable portions of Chapters 6 and 7 before proceeding further.

Generally speaking, economic income/expense statements are preferable to accountants' income/expense statements as a source of historical data on net operating profits of the business whose future level of net operating profit is to be estimated. This is because, as explained in Chapter 7, economic income/expense statements tend to avoid the various distortions that can and frequently do enter into accountants' income/expense statements, affecting the indicated value of net operating profit accordingly.

However, this preferred use of economic income/expense statements as a source of historical data on operating profits is valid from the standpoint of the investment value approach only if it is accompanied by selection of capitalization rate on a corresponding basis. As will be evident from the discussion in the following section of this chapter, there may be some instances in which selection of a capitalization rate to be used in connection with the investment value approach necessarily will be on a basis such that net operating profit as shown on accountants' income/expense statements, rather than on economic income/expense statements, should be used.

Similar considerations apply to the decision of whether expected future net operating profit to be used with the investment value approach should be on a pretax or after-tax basis. Pretax figures are preferable when they can feasibly be used, because pretax figures tend to avoid the inconsistencies and lack of comparability that are frequently present in after-tax figures as a result of differences in the tax situations of otherwise comparable businesses or other investments. Here again, however, the choice of pretax versus after-tax figures must be consistent with the choice of capitalization rate.

After net operating income, perhaps the next most frequent choice of type of income to be used in applying the investment value approach is dividend income to the owner of the business or, in the case of most closely held businesses, dividend-paying capacity.

In estimating the amount of future income to be used in applying the investment value approach, a distinction must be made between actual dividend income on the one hand and dividend-paying capacity on the other hand. Of the two, actual dividend income will be the more appropriate choice in the case of businesses with minority shareholders (who are frequently not otherwise active in the business) and with an actual record of dividend payments. Dividend-paying capacity, on the other hand, will be the more appropriate choice in the case of a business without minority shareholders or without any record of actual dividend payments.

When actual dividend payments are the appropriate choice, the estimated future amount of such payments will be based on the past history of dividend payments, giving appropriate consideration to the expected future trend of the business in question, particularly from the standpoint of profitability.

Dividend payments are made, of course, from after-tax profits, usually determined according to the accountants' income/expense statement. Accordingly, estimates of future profits from which to make dividend payments should be based on accountants' income/expense statements rather than economic income/expense statements, and should be on an after-tax basis.

As compared to estimating future payment of dividends by a business that has a historical policy or record of dividend payments, determining dividend-paying capacity is a more difficult matter.

At best, the determination of dividend-paying capacity requires a judgment by the appraiser. This judgment, however, can benefit substantially from an organized and orderly process for arriving at the estimate.

As a basis for arriving at an estimate of the dividend-paying capacity of a business, the appraiser first must estimate the amount of future profits of the business.

For the present purpose, the desired estimate will be of normal operating profit (that is, excluding nonrecurring items) and after the effect of any appropriate adjustments, such as for owners' excess salary and perquisites in the case of a closely held business. In most cases, this will correspond to the net operating profit as shown on an economic income/expense statement for the business.

However, dividends are distributed to shareholders from the profits of a business after applicable income taxes have been paid by the business. Accordingly, net operating profit after taxes should be estimated by applying the appropriate corporate income tax rate to estimated net operating profit before taxes. In most cases, this will be the corporate income tax rates that apply as of the date of appraisal, unless it is known that tax rates will change in the future.

Since it is generally unsound for a business to disburse all of its profits in the form of dividends, the next step in arriving at an estimate of dividend-paying capacity is to determine what portion of future after-tax profits should be reserved for purposes such as capital expenditures to replace depreciated equipment, expansion of the business, and so on.

If the estimate of future profit has been made by a process that includes provision for eventual replacement of assets subject to depreciation, no other provision need be made for this particular purpose. This will be the case, for example, if estimates of future profit are based on economic income/expense statements that include a reserve for replacements or equivalent expense item.

However, if profit estimates are based on conventional accountants' income/expense statements, there will be a period in the early life of a major asset during which unrealistically high depreciation charges will result in correspondingly unrealistic (low) profits. After the asset has been fully depreciated from a book value standpoint, there will follow a period, typically of several years' duration, during which the asset will continue to be used but without any depreciation or other charges related to its eventual replacement. During this period, the absence of any recorded expenses related to deterioration of the asset in question will lead to unrealistically high profit figures.

Preferably, this phenomenon of profit figures that are first unrealistically low and then unrealistically high should be avoided when determining the amount of income to be used for purposes of the investment value approach. This can be done either by making appropriate adjustments to estimates of future profits as based on accountants' income/expense statements, or by use of profit figures derived from economic income/expense statements.

Finally, that portion of estimated future profit that remains after provision for applicable corporate income taxes, and after provision for possible future capital expenditures, can be taken as representing the dividend-paying capacity of the business.

In those relatively rare cases in which the investment value of a business is to be estimated by capitalizing either gross income or gross profit, the applicable amount of such income or profit usually can be estimated directly from either accountants' or economic income/expense statements for the business, giving consideration to expected future trends as well as actual historical figures.

As previously mentioned, the investment value approach can be used to estimate the value of individual business assets, particularly intangible assets. When this is done, the applicable amount of income attributable to the assets in question can be determined as described in the following section of this chapter.

CHOOSING THE CAPITALIZATION RATE— FACTORS TO BE CONSIDERED

.The third step in applying the investment value approach is to determine the capitalization rate to be applied to the amount of expected future income as determined in the preceding step.

Choosing the capitalization rate is unquestionably the most difficult step in applying the investment value approach. It is also one of the most difficult problems in the entire field of business and property appraisal.

There are, unfortunately, a number of relatively prevalent and persistent misconceptions about capitalization rates.

One of these misconceptions is that capitalization rate is an essentially fixed number that can be applied more or less indiscriminately to any and all situations. The rate that is most often mentioned in this connection is 10%.

It is incorrect to believe that capitalization rate is a fixed number, particularly a number as low as 10%, as is evident from the following.

Capitalization rate as used in connection with the investment value approach represents a yield rate on an investment, namely the investment value of the business or other property that is being appraised. Thus, a contention that capitalization rate is a number that is fixed regardless of circumstances amounts to a contention that all investments producing a given amount of income are of equal value, regardless of other differences among them.

Following this line of reasoning and applying the Principle of Substitution, all investments producing a given amount of income, and therefore having equal value as calculated by application of a fixed capitalization rate, would have to be equally desirable substitutes for one another. This is obviously not the case, since investments, even though they may yield equal amounts of income, differ in many other ways that make some more or less desirable than others. Accordingly, the belief that capitalization rate is a fixed number is a fallacy.

Further, the incorrectness of selecting a capitalization rate as low as 10% to determine the value of a business is apparent from the fact that, at the time this is written, various relatively risk-free investments, such as government-backed securities, are yielding rates of return in the vicinity of 15%. Under such circumstances, no rational and informed investor would accept a yield as low as 10% on a relatively risky investment such as investment in ownership of a business.

Another prevalent misconception is that the capitalization rate to be used in determining the investment value of a given business can be determined from the price-to-earnings ratios of publicly traded stocks. This school of thought holds that the capitalization rate to be used in determining the investment value of a given business is the inverse of the P/E ratios at which stocks of publicly traded companies in the same industry are currently selling.

The P/E ratio approach to selecting capitalization rates holds, in effect, that there is some form of comparability between the business being appraised and other businesses in the same industry whose stocks are publicly traded. The fallaciousness of the P/E ratio approach to determining capitalization rate can be demonstrated in a number of ways, two of which will be mentioned here.

Bearing in mind the Principle of Substitution, the P/E ratio method of determining capitalization rate contains the implied assumption that investment in stock of a publicly owned business and investment in ownership of a closely held business in the same industry (or, for that matter, investment in any two companies in the same industry) are equally desirable substitutes for each other. This is patently not true. Comparability from an investment standpoint requires a great deal more than merely that the two alternative investments be in the same industry.

An investor in the stock of a publicly traded company is, in the great majority of cases, acquiring a very small percentage ownership of a relatively large business. The investor will have little or no control over the future conduct of the business and, in all likelihood, makes the investment with a view toward the anticipated future price of the stock, more so than the future overall performance of the business itself.

The investor in a closely held business, on the other hand, is purchasing a substantial percentage share of ownership of the business (frequently 100%), usually with the expectation that he or she will be active in its future operation, and with the purchase of ownership motivated primarily by the expected future overall performance of the business.

Thus, there is very little comparability from an investment standpoint between purchase of shares in a publicly owned company and investment in ownership of a closely held business in the same industry. In fact, such comparability is limited to the influence that industrywide factors have on the fortunes of individual companies.

Another indication that the P/E ratio approach to determining capitalization rate is wrong is found in the mathematics of the P/E ratio itself.

The price at which shares of publicly traded companies are currently selling is primarily a function of the investing public's perception of the *probable* future performance of the business, or at least of the price of its stock. However, the earnings are *actual* earnings as reported by the company for its most recent fiscal year, which may have ended several months prior to the date of current consideration.

Thus, the earnings figure, which should, according to the philosophy behind the investment value approach, reflect anticipated future normal earnings, actually reflects past historical earnings and may include items of an extraordinary or other nonrecurring nature.

The net result is that, while the current price of the stock may reflect investor knowledge of events that have taken place subsequent to the end of the most recent fiscal year and are expected to influence the future of the company, this price is divided by an earnings figure that is purely historical in nature and that in many cases is distorted by historical circumstances that have little or no significance in terms of the long-term future.

Notwithstanding the foregoing and other fallacies inherent in the P/E ratio approach, this approach continues to be a surprisingly common method for determining capitalization rates to be used in estimating the value of closely held businesses according to the investment value approach.

The fact is that capitalization rate is not a fixed number, nor can it be determined simply from the P/E ratios at which stocks of other companies, publicly traded or not, are selling.

Rather, the capitalization rate that should be used in a given situation depends on a number of considerations, including both internal and external factors. Also—and this fact is frequently overlooked or ignored—capitalization rate changes with time.

While there are a number of considerations that affect determination of the proper capitalization rate in a given situation, and various methods of determining the proper rate, there are two criteria that must be satisfied by the capitalization rate, regardless of the detailed considerations on which it is based and the manner in which it is determined. These two criteria are:

1. The capitalization rate must correspond with the rate of return currently needed to attract capital to the type of investment in question.
2. The capitalization rate must be consistent with the kind of income to be capitalized.

The first criterion is directly related to the Principle of Alternatives and the Principle of Substitution. That is, the capitalization rate to be used in determining the investment value of a given business or other property must correspond with the real investment alternatives of typical potential buyers for the business or other investment being appraised.

The second criterion is a matter of simple logic. If the income to be capitalized as a means of estimating the investment value of a given business is pretax income as estimated from an economic income/expense statement, the capitalization rate will be different from that if the value of the same company was to be estimated using, for example, after-tax income. Likewise, the capitalization rate will differ for income as determined from an accountant's income/expense statement, as compared to income determined from an economic income/expense statement. Similarly, different capitalization rates will be required for estimating value from dividend income and for other types of income that may be used with the investment value approach.

There are a number of factors that, to a great or lesser extent, affect the capitalization rate that should be used in a given situation.

Internal factors include, among others:

Kind of business (whether manufacturing, distribution, or service, and specific industry in which engaged)

Size of business

Quality of management (assumes that existing management is to remain)

Financial condition of business (such as adequacy of existing working capital)

Stability of earnings, especially as evident in historical earnings trends (sometimes referred to as quality of earnings)

Competitive position within industry of business being appraised

General outlook for business being appraised

External factors include, among others:

Competitive situation in industry

General economic conditions in industry

General outlook for industry

Conditions in general economy

Outlook for general economy

It will be evident upon reflection that, whereas each of the factors listed (as well as a number of others) has an influence on the capitalization rate that should be applied in a given situation, there is no simple way of establishing a quantitative relationship between the various factors listed above and the capitalization rate that should be used in a given situation. This is particularly evident when we consider the fact that, however chosen, the capitalization rate is a single number to be applied to a single variable (the income that is to be capitalized) in order to arrive at a result, namely the investment value of the business or other property being appraised.

The number that is chosen as a capitalization rate to be used in a given situation must somehow reflect all the various influences, with the sole exception of the predicted amount of future earnings, that go into determining the value of a business or other investment.

It will be evident from the foregoing that whatever method is used to arrive at a specific capitalization rate, eventual choice of the rate to be used in a given situation will depend heavily on the judgment of the appraiser. Accordingly, there is no substitute, particularly when estimating the value of a business according to the investment value approach, for thorough familiarity on the part of the appraiser with the business or other investment to be appraised.

Aside from the viewpoint that considers the pertinent internal and external factors as previously listed, each of which must be considered and weighed—at least qualitatively—in arriving at a choice of the appropriate capitalization rate, there is another kind of viewpoint that is frequently helpful to the appraiser who is attempting to apply the investment value approach.

This other viewpoint is to consider the business or other property that is being appraised, not so much in terms of its detailed internal and external characteristics as a specific business of a specific type, but rather as one of a variety of alternative investment possibilities, each of which is defined primarily by its investment characteristics. This viewpoint corresponds with the Principle of Substitution as applied to the widest possible universe of equally desirable substitutes.

From the standpoint of comparing various investments to identify those that may be considered as falling within the universe of equally desirable substitutes for a specific investment being appraised, an investment may be thought of as possessing four kinds of attributes, or four dimensions.

One of these dimensions is, of course, rate of return, which is the focus of efforts to determine an appropriate capitalization rate. The other three dimensions of an investment are:

Size of amount invested

Character of the investment

Risk associated with the investment

As for the amount dimension, it is apparent that an investment of, say, $100,000, is generally not a practical substitute for an investment of several times that amount, or $1 million. There are a number of reasons for this, including the fact that an investor who is considering investment of a given amount is generally not in a position to give practical consideration to an investment of many times that amount. Accordingly, possible investments should be considered as substitutes for one another only if they involve invested amounts that, while not necessarily equal, are at least of the same order of magnitude.

A business that could be purchased for a price such as $100,000 is not in any realistic sense an investment alternative to the purchase of another business costing many times that amount, notwithstanding the fact that the two businesses may be in the same industry and may in fact be quite similar in all respects other than their size. (This is one of several reasons why the price of shares of stock in publicly held companies is not a valid basis for determining the capitalization rate to be used in estimating the value of another company in the same industry.)

The second dimension used in comparing investment alternatives, namely the character of the investment, encompasses a number of circumstances and conditions. Principal among these considerations related to the character of an investment are:

Expectation, as intrinsic to the particular investment, of future depreciation (or, conversely, future appreciation) of the capital amount invested

Liquidity

Burden of management

An investment, such as in a mine, oil wells, or other source of natural resources, carries with it the expectation that, as the property is used and existing resources are removed, the value of the investment will decrease. The same is true of an investment in improved real estate to the extent that deterioration over a period of time of the buildings or other improvements is not corrected. When dealing with an investment of such nature that the basic value of the investment can be expected to decline over a period of time, the capitalization rate must include provision, not only for a reasonable return on the initial amount invested, but also for recovery over a period of time of that portion of the initial investment that will be lost as a result of use of the property or, in some cases, simply through the passage of time.

On the other hand, there are some kinds of investments that carry with them the intrinsic expectation of future capital growth. This would be true, for example, of a tree farm planted with seedlings, the value of which would increase as the seedlings matured into full-grown trees. In the case of such an investment, the expectation of future capital growth leads to capitalization rates that are somewhat lower than if the growth expectation did not exist, other things of course being equal.

In the case of most appraisals of ongoing businesses, the means used to forecast future income from the business will include provision, usually in the form of expense allowances for reserve for replacements or the like, for preventing or restoring loss of value that might otherwise occur through the passage of time. In such cases, there is no remaining expectation of either capital depletion or capital growth, and the capitalization rate to be applied to predicted future earnings does not need to include any provision for such capital depletion or growth.

However, there may be cases in which decreases (or increases) in initial capital value are inevitable; the choice of capitalization rate should reflect this fact. This may be the case, for example, with businesses whose earnings are heavily dependent on ownership of consumable natural resources, or businesses a substantial portion of whose assets are in the form of buildings, patents, copyrights, or other assets that have finite useful lives and are not readily subject to renewal, or for which no renewal provision is included in the means used to estimate future profits.

The second element related to the character of an investment is liquidity of the investment. In financial terminology, *liquidity* refers to the ease with which the capital amount of an investment can be converted into cash. Money in a safe-deposit box, or in a demand type of savings account, is highly liquid. An investment in ownership of a closely held business, on the other hand, is relatively nonliquid, since the only way in which the full amount of the investment can be converted to cash is through sale of the business or its assets. Somewhere between these two extremes is investment in stock of a publicly held company, which can be converted to cash with relative ease by selling the stock (provided, of course, that the seller is willing to accept whatever price the stock will bring at the time he or she decides to sell).

Liquidity is a desirable feature of an investment, and, accordingly, the relative liquidity is taken into account when determining the capitalization rate to be used in connection with a given type of investment.

The third element of the character of an investment concerns the burden of management. Ownership of a closely held business carries with it a substantial burden of management for the owner, even in cases in which the owner is not the day-to-day manager of the business. To a lesser extent, there is a burden of management associated with ownership of income-producing real estate or of a portfolio of stocks. An investment in the form of a conventional savings account, on the other hand, involves little or no burden of management for the investor.

In addition to size of amount invested and character of the investment, the third dimension of an investment is the risk associated with the investment.

There are two aspects to investment risk—risk that the predicted return (income) from the investment may not actually be realized, and risk that the full principal amount of the investment may not be recoverable at a future date. Although these two elements of risk are usually considered separately, they are, of course, related.

An investment such as by depositing funds in a savings account, or by purchasing a so-called certificate of deposit backed by guarantees traceable to the federal government, carries with it relatively little risk either that the promised return will not be realized or that the principal amount will not be recoverable at the end of the investment period. An investment in ownership of a closely held business, on the other hand, involves a significant degree of risk, first that the hoped-for future income (profit) may not actually be realized or that the full principal amount invested may not be recoverable, through sale of the business or otherwise, at a future date.

Between these two relative extremes, there are other degrees of risk. Investment in a business that has substantial tangible assets (such as a manufacturing business) involves less risk of loss of principal than investment in a business whose tangible assets are relatively small or nonexistent (such as some service businesses). Similarly, investment in improved real property ordinarily involves somewhat greater risk than investment in savings deposits but frequently less risk than investment in many kinds of operating businesses.

As for risk that the predicted future income from the investment will not be realized, this consideration varies both according to the type of investment and also (except in cases in which the return is essentially guaranteed) according to the specific method used to estimate future return on the investment.

The degree of risk associated with an investment is, of course, a major factor in determining the capitalization rate to be used in determining the investment value of a given amount of predicted future income or, conversely, the rate of return that is acceptable to an investor who is contemplating a given type of investment. This is the principal reason for the relatively low interest rates investors find acceptable in the case of investments involving a high degree of security, as compared to the much higher rates of return investors demand on investments in more speculative forms.

Thus far, we have discussed factors to be considered in choosing the capitalization rate, including two different viewpoints toward an investment. One of these viewpoints looks at a specific business or other investment from the standpoint of various internal and external factors that affect the choice of an appropriate capitalization rate. The second viewpoint considers an investment primarily from the standpoint of certain investment characteristics that affect choice of capitalization rate, namely the size of the amount invested, the character of the investment, and the risk associated with the investment.

It will be evident that, whichever of these viewpoints is chosen, or even if both of them are used, the choice of a specific capitalization rate to be used in a given situation will still be a difficult matter and presumably will benefit from some sort of organized, orderly approach. The following sections of this chapter describe two classes of approaches or methods that are in common use for choosing the capitalization rate.

CHOOSING THE CAPITALIZATION RATE—
SUMMATION METHODS

One class of methods for determining the capitalization rate to be used in a given situation consists of what can be described as summation methods. These are methods in which the capitalization rate is determined as the sum of a number of individual components or elements. (This is in contrast to the second broad class of methods, the direct comparison method, in which the capitalization rate is determined in a single step.)

Summation methods for determining capitalization rates are also sometimes called built-up methods or band of investment methods. Although they are used primarily in connection with estimating the value of improved real property by means of the investment value approach, summation methods are also applicable to appraisals of businesses.

In one form of summation method that is particularly applicable to improved real property, the capitalization rate is calculated as the sum of an interest rate and an equity rate, each of which is weighted according to the portion of the total investment it represents. The interest rate is intended to reflect the interest cost on the portion of the total investment that represents borrowed funds, and the equity rate is intended to reflect the rate of return on an investment that an investor would expect (or would be entitled to receive) on the remainder of the total investment.

Thus, if 20% of the total required investment is to be borrowed at an interest rate of 12% per annum, and if it is concluded that a 15% annual rate of return would be a reasonable rate for the remaining 80% of the total investment, the capitalization rate would be calculated as follows:

	Annual Rate		Portion of Total Investment		Net Contribution to Capitalization Rate
interest component	12%	×	0.2	=	2.4%
equity component	15%	×	0.8	=	12.0%
total capitalization rate					14.4%

If borrowed money is obtained from more than one source and at different rates of interest, the separate interest rates are each reflected in the calculation, weighted according to the portion of the total investment to which the interest rate applies.

Thus, if an investment is to be financed by a combination of a first mortgage for 20% of the total amount at an interest rate of 12% per year, a second mortgage for an additional 30% of the total amount of an interest rate of 14% per year, and the remaining 50% by means of an equity investment at a 16% rate of return, capitalization rate would be calculated as follows:

	Annual Rate		Portion of Total Investment		Net Contribution to Capitalization Rate
interest, 1st mortgage	12%	×	0.2	=	2.4%
interest, 2nd mortgage	14%	×	0.3	=	4.2%
equity component	16%	×	0.5	=	8.0%
total capitalization rate					14.6%

If the character of the investment includes an inherent expectation of decline or depreciation of the original principal amount, a recapture provision for recovery of the initial principal can be included as part of the capitalization rate. Thus, an investment that is expected to have a useful life of 30 years, with a constant rate of decline assumed, requires a rate of 3.3% per year in order for the full amount of principal invested to be returned at the end of the useful life. If this were the case with an investment, such as in the second example given, the total capitalization rate would then be:

capitalization rate for return on investment (as previously calculated)	14.6%
rate required for return of investment	3.3%
total capitalization rate	17.9%

In situations in which the capitalization rate is to include provision for recovery of the initial investment, but in which the investment can be expected to have some residual value at the end of its useful life, the expected residual value, of course, must be taken into account in the calculations. This might be the case, for example, with improved real property, in which the capitalization rate is to include provision for recovery of the value of the improvements, but with recognition of the fact that there will be a remaining value in the land even after the improvements are of no further value.

Recognition of residual value in such situations can be accomplished in any of several ways.

One approach is to calculate the investment value of the depreciating portion of the investment on the one hand, and of the nondepreciating portion on the other hand. The capitalization rates for these two separate calculations will differ at least to the extent that one will include provision for recapture while the other will not, and possibly for other reasons as well. The two separate investment values thus calculated then can be added to determine the total investment value of the complete property.

Another approach is to weight the recapture provision in the total capitalization rate according to the portion of the total investment for which investment recapture is required.

As previously mentioned, however, the need for recapture is somewhat more prevalent in the case of investments involving real property than in the case of typical investments in ownership of operating businesses.

Another approach to determining capitalization rate by summation methods corresponds with the concept of an investment as having certain dimensions as discussed in the preceding section of this chapter.

In this approach, the capitalization rate to be used in a given situation is calculated as the sum of components reflecting, respectively, (1) a so-called safe rate, (2) a premium for lack of liquidity, (3) a burden-of-management premium, and (4) a premium for the amount of risk involved in the investment.

The safe rate, which can be regarded as the base rate when this method of determining total capitalization rate is used, is intended to represent the annual rate of return currently available from investments offering the maximum security (and thus the lowest risk) and the highest degree of liquidity, which at the same time do not impose a burden of management on the investor. Typically, the safe rate used in a given situation will correspond to the rate of return on government-backed securities such as treasury bills or bank certificates of deposit that are insured by the federal government.

To the extent that interest rates on safe investments depend on the size of the amount invested, the rate chosen by the appraiser should be for investments of amount comparable to the value of the property being appraised. This, of course, is consistent with the amount dimension of investments. Also, to the extent that interest rate on a safe investment differs for relatively long-term investments as compared to short-term investments, the long-term rate generally will be the one that will correspond most closely to investment in ownership of a business.

The elements of the total capitalization rate that reflect the considerations of liquidity, burden of management, and risk are premiums that are added to the applicable safe rate to arrive at the total capitalization rate that is appropriate for a specific situation.

To the extent that the liquidity of an investment in the property being appraised differs from that of the investment to which the safe rate applies, a corresponding increment should be added to the safe rate to account for a lesser degree of liquidity or, conversely, should be subtracted from the safe rate to account for a greater degree of liquidity of investment in the property being appraised. The amount of this increment for difference in liquidity is, unfortunately, a matter that the appraiser must determine by what is essentially a subjective judgment.

Similarly, if the investment used to determine the safe rate requires essentially no management by the investor, but if an investment in the property being appraised would impose some burden of management, then a burden-of-management increment should be added to the safe rate. In most business appraisals, especially those in which future income has been estimated from economic income/expense statements or similar means, the estimated future income already will reflect provisions for payment of a reasonable salary to whomever (possibly the owner) manages the business on a day-to-day basis. The burden-of-management increment that is included in the capitalization rate, then, should reflect the burden of managing the investment to the extent that it is not already provided for in the salaries that have been assumed in determining the amount of future income to be capitalized.

Finally, the fact that investment in the property being appraised, in the great majority of cases, will involve greater risk than the safe investment, is reflected in a risk premium increment in the capitalization rate. This risk increment should take account of both (1) risk that the predicted amount of future income from the investment may not actually be realized, and (2) risk of future loss, through unforeseen circumstances, of part or all of the principal amount invested.

Like the increments for nonliquidity and for burden of management, the increment for risk is to a great extent a matter of subjective judgment on the part of the appraiser.

In a typical case, derivation of a capitalization rate by the summation method might be as follows:

safe rate (e.g., currently available rate on long-term certificates of deposit)	12.0%
nonliquidity premium	1.5%

burden-of-management premium	1.0%
risk premium	5.0%
total capitalization rate	19.5%

If the character of the investment required provision for recovery of the principal amount over a period of time, an appropriate increment for this purpose, of course, would be added to the rate resulting from the total of safe rate, together with the premiums for nonliquidity, burden of management, and risk.

The various summation methods for determining capitalization rate are attractive at least from the standpoint of the investment logic that they reflect.

However, these methods have a major disadvantage in that, with the exception of the base or safe rate, the remaining increments that make up the total capitalization rate must be determined by the appraiser by means of a process that is largely a matter of subjective judgment. This is particularly serious for that portion of the total rate that reflects the increased risk associated with the property being appraised as compared to the type of investment from which the base or safe rate was determined.

So long as investment in the property being appraised does not differ greatly, from an investment standpoint, from the safe investment that is used as a reference, the required subjective judgments are not likely to introduce errors of great magnitude. However, the greater the difference from an investment standpoint between the property being appraised and the safe investment, the greater are the possibilities for serious error in arriving at the total capitalization rate.

With some of the riskier types of businesses, where the increment of the total capitalization rate that represents risk premium begins to approach the safe rate in magnitude, and in some cases may even exceed it, the problems of possible errors as a result of the subjective judgment process can become serious indeed.

It might be argued that the judgments the appraiser must make in selecting the various elements of the total capitalization rate when using one of the summation methods can be substantially aided by comparisons of rates that actually apply in other known situations. However, there is really no valid means of breaking down a capitalization rate that is known to apply in a given situation into various elements that can be used for comparison purposes when developing a capitalization rate through one of the summation methods.

The preferable and more direct approach would be to compare, not individual elements of capitalization rates, but the total rates themselves. This is the basis for the second class of methods for choosing a capitalization rate, as discussed below.

CHOOSING THE CAPITALIZATION RATE—
DIRECT COMPARISON METHODS

The second broad class of methods for determining capitalization rate are what can be called direct comparison methods. Unlike the various summation methods, in which the total capitalization rate is built up in the form of a base rate together with a number of increments, direct comparison methods arrive at the final capitalization rate in a single step.

In determining capitalization rates by one of the direct comparison methods, the appraiser searches for investments that are as similar as possible, from an investment standpoint, to the business or other property being appraised and whose yield rate is known. The appraiser then bases the capitalization rate for the business or other property to be appraised on the actual rates of return on these other investments.

The dimensions of an investment already have been discussed in this chapter. These dimensions are, in addition to rate of return:

Size of amount invested

Character of the investment, including:

inherent tendency of principal amount to appreciate, remain constant, or depreciate

liquidity

burden of management

Risk associated with the investment

In using these investment dimensions in connection with direct comparison methods of determining capitalization rates, a search is made for comparable investments whose rates of return are known and which are similar to the business or other property being appraised with respect to the investment dimensions involving size of amount invested and character of the investment.

Desirably, the comparable investments also should represent a degree of risk similar to that of the business or other property being appraised.

This is a practical impossibility, however, inasmuch as there is no meaningful and satisfactory way of measuring risk on an a priori basis. Accordingly, the risk dimension of the investment must be taken into account by other means, which will be described.

It is well established and widely recognized that the greater the risk an investment involves, the greater the rate of return on investment an investor will require. This principle of a relationship between degree of risk and rate of return applies in circumstances ranging from parimutuel wagering to investments in common stocks, and of course includes ownership of closely held businesses.

The converse of this relationship is that, as among a number of different investments that are generally similar in dimensions of amount of investment and character of investment but offering different rates of return, those investments that offer the higher rates of return can be assumed to involve greater risk than those offering lower rates of return. This relationship between risk and rate of return is a key consideration in using direct comparison methods to determine the capitalization rate to be applied in a given appraisal situation.

One form of direct comparison method used by some appraisers to determine capitalization rate involves gathering information, such as from one of the stock reporting services, on actual rates of return of individual publicly owned companies in the same industry as the business being appraised. Typically, the rate of return may be in terms of annual pretax profit as a percentage of stockholders' equity.

The rates of return for the individual companies then are listed in order of rate of return, resulting in what is in effect a risk scale. This done, the appraiser then uses his or her knowledge of the business being appraised to attempt to place it, at least approximately, in its proper relative position on the risk scale. The capitalization rate then is determined according to the rate of return actually offered by other companies in the same region of the risk scale.

While the method just described is attractive from the standpoint of comparing the business being appraised with other companies in the same industry and thus presumably taking account of industrywide factors influencing rate of return, the method has a number of serious deficiencies.

In particular, publicly held companies such as those on which information can be obtained from stock reporting services tend to be much larger than the closely held businesses that are the subjects of most business appraisals. Thus, there is lack of comparability from the standpoint of the amount invested dimension. Also, an investment in a publicly held company is usually much more liquid, at least from the standpoint of the individual investor, than is an investment in a closely held business. There is a lack of comparability in the liquidity element of the character of investment dimension.

For the foregoing and other reasons, direct comparison methods for determining capitalization rate on the basis of rates of return of publicly held companies in the same industry are not particularly recommended. This is in spite of the fact that these methods are, in fact, popular with some appraisers.

A similar but somewhat more desirable method of determining capitalization rate by direct comparison with rates of return offered by other companies in the same industry as the business being appraised uses statistical information that includes small businesses as well as larger ones.

An example of such information is shown in Exhibit 13, which also identifies the source from which the data were obtained. The data in the table happen to pertain to manufacturers of millwork. However, the source identified in the table also contains similar information on a large number of other kinds of businesses.

In Exhibit 13, the information consists of composite rate of return figures for a number of companies. The individual companies have been categorized by size as measured by total assets, the number of companies contributing to the data in each size category indicated in the column "Number of Companies."

Rate of return is measured in terms of pretax profit as a percentage of tangible net worth. For each size category, rate of return percentages are given for the lower quartile, the median, and the upper quartile of all companies included in the data.

For example, 77 companies with total assets between $1 million and $10 million showed a median rate of return of 24.3% of tangible net worth. One-fourth of the companies reported a profit below 8.1% of tangible net worth, and one-fourth reported a pretax profit greater than 36.4% of tangible net worth.

· In using data such as shown in Exhibit 13 to help select a capitalization rate for a business being appraised, the appraiser will attempt to locate the business being appraised in terms of its approximate position on the risk scale represented by the range of rates of return for the companies contributing to the statistical composite data. Thus, if the business being appraised is a manufacturer of millwork with total assets within the range of $1 million to $10 million, and if the study of the business leads the appraiser to conclude that it involves average risk for an investor, the appraiser may select a capitalization

Exhibit 13

PROFITABILITY OF MANUFACTURERS OF MILLWORK

Number of Companies	Size of Business, Total Assets	Profit before Tax as Percentage of Tangible Net Worth		
		Lower Quartile	Median	Upper Quartile
13	Less than $250,000	15.4%	35.6%	64.5%
51	Between $250,000 and $1,000,000	2.1%	17.9%	31.6%
77	Between $1,000,000 and $10,000,000	8.1%	24.3%	36.4%
16	Between $10,000,000 and $50,000,000	6.1%	24.1%	34.7%
157	All sizes combined	7.6%	23.5%	35.4%

Source: Annual Statement Studies (for fiscal years ending 6-30-79 through 3-31-80). Robert Morris Associates, P.O. Box 8500, S-1140, Philadelphia, PA 19178.

rate close to the median rate of return shown in the table, perhaps a rate of 25%.

On the other hand, if the appraiser concludes that the business being appraised involves greater than average risk, he or she may select a rate of return of 30%, 35%, or possibly even higher.

Because it represents actual data on a limited number of companies, statistical information such as shown in the exhibit can have various apparent anomalies. Such an anomaly would appear to exist, for example, in the case of the data in the table for companies with total assets between $250,000 and $1 million. It will be noted that all three rates of return for companies in this size category are lower than the corresponding rates for the other size categories. This normally would not be expected and is probably the result of one or more statistical sports among the 51 companies in the size range in question.

Having become aware of anomalies in the data, an appraiser will use both caution and judgment in applying the data in a specific situation.

Although it is subject to a number of imperfections and uncertainties, use of information such as illustrated in Exhibit 13 does have certain advantages for determining capitalization rate by direct comparison. In particular, the fact that the statistical data are broken down according to size of business permits the appraiser to achieve true comparability with respect to the amount dimension of the investment. The nature and presentation of the information also tends to ensure comparability from the standpoint of the character dimension of the investment.

However, a direct comparison approach based on data as shown in the exhibit also has at least two significant disadvantages. First, limitations of the data available from the indicated source require that rate of return be measured as a percentage of tangible net worth, which is frequently not the same as the total investment value of the business. A second disadvantage is that the information is limited to three different rates of return, representing respectively the lower quartile, median, and upper quartile of the companies included in the statistical composite. This presents the appraiser with what is only a very crude risk scale on which to try to locate, from a risk standpoint, the business being appraised.

Still another direct comparison method of determining capitalization rate uses rate of return information from the widest possible universe of equally desirable substitutes for an investment in the business or other property being appraised. That is, comparability considerations are limited to the investment dimensions as previously discussed.

With this approach, information is gathered about currently available rates of return on a wide variety of different investment alternatives. This information then is ranked according to rate of return, again on the assumption that increasing rate of return corresponds to increasing risk.

An example of such data is shown in Exhibit 14.

It will be seen from the exhibit that types of investment range from long-term U.S. Treasury bonds at one end of the risk scale to large manufacturing and merchandising companies at the other end of the scale. Rate of return information in the exhibit is expressed in terms of annual pretax return as a percentage of investment. For those types of investment in which the raw data are not in this form, they have been converted to equivalent pretax return on investment by means of appropriate calculations.

The data in the table show that, for the point in time to which the data apply, even the lowest-risk investments were providing pretax rates of return in the 12% to 14% range. At the other end of the risk scale, large manufacturing and merchandising companies provided a rate of return on equity ranging from roughly 10% to 30%.

It is interesting to note that, according to the data in Exhibit 14, there is relatively little difference, in terms of return on equity, between manufacturing businesses and merchandising businesses. It could be suspected (and this is to a considerable extent borne out in actual fact) that differences in rate of return tend to be independent of the particular type of manufacturing or merchandising business involved.

A limitation of rate of return data such as those shown in Exhibit 14 is that, because of limitations inherent in available data sources, information on rates

Exhibit 14

RATE OF RETURN ON SOME TYPES OF INVESTMENT

Type of Investment	Typical Annual Rate of Return on Investment (Pretax)
Long-term U.S. Treasury bonds	12.7%
Public utility bonds (Moody Aaa and Aa quality)	14.4%
Bank mortgages on new homes	14.9%
Money market funds (typical)	17.0%
Large manufacturing companies, return on equity (median yield of 500 companies 20.5%)	9.0%–29.0%
Large merchandising corporations, return on equity (median yield of 40 leading companies 20.0%)	11.2%–30.1%

of return from manufacturing and merchandising companies tends to be limited to larger businesses. Considering only the relationship between degree of risk and size of business, it would be expected that the rate of return for most closely held businesses would fall toward the upper end of the range of actual rates of return for the large companies represented by the data in the table.

Thus, an appraiser using data such as shown in Exhibit 14 to determine the capitalization rate for a closely held business that he or she regards as involving relatively low risk, might select a rate in the vicinity of 20% to 25%. If the business involved greater risk, an appropriate capitalization rate might be in the vicinity of 30% to 35%, or in some cases even higher.

A word of caution about using rate of return information such as shown in Exhibit 14 to aid in determining capitalization rate: rates of return tend to vary with time as well as other circumstances, and, accordingly, the appraiser must always take care to ensure that he or she is working with current information about rates of return available from the various comparable investments. The specific rates of return shown in Exhibits 13 and 14 were valid at the dates the respective exhibits were prepared. However, there is no guarantee that they will continue to be valid in the future.

Another precaution that should be observed when determining capitalization rates by this method is to eliminate or adjust for possible sources of noncomparability, such as with respect to amount of investment, liquidity, and so on, between the business being appraised and the individual types of investments represented by the rate of return figures used for comparison purposes.

CALCULATING THE INVESTMENT VALUE

After the preceding steps have been completed, actual calculation of the investment value is a matter of simple arithmetic.

If the amount of the selected type of income to be capitalized has been estimated to be $75,000 per year, and if the appraiser has determined that the appropriate capitalization rate is approximately 30%, the corresponding investment value is calculated as

$$\text{investment value} = \frac{\text{amount of return}}{\text{rate of return}} = \frac{\$75,000}{0.30} = \$250,000$$

This result is the total value of the business or other property being appraised as estimated according to the investment value approach.

Value estimated according to the investment value approach is all-inclusive to the extent that it encompasses all elements of the business, both tangible and intangible, that contribute to the estimated amount of return as used in the calculation of investment value. In the case of the typical operating business, value estimated by the investment value approach will include the value of reasonable amounts of inventory, accounts receivable, and so on. Contrary to the practice that sellers of businesses sometimes attempt to follow, the value of inventory should not be added to the estimated value of the business when this value has been determined according to the investment value approach.

However, if the actual business includes assets (sometimes referred to as surplus or redundant assets) that do not contribute significantly to earnings as estimated for purposes of the investment value approach but do have a market value, then the market value of these surplus or redundant assets should be added to the investment value in order to determine the total value of the business.

In the example previously cited, if there is equipment that is not actually in use and therefore does not contribute to the estimated $75,000 annual return, the fair market value of this equipment should be added to the investment value in order to determine the total value of the business. Assuming that this surplus equipment has a market value (liquidation basis) of approximately $30,000, the total value of the business would then be:

investment value as previously calculated	$250,000
plus liquidation value of redundant assets	30,000

total estimated value of business
    including redundant assets $280,000

Conversely, if there are assets that are normally required for operation of the business but are not a part of the business as appraised, the estimated cost of replacing these assets should be subtracted from the investment value in order to determine the net value of the business.

For example, if a given business with an estimated value of $250,000 as determined by the investment value approach has accounts receivable that are normally approximately $20,000 but if the business is to be sold under terms such that receivables are to be retained by the seller, then the selling price of the business needs to be adjusted accordingly:

total estimated value of business by
    investment value approach $250,000
less normal amount of accounts receivable   20,000

net estimated value of business as
    appraised for sale $230,000

The same principles apply, of course, to other possibilities with regard to surplus or redundant assets, and also other possibilities with regard to normal and necessary assets that, however, are excluded from the business as appraised.

VALUING INTANGIBLES BY THE EXCESS EARNINGS METHOD

In addition to estimating the value of a complete business or other investment, the investment value approach has another application, which involves estimating the value of intangible assets by means of what is termed the excess earnings method. (The excess earnings method is also sometimes called the IRS method, because its use is promulgated by the Internal Revenue Service for application in some situations.)

Use of the excess earnings method to estimate the value of intangible assets may apply to any kind of intangible assets, or grouping of such assets. The excess earnings method may be used to estimate the separate values of such intangible assets as goodwill, patents, copyrights, and so on. (In the case of intangible assets whose useful lives are inherently limited, such as patents, copyrights, and some franchise agreements, a more appropriate method of estimating value may involve use of a discounted future earnings technique as described in Chapter 11.)

Valuation of intangible assets separately from the remainder of a business may be required for any of several reasons. For example, a separate figure for value of intangible assets may be needed when estimating the total value of a business according to the replacement cost approach. In such a case, the value of intangible assets estimated according to the excess earnings method is added to the value of tangible assets determined in the manner described in Chapter 9, to arrive at a figure for the estimated total value of the complete business. Also, separate figures for value of intangible assets—especially goodwill—may be required in appraisals arising out of condemnations by right of eminent domain.

Valuation of intangible assets by means of the excess earnings method may involve either a single figure representing the estimated value of all intangible assets of a business (the big pot theory), or it may involve a value estimate for only a single type of intangible asset, such as goodwill.

Because business goodwill is the kind of intangible asset to which the excess earnings method is applied most frequently, the remainder of this discussion will focus on valuation of goodwill. It should be understood, however, that the methods described also can be used to estimate other intangible asset values by the excess earnings method.

In the present context, *goodwill* can be defined as "those elements of a business that cause customers to return and that usually enable the business to generate profit in excess of a reasonable return on all other assets of the business."

Thus defined, goodwill has a number of attributes, including:

Goodwill is an intangible asset.

Goodwill may be either commercial or personal (commercial goodwill is goodwill attached to or associated with a business enterprise; personal goodwill is goodwill associated with a person rather than with the business enterprise of which that person may be a part).

Goodwill is nonseverable from the business enterprise (commercial goodwill) or person (personal goodwill) with whom it is associated.

In the excess earnings method, the value of goodwill or other intangible assets is estimated from the earnings of the business to the extent that these earnings exceed a reasonable rate of return on the other identifiable (usually meaning tangible) assets of the business. Thus, valuation of an intangible asset by the excess earnings method involves the following steps:

1. First, the total earnings of the complete business or other investment are determined. Most often, this consists of actual historical earnings as determined from an economic income/expense statement.

2. Next, a value is determined for the total assets excluding only the goodwill or other intangible assets whose value is to be estimated by the excess earnings method. Typically, the value of these other assets is determined from an economic balance sheet prepared according to the replacement cost approach.

3. A rate of return is selected as representing a reasonable rate of return on the assets whose value was estimated in the second step. Although there is no widely accepted method for selecting this reasonable rate of return, it will generally correspond to a relatively safe rate of return, or capitalization rate, as determined according to one or more of the methods previously described in this chapter.

4. The estimated value of the tangible assets of the business as determined in the second step is multiplied by the rate of return chosen in the third step. The product then is deemed to be the portion of the total profit that is attributable to the assets in question—that is, all of the assets of the business excluding the assets whose value is to be determined by the excess earnings method.

5. The profit calculated in the fourth step as being attributable to the other assets of the business is subtracted from the total profit as determined in the first step. This profit difference, or excess profit, then is considered to be the profit attributable to the goodwill or other intangible assets being valued by the excess earnings method.

6. Next, a capitalization rate is selected, using one or more of the techniques previously described in this chapter, which is considered appropriate for application to the excess earnings attributed to the goodwill or other intangible assets being valued.

7. Finally, the amount of excess earnings is divided by the capitalization rate applicable to the intangible being valued, to arrive at the estimated value of the goodwill or other intangible asset.

Although the process sounds relatively complex, it is actually fairly simple in practice.

The following is an example of an actual estimate of goodwill value by the excess earnings method:

Total annual profit from entire business		$100,000
Less profit attributable to tangible assets:		
Estimated fair market value of tangible assets	$380,000	
Times reasonable rate of return	× 0.15	
		57,000
Excess profit attributable to intangible assets		43,000
Divided by capitalization rate applicable to intangible assets		0.25
Estimated value of intangible assets		$172,000

The total value of the business is, of course, the sum of the value of tangible assets and the estimated value of the intangible assets.

Thus, in the example given:

Estimated fair market value of tangible assets	$380,000
Plus estimated value of intangible assets	172,000
Estimated total value of business including both tangible and intangible assets	$552,000

Although it is frequently the only method available for estimating the value of some intangible assets, especially goodwill, the excess earnings method presents a number of problems.

For one thing, there is the somewhat philosophical objection that, inasmuch as goodwill is by nature recognized as being nonseverable from the business or person with whom it is associated, there is a certain amount of illogic in attempting to separate the goodwill from the remainder of the business and then to attribute portions of the total profit to each part. While this objection is probably valid, the fact is that the excess earnings method is in wide use and in many cases is the only method available for estimating the value of goodwill.

On a more practical level, the excess earnings method requires difficult determinations both of the rate of return to be attributed to the tangible assets of the business and the capitalization rate to be used in estimating the value of the goodwill or other intangible assets. Selection of a single capitalization rate to be used in a given situation is difficult at best, and the requirement as imposed by the excess earnings method to arrive at two capitalization rates compounds the difficulty.

Although choice of the appropriate rate of return or capitalization rate necessarily will be a matter of judgment by the appraiser according to the circumstances of each situation, it generally will be true that the rate of return to be applied in determining the earnings attributable to tangible assets will be a relatively safe rate of return, inasmuch as the nature of tangible assets is such that they involve less risk than either intangible assets or a complete business enterprise.

As for the capitalization rate to be used in estimating the value of goodwill or other intangibles, it must, of course, be significantly higher than the rate of return that is applied to the tangible assets. How much higher is a matter of judgment, depending in large measure on the appraiser's perception of the relative risk attached to an essentially fragile asset such as goodwill, as compared to the risk attached to tangible assets that have, at least to some degree, a market value independent of the business enterprise.

ADVANTAGES AND DISADVANTAGES OF INVESTMENT VALUE APPROACH

One advantage of the investment value approach is the fact that it reflects a concept that is in itself attractive. It represents the broadest application of the Principle of Substitution as applied to investments. In a sense, it could be said that the investment value approach gets straight to the heart of the matter in relating the value of a business or other investment to the amount of income it produces for its owner.

From the standpoint of the mathematics it requires, the investment value approach could be said to be a single-step method for estimating the value of a complete business. In this respect, it is somewhat less complex and therefore less time-consuming than either the market data approach or the replacement cost approach.

A further advantage of the investment value approach is that it is frequently the only available approach to estimating the value of some intangibles, such as goodwill.

However, the investment value approach also has some important disadvantages. A major disadvantage is the difficulty of selecting an appropriate capitalization rate to be applied to expected future earnings. Selection of capitalization rate inevitably requires that the appraiser exercise a large degree of judgment. The capitalization rate that is finally selected is, at best, an approximation, and the mathematical process used in converting the capitalization rate into an estimate of value is such that the almost inevitable errors in choosing the capitalization rate have a tendency to be magnified in terms of resulting errors in the estimated value of the business or other property being appraised.

In addition to the difficulty of selecting the capitalization rate, the process of arriving at a reasonable estimate of future earnings to be capitalized also contains the potential for errors. All in all, however, the problems involved in estimating the amount of earnings to be capitalized are somewhat smaller in magnitude than the problems in arriving at an appropriate capitalization rate.

11
Analyzing the Facts— Other Approaches

11
Analyzing the Facts— Other Approaches

OTHER APPROACHES TO ESTIMATING VALUE

The preceding chapters have described the three most widely recognized approaches to estimating economic value, namely the market data approach, the replacement cost approach, and the investment value approach.

In addition, there are a number of other approaches to estimating economic value that can be useful in specific situations. Some of these are:

Liquidation value approach

Discounted future earnings approach

Cost to create approach

Justification for purchase test

One additional subject discussed in this chapter concerns discounts for lack of marketability.

253

THE LIQUIDATION VALUE APPROACH

The *liquidation value approach* to estimating economic value is an asset-based approach. In this and other respects, it is similar to the replacement cost approach described in Chapter 9. However, there are important differences between the liquidation value approach and the replacement cost approach, as will be apparent from the following discussion.

As applied to businesses, the concept of liquidation value assumes that operations of the business are terminated and that the assets of the business are then sold or otherwise disposed of for gain. A further assumption is that the liabilities of the business are satisfied, from the proceeds from the sale of assets or otherwise.

In this context, the liquidation value of a business is the net price received from sale or other disposition of the assets, less the cost of satisfying the liabilities. Depending on the function of the appraisal, an estimate of liquidation value also may need to include the estimated cost of the liquidation process, such as brokers' or attorneys' fees, liabilities whose existence may arise from the liquidation itself, and so on.

In the definition of liquidation value as given in Chapter 2, it was pointed out that there are two different types of liquidation value, namely forced liquidation and orderly disposal.

Forced liquidation of a business is the kind of liquidation that occurs when, for reasons usually related to financial insolvency but sometimes for other reasons, the owners of a business—or, in some cases, trustees—are forced to dispose of the assets of the business in a relatively short time, and otherwise under such circumstances that they are frequently not able to obtain the highest price the various assets otherwise would bring. Because of circumstances including the relatively short time available to find buyers for the various assets, together with the fact that the seller is almost always under some degree of compulsion or duress, the value of a business under forced liquidation is almost always substantially less than the value it would have under more favorable circumstances, including orderly disposal.

Orderly disposal is a form of liquidation in which the seller is under no great time pressure or other compulsion and is therefore able to secure prices for the various assets that generally will be somewhat higher than the prices that would apply in the case of forced liquidation. Thus, the liquidation value of a given business under an assumption of orderly disposal is almost always higher than it would be in event of a forced liquidation. Even under the orderly disposal assumption, however, the liquidation value of a business usually will be lower than its value as an ongoing business, for reasons that will be discussed.

For reasons including its wider applicability, the orderly disposal type of liquidation will be assumed in the detailed discussion of liquidation value that follows. However, the reader will recognize that, in estimating the value of a business under forced liquidation circumstances, essentially the same techniques will apply, given the difference in individual asset values to be expected under forced liquidation as compared to orderly disposal circumstances.

The liquidation value approach to estimating the economic value of a business may be applicable in various situations, including some that do not involve the prospect of actual liquidation of the business. Thus, an estimate of liquidation value may be in order:

When actual liquidation of the business is a real and imminent possibility

As an aid in estimating the loan value of the business

To provide a lower limit, or benchmark, for the possible range of values of a business as a going concern

As an indication of the absolute amount of financial risk involved in a going business

In addition to situations involving forced liquidation, a business may be a candidate for orderly liquidation if it is and promises to be unprofitable, or only marginally profitable, in which case it might be more profitable to liquidate the business than to continue its operation.

Another situation that may call for liquidation of a business is one in which the owner–manager of a closely held business has died or is for some other reason unable to continue operating it, and there are no apparent heirs or buyers available to take his or her place.

In any of the foregoing situations, application of the liquidation value approach will be useful in providing an estimate of the actual value of the business in the event of liquidation.

The policies of most lenders are such that the amount they are willing to lend with a business as collateral is more closely related to the liquidation value of the business than to its value from other viewpoints. Accordingly, value as estimated by the liquidation value approach can provide at least a rough indication of the amount a lender might be willing to lend with the business as collateral. Lender policies vary, however, as do the amounts a given lender is willing to lend on various categories of assets. Accordingly, if it is desired to estimate the loan value of a business with as much accuracy as possible, the value estimate should take account of the actual lending policies (e.g., loan-to-value ratios, etc.) of the specific lender.

In the case of businesses for which liquidation is not a real possibility in the foreseeable future, the liquidation value approach still can yield information of substantial value to the appraiser. Because the actual market value of any business that is more than minimally profitable is almost always greater than its liquidation value, an estimate of the liquidation value (orderly disposal basis) of the business can provide the appraiser with a value benchmark in the form of a lower limit on the range of possible values for the business.

Finally, use of the liquidation value approach to estimate the value of a business in event of an orderly disposal can provide a measure of the amount that is at risk in ownership of the business. That is, an investor in the business could not expect to lose, even under the worst circumstances, an amount greater than the difference between the total investment in the business and its liquidation value. Although somewhat limited in terms of its usefulness as part of the appraisal process, such a measure of risk can be helpful in arriving at actual investment decisions.

Application of the liquidation value approach in a given situation is carried out by means of the following steps:

1. A list is prepared showing all assets, either individually or by category, that are included in the business or other property whose liquidation value is to be estimated.

2. An estimate is then made and recorded of the proceeds that would be expected from sale of each asset, or of all the assets in each category, under the assumed circumstances (that is, either forced liquidation or orderly disposal) of the liquidation value estimate.

3. A list is made of all existing liabilities, individually or by category, of the business or other property that is to be liquidated.

4. A dollar value is assigned to each liability, giving consideration to the nature and circumstances of the contemplated liquidation.

5. The total estimated value of all liabilities then is subtracted from the total estimated proceeds from liquidation of the assets, this difference being the net estimated liquidation value of the business or other property.

These steps will lead the appraiser to an estimate of liquidation value that, however, does not include any provision for costs or liabilities of the liquidation process itself. Such an estimate is appropriate for some purposes, as when the estimated liquidation value is to provide an indication of the lower limit of the possible range of values of a business as a going concern, or when it is to be used as an indication of the amount of financial risk involved. However, when the reason for estimating liquidation value makes liquidation a real rather than merely a hypothetical possibility, it is necessary to take one additional step:

6. Those additional liabilities and costs that arise from the liquidation process itself are identified, the amounts of these costs are estimated, and this estimated total is subtracted from the liquidation value as previously determined. This new figure then will be the estimated liquidation value of the business after giving consideration to costs and liabilities arising out of the liquidation process.

In carrying out the steps leading to an estimate of the liquidation value of a business, the list of assets should be prepared in a manner similar to that used in connection with the replacement cost approach as described in Chapter 9. That is, the starting point for preparation of the list of assets ordinarily will be a current balance sheet for the business, either an accountants' balance sheet or, preferably, the economic balance sheet as described in Chapter 7. As with the replacement cost approach, care must be taken to ensure that the list of assets includes all significant assets of the business, even though some of them, for one reason or another, may not appear on the accountants' balance sheet.

Once the list of assets has been prepared, the price each of them would bring at liquidation will be estimated, either for each individual asset or by asset category, in a manner that will vary according to the type of asset. In some cases, the appraiser will be able to estimate the various amounts himself or herself, while in other cases he or she may need help from one or more kinds of specialists, such as appraisers of machinery or real property.

As a general guide for estimating liquidation value, Exhibit 15 illustrates what might be considered typical relationships among the values of various types of assets for different purposes, including the liquidation value approach. The relationships shown in the table are general and should not be used as a substitute for actual estimates pertinent to specific situations.

The listing of existing liabilities, which is the third step in applying the

Exhibit 15

TYPICAL RELATIONSHIP AMONG ASSET VALUES FOR VARIOUS PURPOSES

Basis for Asset Value for Purposes of:

Type of Asset	Accountant's Balance Sheet (book values)	Replacement Cost Approach (economic balance sheet)	Liquidation Value
Cash	Actual amount	Actual amount	Actual amount
Accounts receivable	Actual amount after reserve for doubtful accounts	Actual amount, collectible portion only	Estimated amount collectible in event of liquidation
Marketable securities	(1) Lower of cost or market, or (2) market value	Market value	Market value
Inventory:			
Raw materials	Cost	Cost	(1) Cost less vendor's restocking charge, or (2) scrap value
Work in process	Cost	(1) Cost, or (2) cost plus pro rata profit	Scrap or salvage value
Finished goods	Cost	Market value	Market value but under liquidation conditions
Prepaid expenses	Actual amount	Actual amount	Recoverable portion
Fixed assets	Cost less accumulated depreciation at maximum rate allowable for tax purposes	(1) Normal market value, or (2) estimated cost to replace	Market value under liquidation conditions
Patents and copyrights	Cost, narrowly interpreted	(1) Market value, or (2) estimated contribution to total value of business	Market value if any, otherwise zero
Goodwill	(1) Omitted, or (2)	Estimated contribution	None

258

liquidation value approach, usually will proceed directly from the balance sheet of the business, as already described in Chapters 6 and 7.

Likewise, the dollar amounts of the various liabilities for purposes of the liquidation value estimate in most cases will be identical with the amounts shown on the accountants' or economic balance sheet of the business. As in the case of the replacement cost approach, however, there may be exceptions in the case of liabilities involving transactions with the owner of the business. Thus, the estimated amount of liabilities for liquidation value purposes should include debts to the owner of the business only to the extent that such debts actually would be repaid upon liquidation of the business.

As already stated, there is one additional step to be taken when the circumstances of the liquidation value estimate are such that liquidation of the business is a real possibility. This step is to identify the costs and liabilities that will arise out of the liquidation process, to estimate the dollar amount of each, and then to subtract the total of such estimates from the estimated liquidation value as determined from the results of the preceding steps. The nature of these liabilities and costs arising out of the liquidation process will vary somewhat from situation to situation and may include such items as:

Brokers' commissions, such as in connection with sale of real estate, machinery and equipment, and so on

Attorneys' fees

Possible tax liabilities arising out of the liquidation, such as possible capital gains taxes on assets sold for a liquidation price that exceeds their basis cost less accumulated depreciation, changes in income tax liability as a result of the liquidation, and so on. (It is also possible that liquidation of a business could produce tax benefits in some circumstances.)

Termination pay to employees

Cost of completing funding of pension plans

Short rate or cancellation charges for insurance

By the way of illustration, Exhibit 16 presents a comparison for the fictitious XYZ Corporation of values of individual assets and liabilities as shown on the accountants' balance sheet, the economic balance sheet, and a liquidation balance sheet. While these values are hypothetical, the relationships they illustrate are more or less typical of what may be found in actual situations.

Reviewing the hypothetical comparisons in the table, it will be noted that the total estimated liquidation value of XYZ Corporation is substantially less than its value as shown on the economic balance sheet (which corresponds closely with estimated value according to the replacement cost approach). In this particular situation, total estimated liquidation value is also less than total book value as shown on the accountants' balance sheet. However, this will not necessarily be the case in all situations.

In the situation illustrated by Exhibit 16, the asset that represents the greatest individual difference between liquidation value and value as shown on the economic balance sheet is work in process. This is because the total amount of work in process was itself substantial, and the liquidation value of work in process was estimated in terms of a salvage value equal to only 50% of total cost. This relationship would vary depending on the kind of products involved, of course, and in some cases the salvage value may be less than 50% of total cost, as when costs include high labor content or when materials have been modified in such a way as to have little or no salvage value.

In the hypothetical case of XYZ Corporation, other significant differences between liquidation value and value as shown on an economic balance sheet will be found in the asset categories for patents and copyrights, finished goods, raw materials, and accounts receivable. And, of course, whatever goodwill value a business may have as an ongoing business is totally lost in event of liquidation. This follows from the nature of goodwill as an asset that is non-severable from the business of which it is a part. (This will not necessarily be true of some other intangible assets, such as trademarks, customer lists, and so on. Such other intangible assets may sometimes be saleable to other businesses in the same industry, though frequently at a price substantially lower than their original value as part of the ongoing business whose liquidation value is being estimated.)

Exhibit 16
XYZ CORPORATION
COMPARISON OF VALUES AS OF DECEMBER 31, 19X1

	Accountants' Balance Sheet[a]	Economic Balance Sheet[b]	Liquidation Value
ASSETS			
Cash	$ 126,845	$ 126,845	$ 126,845
Accounts receivable	$ 482,005	$ 482,005	$ 482,005
Less estimated uncollectible	25,000	25,000	50,000 [c]
Net receivables	$ 457,005	$ 457,005	$ 432,005

Exhibit 16 *(Continued)*

	Accountants' Balance Sheet[a]	Economic Balance Sheet[b]	Liquidation Value
Marketable securities	$ 155,977	$ 216,631	$ 216,631
Inventory:			
Raw materials	$ 154,136	$ 154,136	$ 131,016 [d]
Work in process	540,165	604,985	270,082 [e]
Finished goods	351,971	394,208	354,787 [f]
Total inventory	$1,046,272	$1,153,329	$ 755,885
Prepaid expense	$ 4,924	$ 4,924	$ 4,924
Fixed assets	430,889	515,744	464,170 [f]
Patents and copyrights	45,680	96,280	5,000 [g]
Goodwill	1	15,400	0
Total assets	$2,267,593	$2,586,158	$2,005,460
LIABILITIES			
Accounts payable	$ 446,102	$ 446,102	$ 446,102
Notes and loans payable	833,436	783,436	783,436
Mortgages on land, buildings	610,286	610,286	610,286
Accrued expenses	26,240	26,240	26,240
Reserve for taxes	52,000	52,000	52,000
Other liabilities	45,996	45,996	45,996
Total liabilities	$2,014,060	$1,964,060	$1,964,060
Net, assets less liabilities	$ 253,533	$ 622,098	$ 41,400

[a] Figures are from Chapter 6, Exhibit 3.
[b] Figures are from Chapter 7, Exhibit 6.
[c] Includes provision for additional uncollectibles resulting from liquidation.
[d] Cost less provision for 15% restocking charge by vendor.
[e] Salvage value estimated as 50% of total cost.
[f] Normal market value less provision for 10% liquidation discount.
[g] Estimate of price at which certain patents or copyrights might be sold to competitors.

THE DISCOUNTED FUTURE EARNINGS APPROACH

The *discounted future earnings approach* to estimating economic value is an income-based approach. In this respect it is similar to the investment value approach described in Chapter 10. However, there are substantial differences between the discounted future earnings approach and the investment value approach, as will be apparent from the following discussion.

The discounted future earnings approach has its basis in the fact that a sum of money that is expected to be received at some time in the future has less present value than the same amount of money in hand today.

A given sum of money in hand today can be invested so as to earn interest, with the result that its total value in the future will be greater than the initial principal amount to an extent that depends on the interest rate, or yield, on the original principal. However, if the principal amount is not in hand today but instead is promised for some time in the future, then its present value is less than the future principal amount, because of the interest that it will not be earning in the meantime.

Very briefly, the foregoing is the basis for the discounted future earnings approach to estimating economic value.

In applying the discounted future earnings approach to estimating economic value, the amount of future earnings from the business or other investment is estimated for each of a number of years into the future. The estimated earnings for each year are then discounted at the appropriate rate to determine their present value, and the present values of estimated earnings for all future years are then added to determine the total present value. Finally, the residual value of the property at the end of the period of years is estimated, and this value as discounted to its equivalent present value is then added to the present value of estimated future earnings to determine the total present value of the business or other property.

This approach is in contrast to the investment value approach as described in Chapter 10. In the investment value approach, a single figure for estimated annual earnings is capitalized (the converse of discounting) to determine the investment value of the business or other property. This single-step method as used in the investment value approach is frequently referred to as straight capitalization. It is in contrast to the multistep method that is required by the discounted future earnings approach.

Partly because of its relative simplicity, the investment value approach, or straight capitalization, is preferred by most appraisers when circumstances permit its use. These circumstances include the likelihood of a more or less constant stream of future earnings, availability of the necessary information from which to predict the amount of these earnings, and availability of information from which to determine an appropriate capitalization rate.

However, there are situations in which not all of the requirements for application of the investment value approach are met. In such situations, the discounted future earnings approach can provide a useful alternative, though one that is somewhat more tedious from the standpoint of the required calculations.

The discounted future earnings approach is particularly applicable when estimating the economic value of a business or other property on the basis of anticipated future earnings that are not expected to remain relatively constant from year to year.

Such a situation can arise, for example, with a business whose earnings are related to wasting (that is, nonrenewable) resources such as mineral deposits, short-term licenses of one kind or another, and so on. In such cases, earnings can be expected to decline at a relatively rapid rate or to terminate altogether within a relatively few years. Whereas the straight capitalization method of the investment value approach is not applicable in such situations, the discounted future earnings approach can be used.

Another kind of situation that may call for application of the discounted future earnings approach is one in which future earnings are expected to increase other than at a moderate and relatively steady rate. Such a situation may result, for example, from a major new product whose market debut is imminent but that has not had a significant impact on earnings up to the date of the appraisal. Another possible cause of a sharp increase in future earnings is the end of some situation that has had a depressing effect on past earnings but is scheduled to terminate at some definite date in the future. An example of the latter might be heavy payments under a noncompete or similar agreement with a former owner of the business.

There are two principal forms of the discounted future earnings approach to estimating economic value. Though similar in concept and method, the two forms differ from the standpoint of the kind of future earnings that are discounted as part of the process of estimating economic value.

One of the two forms of the discounted future earnings approach is based on estimated future profit. The second form is based on estimated future cash flow from the business or other property. This second form, which is frequently referred to as the discounted cash flow approach, is more common.

Depending on circumstances, either the discounted future profit or the discounted cash flow form of the discounted future earnings approach can be used to estimate the economic value of a business or other property. This assumes that the necessary information is available from which to estimate the amount of future profit or cash flow, as the case may be, and that the discount rate used is consistent with, among other things, the kind of earnings on which the calculations are based.

Whichever form is used, application of the discounted future earnings approach involves the following steps:

1. An estimate is made of the amount of future earnings, year by year for at least several years into the future.
2. A discount rate is selected by the appraiser as the appropriate rate to apply in the situation at hand.
3. The amount of estimated earnings for each future year is discounted at the selected rate to arrive at a figure for the present value of that year's estimated earnings.
4. The present value figures for all future years' earnings then are added to determine the total present value of all future earnings
5. The estimated residual value of the business or other property at the end of the period of years is discounted to the present and added to the total present value of earnings to arrive at a final figure for the total present value of the business or other property.

The year-by-year estimate of future earnings is, of course, based on the information the appraiser has gathered about the business or other property being appraised and about the business environment in which it operates.

If the discounted future profit form of the approach is to be used, the various annual estimates of future profit may be based on techniques at least analagous to the economic income/expense statement discussed in Chapter 7. Rather than using estimated figures for net operating profit before taxes, however, it frequently will be desirable to estimate the effect of applicable income taxes on each year's estimated profits. One reason is that use of estimated after-tax figures will greatly facilitate selection from available data of a truly meaningful discount rate.

If the cash flow form of the discounted future earnings approach is to be used, the amount of each year's earnings will be estimated by techniques similar to those that would be used to estimate profits, except that the estimates will be of each year's cash flow rather than profit. For purposes such as the present one, cash flow can be defined as net profit after being adjusted for accounting items of a noncash nature. Such items include, for example, depreciation and amortization, which are noncash expenses that result in upward adjustment of the figure for net profit. Downward adjustment of the net profit figure may be in order to reflect such items as loan amortization and capital expenditures, which do not affect profit as shown on the income/ expense statement but do place demands on available cash.

The second step in applying the discounted future earnings approach is to select the appropriate discount rate. This is done in a manner similar to that used to arrive at a capitalization rate in connection with the investment value approach, as discussed in Chapter 10. That is, the discount rate selected will be a result of considerations including anticipated future interests rates, together with the degree of risk involved in the particular buisness or other investment being appraised.

Although the capitalization rate for use with the investment value approach and the discount rate for use with the discounted future earnings approach are selected by similar processes, they are not necessarily identical figures in a given situation. This is because of differences in the respective mathematical processes with which they are used. In the great majority of cases, however, capitalization rate and discount rate should be of at least similar magnitude for a given set of investment circumstances.

The third step in applying the discounted future earnings approach is to apply the selected discount rate so as to determine the present value of each year's predicted earnings.

The mathematical relationship is:

$$P_n = \frac{E_n}{(1 + d)^n}$$

where P_n = present value of the nth year's earnings,
$\qquad E_n$ = estimated amount of earnings for the nth year,
$\qquad d$ = discount rate

To save the appraiser the labor of making calculations using the above formula, tables are available that show the present value of a future payment as a function of the discount (or interest) rate and the number of years in the future in which the payment is to be received. The data in such tables are customarily normalized in terms of the present value of the sum of one dollar; the present value of future payments of other amounts then can be determined by simple multiplication.

Exhibit 17 shows the present value of one dollar to be received at various times from one to 13 years in the future, and at discount rates ranging from 5% to 60% in increments of 5%. This table should be adequate for most appraisal-related purposes. For appraisers who require information extending over a period greater than 13 years, or for discounts in increments finer than 5%, various books of mathematical and financial data include present value tables extending for as long as 100 years into the future and for discount (interest) rates in increments of a fraction of a percent.

It will be seen in Exhibit 17 that the present value, at a discount rate of 20% per year, of one dollar to be received five years from now, is $0.402. Thus, the present value of $1,000, at the same discount rate and to be received at the same time, would be $402.

Similarly, the exhibit shows that the present value at a discount rate of 30% of a payment to be received in six years would be $0.207 per dollar or $207 per thousand dollars of future payment.

The fourth step in applying the discounted future earnings approach is to add the present values, as determined with the aid of a table such as Exhibit 17, of expected earnings for all future years. The manner in which this is done is best explained by means of an example, as also is the final step in applying the discounted future earnings approach, which is to determine the present value of the business or other property as it will exist at the end of the period of years, and to add this amount to the total present value of future earnings.

Assume that we are to use the discounted future earnings approach to estimate the economic value of a business (or of any other kind of investment, for that matter) that is predicted to produce the following amount of earnings for each of the next five years:

	Estimated amount of earnings
First year	$50,000
Second year	$40,000
Third year	$35,000
Fourth year	$20,000
Fifth year	$15,000

Further, assume that it has been determined that a discount rate of 25% would be appropriate and that the business is estimated to have a residual value (such as in terms of its net tangible assets at that time) of approximately $100,000 at the end of the fifth year.

Exhibit 17

PRESENT VALUE OF ONE DOLLAR TO BE RECEIVED IN THE FUTURE

Discount Rate per Annum

Years Hence	5%	10%	15%	20%	25%	30%	35%	40%	45%	50%	55%	60%
0	1.000	1.000	1.000	1.000	1.000	1.000	1.000	1.000	1.000	1.000	1.000	1.000
1	0.952	0.909	0.870	0.833	0.800	0.769	0.741	0.714	0.690	0.667	0.645	0.625
2	0.907	0.826	0.756	0.694	0.640	0.592	0.549	0.510	0.476	0.444	0.416	0.391
3	0.864	0.751	0.658	0.579	0.512	0.455	0.406	0.364	0.328	0.296	0.269	0.244
4	0.823	0.683	0.572	0.482	0.410	0.350	0.301	0.260	0.226	0.198	0.173	0.153
5	0.784	0.621	0.497	0.402	0.328	0.269	0.223	0.186	0.156	0.132	0.112	0.095
6	0.746	0.564	0.432	0.335	0.262	0.207	0.165	0.133	0.106	0.088	0.072	0.060
7	0.711	0.513	0.376	0.279	0.210	0.159	0.122	0.095	0.074	0.059	0.047	0.037
8	0.677	0.467	0.327	0.233	0.168	0.123	0.091	0.068	0.051	0.039	0.030	0.023
9	0.645	0.424	0.284	0.194	0.134	0.094	0.067	0.048	0.035	0.026	0.019	0.015
10	0.614	0.386	0.247	0.162	0.107	0.073	0.050	0.035	0.024	0.017	0.012	0.009
11	0.585	0.350	0.215	0.135	0.086	0.056	0.037	0.025	0.017	0.012	0.008	0.006
12	0.557	0.319	0.187	0.112	0.069	0.043	0.027	0.018	0.012	0.008	0.005	0.004
13	0.530	0.290	0.163	0.093	0.055	0.033	0.020	0.013	0.008	0.005	0.003	0.002

The calculations leading to the estimate of the present value of the business are shown in Exhibit 18, which the reader should find self-explanatory.

Before concluding discussion of the discounted future earnings approach, two points should be mentioned in connection with present value tables such as Exhibit 17.

Exhibit 17 includes a line of figures for year 0. This line of figures, showing a present value of 1.000 regardless of discount rate, is included in the exhibit to emphasize that 1.000 is the starting point for present values at all discount rates. Figures for year 0 are, of course, not included in actual calculations of the present value of a stream of earnings. If not already obvious, this will be apparent from the example of Exhibit 18.

The second point to be mentioned regarding the figures in present value tables concerns their relationship to the straight capitalization process as used with the investment value approach.

The total present value of a constant stream of income, in perpetuity, can be determined by adding the present value factors for the applicable discount rate, beginning with year 1 and continuing—at least in theory—indefinitely.

Exhibit 18
PRESENT VALUE OF FUTURE EARNINGS
EXAMPLE OF CALCULATIONS

Assumptions: (1) Earnings each year for five years in amounts shown below
(2) Residual value $100,000 at end of fifth year
(3) Discount rate 25% per annum

Year	Annual Earnings		Present Value Factor		Present Value
1	$ 50,000	×	0.800	=	$ 40,000
2	$ 40,000	×	0.640	=	25,600
3	$ 35,000	×	0.512	=	17,920
4	$ 20,000	×	0.410	=	8,200
5	$ 15,000	×	0.328	=	4,920
Earnings total					$ 96,640
Plus present value of residual:					
5	$100,000	×	0.328	=	32,800
Total present value					$129,440

As a practical matter, the present value factor at a given discount rate becomes progressively smaller the more distant the year in question, so that the contribution to total present value on the part of very distant years tends to be negligible.

Thus, the sum of the present value factors for a discount rate of 35% beginning with year 1 and continuing through the thirteenth year is 2.799. This means that a constant stream of income of, say, $1,000 per year for 13 years, would have a present value of $2,799 at the discount rate of 35%.

This corresponds with an investment value as calculated by the investment value approach, and using the rate of 35% as a capitalization rate, of

$$\text{investment value} = \frac{\$1,000}{0.35} = \$2,857$$

This illustrates the tendency of the total present value of a constant stream of income as calculated according to the discounted future earnings approach to converge with the investment value as calculated according to the investment value approach. If the calculations of present value are carried out for an infinite number of years, then the results obtained by the two methods will be in exact agreement. However, the agreement between the results produced by the two methods becomes sufficiently good for practical purposes when the calculations by the discounted future earnings approach are carried out for a number of years that, depending on the applicable discount or capitalization rate, is relatively small.

THE COST TO CREATE APPROACH

Although it has only very limited application in appraising and is generally not recognized as an acceptable appraisal method, the *cost to create approach* deserves at least brief mention.

In the cost to create approach, the value of an asset or group of assets is estimated directly from the cost that was incurred to create or acquire the assets. This is in contrast to the replacement cost approach, which bases the value estimate on the cost to replace, rather than to originally create or acquire, the property.

The appraiser occasionally will encounter situations in which the owner of a business or other property values it on the basis of what is, in effect, the cost to create approach. This may happen, for example, with owners who are thinking of selling their businesses.

If the business is not doing well financially, the owner very well may attempt to establish its value on a cost-to-create basis. This is, of course, an incorrect approach and results primarily from failure to make a proper distinction between historical cost on the one hand and value (particularly as related to the Principle of Future Benefits) on the other hand. Such a situation should not be of concern to the appraiser, except to the extent that he or she may find it necessary to dissuade the owner from the incorrect viewpoint.

However, there sometimes can arise situations in which the cost to create approach may have legitimate applications in appraising.

In particular, this can happen with assets whose value cannot be estimated readily by other means, so that the cost to create approach becomes a method of last resort. Such situations are more likely to involve intangible assets, whose value is difficult to estimate under the best of circumstances, as compared to tangible assets whose value usually can be estimated by one of the other methods such as the replacement cost approach or the market data approach.

Thus, if an asset such as a copyright is quite evidently making a positive contribution to the profitability of an overall business, but in such a way that the amount of this contribution cannot be determined by any more direct means, the cost of originally creating the copyrighted material and obtaining the copyright itself can be used as an indication of the value of the copyright. The same might be true of a patent, in which case the estimate of cost to create should include not only the legal fees and patent office filing fees to obtain the actual patent but also the research or other effort that produced the invention in the first place.

In the case of limited-life assets such as copyrights and patents, the original cost to create, of course, should be reduced proportionately over the life of the asset in order to arrive at a figure for remaining value at any given valuation date.

Various proprietary items, such as trade formulas or processes, or various kinds of customer and/or prospect lists, are other examples of assets that can be valued by means of the cost to create approach.

In applying the cost to create approach to estimate value, it is important to distinguish between historical costs that actually have contributed to the value of the asset and other costs that, for one reason or another, may have contributed little or nothing to value. The need for this distinction becomes particularly evident when applying the cost to create approach to estimate the value of goodwill.

The cost to create approach is sometimes used as a basis for estimating the value of goodwill, either when no other method of valuing goodwill seems to apply or as a check on the results obtained by another method, such as the excess earnings method described in Chapter 10.

Historical costs that might reasonably be regarded as having contributed to the goodwill of a business might include:

Advertising costs of various types

Costs to acquire assets of such nature that they have essentially no intrinsic value except as goodwill (examples might be trademarks or celebrity endorsements)

Unusual services performed for special customers, the cost of which exceeds any income derived directly from the services

Costs of certain kinds of charitable or community service programs, provided the program is of such nature as to contribute significantly to goodwill, rather than merely satisfying a perceived public service obligation.

It will be evident that not all activities such as those listed above are fully cost-effective in the sense of producing a full measure of goodwill in return for each dollar expended.

Provided they are part of a well-thought-out and competently executed marketing program, expenditures for such purely goodwill purposes as acquiring trademarks or celebrity endorsements are among those most likely to produce a full measure of goodwill in return for costs incurred. Even advertising costs, however, frequently fall short of the hoped-for results and thus represent a cost that is only partially effective in terms of the goodwill produced.

As for such expenditures as community service programs, the nature of most such programs is such that, for reasons such as the targets at which the programs are directed or lack of close identification of the business contributor with the benefits, the return in terms of actual goodwill value is relatively small.

It will be apparent that, when the cost to create approach is employed to estimate the value of goodwill or other intangibles, it frequently will be appropriate to discount the historical costs substantially in order to arrive at a reasonable estimate of the value of the resulting goodwill.

THE JUSTIFICATION FOR PURCHASE TEST

The approach called the *justification for purchase test* sometimes is called by other names, including the business broker's method, the acid test, and the ability formula.

The justification for purchase test is not, strictly speaking, a method for estimating the value of a business or other property, as are the various approaches that have been described in Chapters 8, 9, and 10 and in the preceding portions of this chapter. Rather, the justification for purchase test provides a means to test the reasonableness of value estimates that have been made by one or more of the other approaches. An especially important application of the justification for purchase test is to determine the reasonableness of the proposed selling price for a business or other property that is actually to be offered for sale.

In essence, the justification for purchase test consists of (1) assuming that the business or other property is actually purchased by a buyer who pays a price equal to the appraised value, and then (2) examining the transaction from the buyer's viewpoint to determine whether the purchase was, in fact, an economically sound move. Generally speaking, the purchase of a business or other income producing property can be considered to be economically sound if the income produced is sufficient to permit the property to pay for itself over a reasonable period of time and if the buyer's rate of return on investment compares favorably with rates of return available on other, alternative, investments within the universe of equally desirable substitutes.

A noteworthy difference between the justification for purchase test and much other appraisal methodology is that, whereas most appraisals are based on a market value definition that assumes, either implicitly or explicitly, an all-cash transaction, the justification for purchase test makes no such assumption. Rather, the justification for purchase test attempts to apply real world considerations, which usually include purchase of a business on a basis that includes a down payment together with subsequent installment payments, each of which bears interest at a specified rate.

The basic concept underlying the justification for purchase test, namely to explore the implications of a given estimated value under real world conditions, is applied in various ways depending on the circumstances of each individual situation.

Of particular interest in connection with appraisals of closely held businesses is application of the justification for purchase test as illustrated by the following example.

Assume that the fictitious ABC Company mentioned in Chapters 6 and 7 has been appraised, with the result that the company is estimated to have a fair market value of $320,000.

Further assume that ABC Company has an estimated future net operating profit of $81,484 per year as determined from the economic income/expense statement shown in Exhibit 8, and that this estimated net operating profit is after provision for expenses including an owner's salary of $30,000 per year. (It might be noted at this point that the assumed fair market value estimate of $320,000 for ABC Company could be the result of an appraisal by means of the investment value approach, with a 25% capitalization rate having been applied to the estimated net operating profit of $81,484 per year.)

Application of the justification for purchase test also requires information about the terms of payment in event of sale of the property being appraised. When the situation involves an actual (contemplated) sale, the proposed actual terms of payment should be used in applying the justification for purchase test. Otherwise, hypothetical terms of payment can be assumed, on the basis of what is considered to be common practice in the industry, locality, and so on.

In the present example it will be assumed that the total price of $320,000 will be paid by means of a down payment of 30% at the time of sale, with the balance to be paid in equal monthly installments over a period of five years, interest on the unpaid balance at the rate of 10% per year being added to each principal payment.

This results in a proposed transaction as follows:

Proposed Sale of ABC Company

Total price	$320,000
Terms of payment:	
down payment at time of sale 30% of total price	96,000
balance of purchase price to be financed	$224,000
Financed portion of total price	

to be paid in 60 monthly installments, each consisting of a principal payment of $3,733.33 (equivalent to $44,800 per year) plus interest on the unpaid balance at the rate of 10% per year

Projected future annual net operating profit,

after provision for all operating expenses including owner's salary but before income tax (from economic income/expense statement)	$ 81,484
Owner's annual salary, in addition to net operating profit as above	$ 30,000

On the basis of the foregoing information, it is now possible to carry out a series of calculations as shown in Exhibit 19.

The table includes a set of calculations for each year beginning with the date of sale and continuing until the results of the calculations stabilize, which occurs when the total purchase price has been paid and there are no further annual payments of principal and interest.

The upper part of the exhibit is devoted to calculations involving the principal and interest on the purchase price. The lower part of the table is devoted to calculations related to determining profits, including the buyer's net income after all expenditures including both principal and interest payment on the unpaid indebtedness, and also including the effect of estimated income tax.

Although the various calculations in the table should be self-explanatory, the reader may find the following discussion helpful.

Referring to the figures in Exhibit 19 for year 1, the upper part of the table shows that the outstanding balance of indebtedness, which stands at $224,000 at the beginning of the year, will be reduced by means of monthly principal payments totaling $44,800, to a new balance of $179,200 at the end of the year. As calculated from the average principal balance during the year, total interest payments during the year at the applicable rate of 10% of the unpaid principal balance will amount to $20,160.

Proceeding to the lower part of the exhibit, the first step in the profit-related calculations is to add the owner's salary to the net operating profit before tax, thus arriving at the owner's proprietary income. (This addition of owner's salary to operating profit is applicable in a closely held business, either a proprietorship or a so-called subchapter S corporation, in which the operating profit and owner's salary are combined for tax purposes. Otherwise, as in the case of larger businesses or businesses with several owners, calculations such as those in the exhibit would be based on business operating profit only, without adding back the owners' salaries.)

Continuing with the profit-related calculations in the table, the annual interest payment on the indebtedness is deducted from owner's proprietary

Exhibit 19

JUSTIFICATION FOR PURCHASE TEST—ABC COMPANY

Year	1	2	3	4	5	6 on
Principal balance at beginning of year	$224,000	$179,200	$134,400	$89,600	$44,800	$ 0
Less payment on principal	44,800	44,800	44,800	44,800	44,800	0
Principal balance at end of year	$179,200	$134,400	$89,600	$44,800	$ 0	$ 0
Interest on average balance	$20,160	$15,680	$11,200	$6,720	$2,240	$ 0
Net operating profit pretax	$81,484	$81,484	$81,484	$81,484	$81,484	$81,484
Plus owner's salary	30,000	30,000	30,000	30,000	30,000	30,000
Owner's proprietary income	$111,484	$111,484	$111,484	$111,484	$111,484	$111,484
Less interest	20,160	15,680	11,200	6,720	2,240	0
Owner's taxable income	$91,324	$95,804	$100,284	$104,764	$109,244	$111,484
Less estimated tax	31,661	33,870	36,249	38,628	41,006	42,328
Net income after tax	$59,663	$61,934	$64,035	$66,136	$68,238	$69,156
Less payment on principal	44,800	44,800	44,800	44,800	44,800	0
Owner's net cash flow	$14,863	$17,134	$19,235	$21,336	$23,438	$69,156

275

income (or from net operating profit before tax in the case of larger or widely held businesses) to determine the net taxable income. Income tax on this taxable income then is estimated using applicable tax rate tables, and is deducted from total taxable income to determine net income after tax. (In the table, taxes have been estimated on the basis of assumptions including (1) that the business is either a proprietorship or a subchapter S corporation, with the result in either case that the net operating profit from the business and the owner's salary are treated as a single item for tax purposes; (2) that the owner has no other significant source of income; (3) that the owner's personal deductions from gross income to determine taxable income are what might be considered normal, and (4) that applicable tax rates are those in effect at the time this is written.)

Next, the annual payment on the principal of the indebtedness is deducted from the net operating profit after tax, the resulting difference being the owner's net cash flow from the business. The reader will understand, it is assumed, that annual payments of interest on the indebtedness were deducted from profit *before* tax because interest is considered a deductible expense for tax purposes, whereas payments on the principal amount were deducted from the profit *after* tax because principal payments are not considered a deductible expense for tax purposes.

The bottom figure in each column of the table represents the owner's net cash flow income for the corresponding year. This figure is inclusive of the owner's salary (nominally $30,000 per year), which was added to the business operating profit as the first step in the profit calculations. Thus, the owner's total after-tax income from the business during the first year is somewhat less than $15,000.

Although this figure may at first seem disappointing when compared with the annual salary of $30,000 that was assumed in the economic income/expense statement, two points must be kept in mind. First, in addition to the owner's net income, the business also has provided the funds to make a payment of $44,800 to reduce the principal amount of the indebtedness. Second, the owner's nominal salary of $30,000 is a pretax figure that, in any event, would have been reduced somewhat as a result of income tax.

As shown by the figures in the exhibit, the owner's net cash flow can be expected to increase gradually from year to year through the end of the fifth year, at which time the final payment on the principal of the indebtedness will have been made. Then, beginning with the sixth year, the owner can look forward to an after-tax income of almost $70,000 per year, continuing for as long as the assumptions on which the calculations are based remain valid.

What has the justification for purchase test proved? Is the business a good buy under the assumed conditions?

The answer to that question depends, of course, on a number of considerations, including the buyer's alternatives at the time purchase of the business is assumed to have occurred, and also on whether the buyer is able to meet personal expenses at the (reduced) income levels shown in the table for the five years immediately following the date of purchase.

Generally speaking, most prospects for purchase of a business of a size similar to ABC Company would feel that they were getting a reasonably good buy under the circumstances of the example and as illustrated in Exhibit 19.

DISCOUNTS FOR LACK OF MARKETABILITY

The matter of possible value discounts for lack of marketability is one that sometimes arises in connection with business appraisals.

Although there are a number of possible reasons for discounting the value of business interests, the two that arise most frequently involve minority interests in closely held companies, or so-called restricted or letter stock, sale of which is limited by the terms under which the stock is issued.

Stock representing a minority interest in a widely owned company whose stock is publicly traded ordinarily has a ready market. Further, the value of such stock usually can be determined directly from recent market transactions in the stock, independently of the value of the company as a whole except to the extent that the stock market tends to reflect total company value.

In a closely held business, however, the situation of a minority owner is such that the value of his or her ownership interest is frequently less than the corresponding pro rata share of total company value. In most cases, the minority shareholder lacks the opportunity to exert significant influence on decisions such as determining executive salaries, declaring stock dividends, and generally determining the future course of the business and the manner in which it is conducted.

Unlike the situation of a majority stockholder who is able to exert control over the conduct of the business, the value of a minority owner's interest in a business depends to a considerable extent on the existence of dividends (actual or prospective) and on the right to participate pro rata in the proceeds of possible future sale or liquidation of the business.

Because of these and other disadvantages of a minority ownership position, the market for minority interests in closely held businesses is quite limited in scope, and minority interests usually sell at a significant discount from the pro rata value of the total business of which they are a part.

The amount of discount for lack of marketability that is appropriate in a given situation is a complex question regarding which there is no close agreement, either among appraisers or among judicial authorities who have rendered decisions on such matters. In a given situation, the discount from pro rata market value may range from a few percent to as much as 50% or more. The majority of such discounts, however, appear to fall within the range of from roughly 10% to 35%.

An exception exists, of course, in the case of business interests that, though representing less than 50% of total ownership, constitute effective control of the business. Such a situation can result from the distribution of total ownership of the business over a number of stockholders, together with the relationship (such as in terms of family ties) among the various partial owners. Rather than being subject to a discount, a minority interest that represents effective control may, in fact, carry a premium value.

The second major reason for discounting market value of ownership interests concerns stock—which may be in either a closely held or a publicly held corporation—whose sale is restricted by the terms under which the stock was issued. Such restrictions may prohibit, for example, sale of the stock under any circumstances before a specified date. Another type of restriction, particularly in closely held businesses, is that if stock is to be sold it must first be offered to existing shareholders at a price determined by some formula set forth in the restrictive agreement.

Ownership interests whose sale is limited in such a manner are frequently referred to as restricted stock or letter stock. Because of the restrictions on their sale, such ownership interests usually are considered to have a value that is substantially less than the pro rata value of the ownership interest they represent.

As with the case of minority interests in closely held companies, discounts on ownership interests whose sale is restricted by the terms under which they were issued vary widely. As determined by court cases and other means, discounts on such restricted or letter stock appear to fall generally within a range from roughly 25% to 50%, although they may sometimes be even higher, possibly as great as 90% in some instances.

The reader who wishes to learn more about discounts for lack of marketability will find it helpful to consult some of the references listed in the following section.

BIBLIOGRAPHY ON VALUATION OF MINORITY INTERESTS AND RESTRICTED STOCK

Books

Business and Securities Valuation, by George Ovens and Donald I. Beach. Methuen Publications, 2330 Midland Ave., Agincourt, Ontario M1S 1P7, Canada. Pages 26–8, 56–7, 282, 298–99.

Business Valuation Handbook, by Glenn M. Desmond and Richard E. Kelley. Valuation Press, Inc., P.O. Box 1080, Marina del Rey, CA 90291. Chapter 11, pages 231–41.

Canada Valuation Service, by Ian R. Campbell. Richard DeBoo, Ltd., 70 Richmond St. E., Toronto, Ontario, M5C 2M8, Canada. Section 7, pages 47–71, 151, and 155–59.

Valuation of Businesses—A Practitioner's Guide, by Peter McQuillan, Phillip Doherty, and Graham Donald. CCH Canadian, Ltd., 6 Garamond Ct., Don Mills, Ontario, M3C 1Z5, Canada. Pages 19–23, 66–7.

Valuing a Business—The Analysis and Appraisal of Closely Held Companies, by Shannon Pratt. Dow Jones–Irwin, 1818 Ridge Rd., Homewood, IL. Chapter 10, pages 147–55.

Valuing a Company—Practice and Procedures, by George D. McCarthy and Robert E. Healy. John Wiley and Sons, Inc., 605 Third Ave., New York, NY 10016. Pages 123–24, 137, 145–46, 148–49, 153.

Other Sources

"Discounts for Lack of Marketability for Closely Held Business Interests," by J. Michael Maher. *Taxes*, September 1976.

"Discounts Involved in Purchases of Common Stock," *Institutional Investor Study Report of the Securities and Exchange Commission*, March 10, 1971, U.S. Government Printing Office, document 92–64, part 5.

"Factors the IRS and the Courts Are Using Today in Valuing Closely Held Shares," by S. J. Martin. *Journal of Taxation*, February 1972.

"How to Use and Invest in Letter Stock," by Benjamin R. Makela. President's Publishing House, Inc., January 1, 1970.

"Judicial Valuation of Dissenting Shareholder Interests," by Edwin M. Rams. *The Appraisal Journal*, January 1975, pages 105–18.

"Most Courts Overvalue Closely Held Stocks," by Robert E. Moroney. *Taxes*, March 1, 1973.

Revenue Ruling 77–287, 1977–2 C.B. 319.

"Valuation of Business Interests," by G. T. Finnegan. *Trusts and Estates*, April 1, 1939, page 473.

"Valuation of Closely Held Stock," by Alexander D. Schiach. Valutape Audio Library Series, American Society of Appraisers, January 1, 1973.

"Valuation of Closely Held Stock for Federal Tax Purposes: Approach to an Objective Method," by Lyle R. Johnson, Eli Shapiro, and Joseph Olmeara Jr. *Law Review*, University of Pennsylvania, November 1, 1951, page 170.

"Valuation of Closely Held Stocks in Trusts and Estates," by J. E. Stone. *American Society of Appraisers Valuation Manual*, February 1956, pages 116–18.

"Valuation of Preferred Stocks of Closely Owned Businesses," by Robert M. Meyers. *Valuation*, December 1, 1973, pages 22–3.

"The Valuation of Stock Options," by H. Bierman Jr. *Journal of Finance and Quantitative Analysis*, 1967, pages 327–34.

"Valuing Closely Held Corporations and Publicly Traded Securities with Limited Marketability: Approaches and Allowable Discounts from Gross Value," by William P. Lyons and Martin J. Whitman. *Business Lawyer*, July 1978.

"Valuing Restricted Securities: What Factors Do the Courts and Service Look For?" by Thomas A. Solbeg. *Journal of Taxation*, September 1979.

"Why 25 Percent Discount for Nonmarketability in One Valuation, 100 Percent in Another?" by Robert E. Moroney. *Taxes*, May 1977.

12

Making the Final
Value Estimate

12

Making the Final Value Estimate

E PLURIBUS UNUM

In preceding chapters we have discussed various approaches to estimating the value of businesses and business assets.

Because appraising is not an exact science, it is to be expected that estimated values of a business or other property as determined by different approaches will not be in exact agreement, but instead will differ from each other to a greater or lesser extent.

However, almost all appraisal situations call, not for a number of different estimates as to the value of the property being appraised, but instead for a single figure for estimated value. The question then arises of how the appraiser should go about determining the single figure for estimated value to be reported to his or her client—presumably the figure that represents the appraiser's best overall estimate of the actual value of the business or other property appraised.

CHOICE OF VALUATION APPROACHES

The choice of valuation approaches to be used in a given situation will depend on the circumstances of the situation. In particular, the choice of approaches will be influenced heavily by the nature of the business to be appraised and by the availability of the information needed to apply the various approaches.

In most cases the appraiser will find it desirable to appraise a business or other property by as many of the different approaches as fit the situation and for which the necessary information is available or can be obtained within reasonable limits of effort and cost. Even though the values estimated by several different approaches will tend to differ from each other to a greater or lesser extent, the availability of two or more different value estimates, reached through application of an equal number of different appraisal approaches, can be very useful to the appraiser. Each approach serves as a check on the results reached by the other approaches, and the ensemble of value estimates can help to establish a range of possible values of the business or other property appraised.

Further, the several different estimated values reached by different approaches should be of substantial use to the appraiser in arriving at the final estimate of value to be reported to the client.

Although it is desirable to use as many valuation approaches as may apply in a given situation, there is no useful purpose to be served in going through the motions of applying approaches that do not fit the situation or for which the necessary information is not available. To do so would be a waste of time and effort at best, and at worst could be considered foolish.

SUMMARY OF AVAILABLE APPROACHES

It is useful at this point to summarize the various approaches to estimating economic value that have been described in detail in preceding chapters.

The *market data approach* is a market-oriented method of estimating value. In the majority of appraisal situations, in which concern is with the market value of the property being appraised, the market data approach represents the most direct approach to arriving at a value estimate. However, successful application of the market data approach depends on availability of a statistically significant quantity of information on actual comparable sales.

Although the market data approach is an extremely powerful method of appraising property such as residential real estate, the relative lack of information on actual comparable sales of businesses severely limits efforts to apply the market data approach in business appraisal. However, it is still a valuable approach for appraising businesses in those situations in which comparable sales information is available. Also, the market data approach is frequently a useful approach for estimating values of individual business assets, either as part of one of the other approaches or in situations calling for appraisal of business assets other than as part of a complete business.

The *replacement cost approach* is an asset-oriented approach. While the other principal approaches to estimating value lead directly to a single figure for the estimated total value of a business, the replacement cost approach reaches a figure for total value through a process of summation of estimated values of individual assets. While potentially applicable to estimating the value of any business, the replacement cost approach is most effective in applications involving businesses a major portion of whose total value is made up of values of individual tangible assets.

A major shortcoming of the replacement cost approach is that, in the great majority of cases, it cannot be used to estimate values of intangible assets. Accordingly, estimates of total value as reached through application of the replacement cost approach usually omit value attributable to intangible assets, whose values must be estimated by other means and added to the figure for estimated value as determined by the replacement cost approach.

The *investment value approach* is an income-oriented method of estimating economic value. It is applicable to appraising essentially any kind of property whose purpose is to produce income for its owner. However, it is not applicable to non-income-producing property.

Reflecting the broadest interpretation of the Principle of Substitution, the investment value approach is both attractive in concept and simple in mathematical form. However, the approach suffers from practical limitations, including the requirement for the appraiser to make an estimate of the amount of future income from the business or other property being appraised and the difficulty of selecting an appropriate capitalization rate to be applied to this estimated future income. As a result of these limitations, the investment value approach is not considered a particularly accurate method of determining the economic value of a business or other investment. Notwithstanding these disadvantages, however, the investment value approach is frequently the best method—and sometimes the only one available—for estimating the value of at least some kinds of intangible assets, particularly business goodwill.

The *liquidation value approach* is another asset-based approach to estimating economic value. It differs from the replacement cost approach in that, whereas the replacement cost approach is concerned with the cost of replacing the various assets, concern in the liquidation value approach is with the actual market value of the assets.

The liquidation value approach may be used to estimate the value of a business or other property in event of either forced liquidation or orderly disposal. In addition to its use in situations in which actual liquidation of the property being appraised is a real possibility, the liquidation value approach also can be used for other purposes. These include estimating the loan value of the business or other property and establishing a probable lower limit for the range of possible values of an ongoing business.

The *discounted future earnings approach* is an income-oriented method of estimating economic value. Most often, the discounted future earnings approach is used in connection with the estimated future cash flow of a business. However, it also can be applied using other definitions of future earnings.

Like the investment value approach, the discounted future earnings approach requires an estimate of the amount of future earnings of the business and also a decision about the appropriate rate of return on investment in the given situation. However, the discounted future earnings approach differs from the investment value approach in that, while the investment value approach involves a single capitalization calculation of an estimated amount of future income that is assumed to remain essentially constant for at least the next several years, the discounted future earnings approach consists of a series of calculations, one for each of several years in the future, and involving estimated future earnings that may vary from year to year. Accordingly, while the discounted future earnings approach is somewhat more complex mathematically, it is applicable to situations in which future earnings can be expected to vary substantially with time, while the investment value approach is essentially inapplicable to such situations.

The *cost to create approach* is essentially trivial in terms of application to business appraising. Although it sometimes may represent an acceptable means for estimating the value of certain kinds of intangible assets, the cost to create approach is, in most circumstances, little more than a fallacious viewpoint held by some persons who lack an understanding of value principles.

The *justification for purchase test* is not, strictly speaking, actually a method for estimating value. Rather, it is a method of judging the reasonableness of a given value estimate, either an assumed value or a value estimate arrived at by one of the other approaches.

Essentially an income-based approach, the justification for purchase test is potentially applicable to almost any income-producing property, particularly businesses that are actually being offered for sale or considered for purchase.

APPRAISING BUSINESSES OR PROPERTY OF VARIOUS TYPES

It was mentioned previously that choice of the appraisal approaches to be used in a given situation will be influenced by the nature of the business or other property to be appraised.

From the standpoint of choosing the approaches to be used in business appraisals, it is useful to categorize property to be appraised as consisting of either complete businesses or individual assets.

Complete businesses can be classified further by type, according to whether they are predominantly manufacturing businesses, distribution businesses, or service businesses.

In addition to falling into one of the above classifications of type of business, some businesses exhibit special characteristics that affect choice of the appraisal approach. Businesses exhibiting such special characteristics include unprofitable businesses and businesses not exhibiting identifiable historical trends.

Manufacturing businesses tend to be characterized by a relatively high proportion of tangible assets, including manufacturing equipment, in some cases the real property where the business is located, and, of course, inventory and accounts receivable. Because it is an asset-oriented method, the replacement cost approach is especially useful when applied to manufacturing businesses, and the value estimate it yields usually will be a major consideration in the appraiser's choice of the final value estimate.

If the business is more than nominally profitable, the investment value approach is also applicable to estimating the value of manufacturing businesses, as is the market data approach if the comparable sales information required for its application is available.

Distribution businesses tend to be characterized by tangible assets that, though usually somewhat smaller in proportion to business size than in the case of manufacturing businesses, are nevertheless substantial in comparison with the total size and value of the business. Accordingly, the replacement cost approach is usually of major importance in appraising distribution businesses, as it is with manufacturing businesses.

In distribution businesses, however, tangible assets tend to be more in the form of inventory and somewhat less in the form of equipment than is the case with manufacturing businesses. Most of the inventory in distribution businesses is obtained from outside sources in essentially its final form and for that reason is usually somewhat easier to appraise than inventory in manufacturing businesses, a substantial portion of whose value arises from operations performed within the manufacturing business, the value contribution of which is sometimes difficult to estimate.

Other inventory differences between manufacturing businesses and distribution businesses are that inventory levels in distribution businesses may vary more widely from time to time, and, especially in the case of certain types of distribution businesses, some portion of the total inventory may not actually be owned by the business but instead may be on consignment from suppliers. For these and other reasons, application of the replacement cost approach represents a somewhat different matter with distribution businesses as compared to manufacturing businesses.

As in the case of manufacturing businesses, the investment value approach and the market data approach are also applicable to distribution businesses, provided the necessary requirements, namely more than marginal profitability in the case of the former and availability of comparable sales information in the case of the latter, are met.

Unlike manufacturing businesses, and to a slightly lesser extent distribution businesses, *service businesses* usually have tangible assets that are relatively small in comparison with the total size and value of the business. Although the replacement cost approach can be applied to service businesses, of course, the figure it yields for total estimated value of tangible assets usually will be substantially less than the total actual value of the complete business.

In appraisals of service businesses, the investment value approach tends to be the dominant method. The market data approach is also applicable, of course, if the required comparable sales information is available.

When applying the replacement cost approach to any type of business, it is necessary, of course, to add estimates for any intangible values—determined by an appropriate method such as the excess earnings application of the investment value approach—to total tangible asset value as determined by the replacement cost approach.

For any of the three types of businesses—manufacturing businesses, distribution businesses, and service businesses—approaches in addition to the three principal approaches may be useful for specific purposes.

Thus, the liquidation value approach (orderly disposal basis) can be used to establish a lower limit on the range of possible values of a business that is not actually a candidate for liquidation. Likewise, the discounted future earnings approach can be substituted for the investment value approach in the case of businesses whose future income is expected to follow a varying but nevertheless predictable trend. And the justification for purchase test is useful as a check on the reasonableness of market value estimates made by any of the approaches, especially in the case of businesses that are actually being offered for sale or considered for purchase.

As previously mentioned, businesses of any of the three types sometimes may exhibit special characteristics that affect choice of valuation approaches. Such special characteristics include lack of profitability and absence of any identifiable historical trends.

An unprofitable business may be so either because it was planned that way, as in the case of various kinds of nonprofit businesses or, more frequently, inadvertently. Businesses that were never intended to be profitable are similar from an appraisal standpoint to so-called special-purpose real property, such as churches, schools, and various types of government buildings.

Regardless of the reason why a business is unprofitable, the most powerful of the three approaches to estimating economic value almost always will be the replacement cost approach. (The market data approach is also theoretically applicable, of course. However, it is difficult enough to find comparable sales information for normal businesses without adding the requirement that comparability also extend to absence of profit.)

In the case of businesses that are intended to be profitable but are not actually so, the investment value approach also may be useful. If present lack of profitability appears to represent only a temporary departure from a historical record of profits, then the investment value approach can be applied on the basis of the prediction by the appraiser of a future return to profitability. Even so, use of the investment value approach in such a situation is somewhat speculative, and the appraiser may wish to select a higher capitalization rate, thus leading to a lower estimated value, than would apply otherwise.

In the case of a business that has never been profitable, the prediction of future profitability on any basis other than the existence of unusual and compelling facts and circumstances would appear to be extremely unrealistic.

One situation involving an unprofitable business in which a prediction of future profits nevertheless might be appropriate concerns relatively new businesses—that is, businesses that were started relatively recently and primarily for that reason have not yet established a record of profitability.

In the case of relatively new businesses that have not yet shown profits, the appraiser will need to examine carefully all of the available facts, including both internal and external facts affecting the business, and thus arrive at a determination of whether he or she might reasonably predict that the business will be profitable within the foreseeable future. If the appraiser concludes that such is the case, he or she then may wish to apply the investment value approach (or alternatively the discounted future earnings approach), frequently using a high capitalization rate to reflect the fact that any relatively young business, and particularly one that has not yet shown profits, involves greater risks than an older and longer-established business that otherwise may be similar.

The problem of appraising relatively new businesses that have not yet shown profits is one of the most difficult ones in the entire field of business appraisal. In arriving at the final value estimate in such a situation, the appraiser should carefully consider value estimates by as many different approaches as seem to fit the situation, including, in addition to the investment value approach, the replacement cost approach and, if the necessary information can be obtained, the market data approach.

Another case of special characteristics involves businesses that, though quite possibly profitable in the past, fail to exhibit any identifiable historical trends. Application of the investment value approach in such circumstances is particularly difficult, since even though existence of profits in the past may be strongly indicative of profitability in the future, lack of identifiable historical trends provides little or no basis for estimating the amount of such future profits. Although the investment value approach is frequently applied in such situations, the estimate of future profits needs to be made with utmost care and caution, and the capitalization rate should be chosen so as to recognize the uncertain nature of the prediction of future profitability.

From the standpoint of estimating the economic value of individual assets, whether as a step in applying one of the asset-based methods of estimating the total value of a business or from the standpoint of appraising assets by themselves, it is particularly helpful to classify each asset as being either tangible or intangible.

With some kinds of tangible assets, market values frequently can be estimated directly by use of the market data approach, the required information on comparable sales being somewhat more readily available in the case of individual assets than in the case of complete businesses.

In other cases, as when the asset is of a more or less unique type for which there is no market comparability, or when the effects of age and deterioration cannot readily be taken into account directly from market data, the replacement cost approach will be useful.

The nature of intangible assets, on the other hand, is such that their value usually must be estimated from one of the earnings-based approaches, either the investment value approach or, in the case of certain kinds of intangible assets—particularly those of limited earnings life—the discounted future earnings approach.

Business goodwill is an intangible asset whose valuation is frequently required, such as when estimating the total value of a business whose tangible asset values have been estimated by the replacement cost approach. Although attempts sometimes are made to estimate the value of business goodwill by other approaches, the excess earnings method, which is in effect a form of the investment value approach, is by far the most frequently applied.

Earnings-based methods are also frequently applicable to estimating values of other kinds of intangible assets. In the case of certain intangible assets, such as patents, copyrights, franchises, and so on, other approaches including the market data approach or the replacement cost approach may sometimes apply. Even the cost to create approach, though not generally recognized as a valid method of estimating value for most purposes, sometimes may apply to estimating values of intangible assets such as copyrights and special lists.

RECONCILIATION OF VALUE ESTIMATES

Having several different estimates of the value of the business or other property being appraised, these estimates being the result of application of as many different approaches as were considered applicable in the circumstances, the appraiser somehow must use the several different value estimates as the basis for arriving at a single value estimate to be reported to the client.

The process of arriving at a single final estimate of value from several different estimates is termed reconciliation.

This process is also sometimes called correlation of value estimates. However, the term *correlation* also refers to a specific mathematical process, while the process of arriving at a single final estimate of value is essentially one of judgment rather than mathematics. Accordingly, the term *reconciliation* is the preferable one in the present context.

While it would certainly be possible to calculate a final value estimate by taking an average (arithmetic mean) of the different values arrived at through application of the various approaches, there is essentially nothing to justify such an averaging process. In fact, a simple average would tend to give more emphasis to estimates resulting from some of the approaches than they actually deserve. While some form of weighted average might seem to overcome this problem, it would be difficult or impossible to justify, on grounds of logic, any particular weighting arrangement that might be employed.

Rather than being an exercise in mathematics, determination of the final value estimate should be essentially a matter of reason and judgment. The appraiser should consider each of the different value estimates that has been derived, the background of each, and the relative degree of confidence he or she has in each of the various approaches under the given circumstances.

It usually will be helpful to begin the reconciliation process with a detailed review of each of the approaches used, as applied to the particular business or other property being appraised. In addition to checking for possible mathematical errors, the appraiser should objectively consider each approach and the value estimate it produced from such standpoints as:

The nature and source of the input data used in applying the approach

The extent to which the value estimate resulting from application of the approach is a function of estimates and judgments, including judgments on the part of the appraiser, as contrasted to known, verifiable facts

The relevance of the approach in question to the type of business or other property being appraised

Possible preoccupation during the estimating process with particular aspects of the business or other property being appraised, or with procedural aspects of the appraisal process itself, either of which can affect the result significantly

The purpose of this review of the individual approaches as applied to the business being appraised is not to alter the value estimates, although any mathematical errors that may be discovered should, of course, be corrected. Rather, the purpose of the review is to put the result arrived at by each approach in context of the appraisal assignment as a whole, to give the appraiser a feeling for the relative confidence that should be placed in the result reached by each approach, and ultimately to contribute to an objective judgment leading to the final value estimate.

Following detailed review of the steps leading to each of the individual value estimates, it will be helpful to record the several different estimates in order according to the amount of estimated value. This done, the appraiser will have not only a listing of the individual estimates but also an indication of the range between maximum and minimum estimated values.

For example, such a listing of estimated values, arranged in descending order by the size of the value estimate, might appear as follows:

	Estimated Total Value of Business
Investment value approach	$750,000
Replacement cost approach	$635,000
Market data approach	$580,000
Liquidation value approach (orderly disposal)	$540,000

Use of a simple table such as the above, in which the various value estimates are arranged in order, could be called the value limit approach to arriving at the final estimate of value. In other words, in almost every instance the final value estimate will lie somewhere between the highest and the lowest figures in the table. Just where the final value lies within this range is a decision requiring more information than is given in the table. This will be evident from the discussion of actual examples as given in the last section of this chapter.

ROUNDING

Once the final value estimate has been selected, it is almost always rounded, to the nearest $100, nearest $1000 and so on. Rounding is appropriate because, to carry out the final value estimate to the last dollar, or worse yet to the last cent, would imply a degree of accuracy that is simply not found in appraisal results.

Whether the rounding is to the nearest $100, the nearest $1000, or even the nearest $10,000 will depend both on the appraiser's judgment of the probable accuracy of the result and on the magnitude of the result itself.

In deciding how to round, the appraiser might bear in mind the general rule that the number of significant (that is, nonzero) digits used to express a result should correspond, at least roughly, with the estimated accuracy of the result.

Thus, if the indicated final value estimate is $173,089, and if the appraiser believes that the estimate is accurate to within about 10%, he or she might round the figure to a final estimate of $170,000. On this basis, an indicated final value of $1,730,890 would be rounded to $1,700,000.

If the appraiser concluded that the value estimate was accurate to within as close as 1% or 2% (which, in fact, is very unlikely), an estimate of $173,089 would be rounded to $173,000, and an estimate of $1,730,890 would be rounded to $1,730,000.

TESTING OF FINAL VALUE ESTIMATES

After a final value estimate has been selected tentatively, it is sometimes useful to test this estimate before actually deciding upon it.

One method of testing a tentative final value estimate is to apply the justification for purchase test described in Chapter 11. This is particularly applicable when making estimates of market value of businesses that are actually being offered for sale or considered for purchase.

A second possible method of testing is sometimes enlightening in situations in which an appraisal is being made for a client who is in an adversary position. In such cases, the appraiser can put himself or herself—hypothetically, of course—in the position of the client's adversary and then reexamine the appraisal from the standpoint of the view that the adversary might take of it. This can be a particularly valuable step for the appraiser who may subsequently find himself or herself on a witness stand, facing an opposition attorney who is attempting to discredit the appraiser's results.

EXAMPLES OF RECONCILIATION
OF VALUE ESTIMATES

The following examples, taken from actual cases, illustrate the reconciliation process and should therefore add to the reader's understanding. If some of the following examples seem unusual, the reader should bear in mind that, at least when it comes to appraising businesses, there are very few normal appraisal situations.

Example 1.   Unprofitable Service Business

This appraisal concerned a small restaurant, or diner, that had changed ownership approximately two years before the date of the appraisal and had proved to be unprofitable under the new ownership. The appraisal was requested by a major creditor of the business, who was considering purchasing it.

The appraisal approaches used and the estimated value resulting from each were as follows:

	Estimated Total Value
Market data approach	$105,000
Investment value approach (assumes return to profitability under future ownership)	$ 87,777
Replacement cost approach	$ 34,000
Liquidation value approach (orderly disposal)	$ 25,000

The estimate of value by the market data approach was the result of using information on sixteen sales of other restaurants, the selling price in each case being normalized on the basis of gross volume. Although this was one of the rare cases in which presumably comparable sales information was available, no detailed information was available on any of the other sales, and normalization of purchase price on the basis of gross volume (rather than on the basis of profit) was necessary because the business being appraised was not profitable. The appraiser concluded that the estimate of value by the market data approach should not be regarded with much confidence.

The value estimate by the investment value approach was based on the assumption, which seemed credible in view of the history of the business under previous ownership, that improved management could produce a return to profitability. However, in reviewing the estimate by the investment value approach, the appraiser concluded that the capitalization rate of 25% that had been used might be somewhat low in view of the risks involved.

Application of the replacement cost approach was on the basis of an ongoing business and reflected only the estimated costs of replacing tangible assets. Although the location, past history, and current patronage of the business suggested the possible existence of goodwill, the recent history of unprofitability indicated that the economic value of such goodwill was small or nonexistent.

The liquidation value approach assumed an orderly disposal of the saleable tangible assets of the business and was applied primarily as a test of the other estimates.

Considering the facts and circumstances as summarized above, the appraiser concluded that neither the estimate by the market data approach nor that by the investment value approach should be accorded a high degree of credibility. Instead, it was apparent that the replacement cost approach was the most appropriate one under the circumstances, and that the value as estimated by this approach was, of the several different estimates, the one that was most likely to be valid.

Accordingly, the appraiser selected a final value estimate of $40,000, based primarily on the estimate reached by the replacement cost approach, with a small upward adjustment to reflect the possible existence of commercial goodwill, notwithstanding the recent history of unprofitability.

Example 2.   Manufacturing Business

The subject of this appraisal was a manufacturing business, making a wide range of wood products and components on special order for customers many of whom had been repeat customers over a number of years. In addition to a substantial amount of manufacturing machinery, the business also owned the buildings in which manufacturing operations were conducted.

The appraisal was made for the owner of the business, the principal function of the appraisal being to aid in establishing a value figure for a contemplated buy–sell agreement between the owner and a key employee of the business.

Approaches used and the resulting value estimates were as follows:

	Estimated Total Value
Market data approach	$720,000
Replacement cost approach	$667,000
Liquidation value approach	$495,000
Investment value approach	$330,000

The estimate by the market data approach was based on information on actual sales of six other businesses, of varying size but each manufacturing custom wood products. As with most applications of the market data approach in appraising businesses, detailed information on the comparable sales was lacking, and it was necessary to make a number of assumptions and approximations in arriving at a figure for estimated value by this approach.

Value as estimated by the replacement cost approach reflected the estimated costs of replacing tangible assets less liabilities, without any explicit provision for goodwill.

The estimate by the liquidation value approach included estimated values of the same assets and liabilities but estimated on the basis of orderly disposal liquidation of the business, rather than on the basis of replacement cost.

The fact that the estimate of value reached by the investment value approach was the lowest of the four, lower even than the value estimated by the liquidation value approach, was an unusual aspect of this appraisal and caused the appraiser to review all of the value estimates, and especially the assumptions behind them, before arriving at a final value figure.

As shown in the preceding table, value as estimated by the investment value approach reflects actual profits beyond a reasonable owner's salary, capitalized at 25%. In reviewing the estimates, the appraiser concluded that a capitalization rate lower than 25% would be too low in view of the inherent risks involved in the business. A higher capitalization rate, of course, would have resulted in an even lower figure for estimated value by the investment value approach.

After reviewing the various estimates, the appraiser reached the conclusion that the apparently anomalous relationship between value estimated by the investment value approach and that estimated by the liquidation value approach resulted from the fact that the business, though profitable, was somewhat less so than might be considered normal for the amount and value of fixed assets it employed.

Because of the assumptions and compromises involved in arriving at a figure for estimated value by the market data approach, the appraiser placed relatively little confidence in this figure.

Recognizing the unquestionable value of the business, both to its present owner and to the key employee who was interested in the possibility of purchasing it, the appraiser concluded that value as estimated by the replacement cost approach was most appropriate under the circumstances. Accordingly, this estimated value was rounded upward slightly, and the appraiser arrived at a final value estimate of $675,000 for the business.

Example 3.   Distribution Business

The next appraisal subject was a specialized distribution business with a relatively long and profitable history. The appraisal was requested by the owner, who planned to offer the business for sale and wanted the appraisal both to compare with his own opinion of what the business was worth and in the hope of gaining some ammunition that could be used to help convince potential buyers.

Information on comparable sales not being available, the appraisal employed the replacement cost approach and the investment value approach, with the following results:

	Estimated Total Value
Replacement cost approach	$265,409
Investment value approach	$262,707

The estimate by the replacement cost approach represented the estimated cost of replacing net tangible assets, together with an estimate for the amount of goodwill by the excess earnings method.

The estimate by the investment value approach reflected anticipated future profits (in addition to owner's salary at estimated market), capitalized at 25%.

Upon discussing the preliminary appraisal results with the owner of the business, the appraiser learned that the owner had intended to offer the business for sale at a price almost three times the value as estimated by the appraiser. The appraisal methods and figures used were discussed with the owner of the business in an effort to determine, if possible, the reasons for the wide discrepancy between the value conclusions of the appraiser and those of the owner.

With respect to the replacement cost approach, the owner's principal objection appeared to center on the value assigned by the appraiser to existing field samples of the products distributed. Relative to the investment value approach, the owner disagreed with the appraiser regarding both the probable amount of future profits and the present value of such profits.

In an effort to resolve the question, at least to the appraiser's satisfaction if not to that of the owner, the justification for purchase test was then applied. According to this test, the highest price that could be justified by a buyer purchasing the business on conventional terms of payment was approximately $265,000. (The very close agreement between the maximum price determined by the justification for purchase test and values estimated by the other two approaches is probably a coincidence.)

On the basis of the foregoing, the appraiser's final conclusion was that the value of the business was approximately $265,000.

Although the owner remained unconvinced, the appraiser was satisfied that a proper job had been done in estimating the fair market value of the business.

Example 4. Unprofitable Service Business

The owner–operator of this small service business had died. Although the business had never been profitable, providing the owner with less than an adequate living in return for her full-time efforts, one of the heirs was interested in purchasing the business from the estate. The business was appraised for the estate, the administrator of which needed a figure for the value of the business that would be fair from the standpoints of all of the heirs.

No data could be found on sales of comparable businesses, so the market data approach was not used. Because the business had never been profitable, the investment value approach was not appropriate.

Accordingly, the business was appraised by the replacement cost approach and the liquidation value approach.

	Estimated Total Value
Replacement cost approach	$996
Liquidation value approach	($582)

Value as estimated by the replacement cost approach consisted of the estimated cost of replacing existing assets, less existing liabilities, without any provision for business goodwill, which was concluded to be nonexistent or at least to have no value.

Value as estimated by the liquidation value approach was negative, as a result of the fact that existing liabilities exceeded the estimated market value of assets on an orderly disposal basis.

In view of the fact that one of the heirs was interested in actually purchasing the business in spite of its limitations, the appraiser concluded that the appropriate estimate would be that based on the replacement cost approach. Accordingly, the estimated value of $996 by the replacement cost approach was rounded to a final value estimate of $1,000.

Example 5. Assets Only, Not Part of Operating Business

Rather than a complete operating business, this appraisal concerned only assets, consisting of a supply of printed and bound copies of a consumer-oriented book, together with the copyright to the book. The appraisal was made for a buyer who was considering purchasing the inventory and copyright, the books subsequently to be marketed by direct mail.

Appraisal methods used were the investment value approach and the replacement cost approach, with the following results:

	Estimated Total Value
Investment value approach	$11,300
Replacement cost approach	$ 6,600

Application of the investment value approach involved determining an appropriate selling price for individual copies of the book by a process of market comparison and then making a number of assumptions and estimates of the income, operating costs, and resulting profit of a mail order business based on the book. The resulting estimated profits were capitalized at a relatively high rate to reflect both the essentially risky nature of the venture and the numerous assumptions that were required in arriving at any figure for estimated profit.

Value estimated by the replacement cost approach represented primarily the estimated cost of reproducing the existing inventory of completed copies. The copyright was concluded to have relatively little value, inasmuch as it was soon to expire.

Recognizing that the value estimated by the investment value approach could not be relied on in view of the numerous assumptions on which it was based, the appraiser concluded that the replacement cost approach was the more appropriate. Accordingly, a final value figure of $7,000 was selected.

13

Preparing
the Appraisal Report

13

Preparing
the Appraisal Report

FUNCTIONS OF THE APPRAISAL REPORT

The most obvious function of an appraisal report is to communicate the appraiser's value conclusion to the client and to any other person who might have a legitimate interest in it.

However, communicating the value conclusion is seldom the only function of the report. Other functions of an appraisal report can include:

Avoiding or eliminating possible errors of understanding with respect to the appraiser's value conclusion, or avoiding or eliminating misunderstandings regarding the conditions and circumstances under which the value conclusion applies

Providing the client or other person reading the report with background information that will contribute to a grasp of the full significance of the appraisal results from the standpoint of the interest that led to commissioning the appraisal in the first place

Inspiring confidence on the part of the client and others reading the report in the results of the appraiser's work

Establishing or enhancing the appraiser's credibility in the eyes of the client

Generally contributing to the appraiser's reputation as a competent professional

This chapter is devoted to a discussion of appraisal reports and how they can be made to fulfill the foregoing functions. Chapters 14 and 15 are examples of actual written appraisal reports.

TYPES OF APPRAISAL REPORTS

From the standpoint of business appraisals, there are two principal types of appraisals reports:

So-called letter reports, or short-form reports

Formal reports, sometimes called long-form or narrative reports.

In some fields of appraising, use is sometimes made of so-called standard or form reports. These are essentially short-form appraisal reports in which much of the information that remains constant from appraisal to appraisal, such as definitions of value, forms for recording data, appraiser's certification, and so on, is preprinted on a form. Such standard or form appraisals are especially common in appraisals of residential real estate. Some lending institutions, in fact, have their own standard forms for use with appraisals made in their behalf.

Unlike appraisals of residential real estate, appraisals of businesses and business assets tend to vary from one appraisal to another to such an extent that standard form appraisals are not applicable or, if used, offer little or no practical advantage. Some business appraisers, however, do develop standard data forms or standard language that they incorporate in their appraisal reports.

In theory, an appraiser's value conclusion could be reported to the client orally rather than in writing. However, such a practice is definitely not recommended, as it easily can result in errors or misunderstandings leading to problems for the appraiser, the client, or both. If the appraiser's value conclusion is reported to the client orally, as may happen when the client needs to know the estimated value before the appraisal report has been completed, it should always be confirmed in writing and as promptly as possible.

REQUIREMENTS COMMON TO ALL APPRAISAL REPORTS

Regardless of the length or form of an appraisal report, there are certain requirements that each report should meet.

The most basic requirement is that the appraisal report should satisfy the requirements of the situation. That is, it must be appropriate to the function for which it was prepared and also to any subsequent functions or applications for which it reasonably might be expected to be used in the future.

If the function of the appraisal report involves governmental agencies or judicial authorities, the report must be consistent with the known requirements of such agencies or authorities. For example, the definition of value used in the appraisal report should be one that is known to be acceptable to, and in some cases may be a requirement of, the cognizant agency or authorities. Likewise, appraisal concepts and methods must be acceptable to such officials, even though they may not be the ones the appraiser might have preferred.

If the situation involves or is likely to involve litigation, the appraiser must remain conscious when preparing the report that it may be reviewed eventually by a judge or jury during the course of deciding the case.

Especially in situations involving litigation, the appraiser should pay careful attention to the instructions or suggestions of the attorney for whom the report is being prepared. While decisions on important questions involving the format and content of the report should be the result of joint discussion and consideration by the appraiser and the attorney, the attorney's word should be accepted as final on such matters as the overall structure of the report, interpretation of whatever laws are involved, and the extent of detail to be included in the report. While the appraiser is assumed to be the expert on matters that are purely of an appraisal nature, the attorney is the expert on matters of law and also has responsibility for legal strategy and tactics.

For example, the attorney may plan to try for an out-of-court settlement, in which case he or she may wish to limit the amount of detail in the appraisal report, so that there will be some remaining bargaining power to use later if needed. Or the attorney may be thinking of the possibility of being required to furnish a copy of the report to an adversary attorney, in which case he or she will not want the report to include any unnecessary detail that could provide the opponent with a starting point for efforts to discredit the appraiser's work.

As for content, the following requirements for the minimum acceptable content of an appraisal report are adapted from the Code of Ethics of The Institute of Business Appraisers.

All appraisal reports shall be in writing, shall be signed by the appraiser, and shall include the following as a minimum:

1. A statement of the purpose for which the appraisal was made and a definition of the value estimated

2. A description of the business, business interest, or other property being appraised

3. A summary of the facts upon which the appraisal is based

4. At least a brief description of the appraisal method or methods employed

5. A statement of the conclusions reached, together with any applicable qualifications or limitations on the conclusions

6. A statement of at least the principal assumptions and conditions applicable to the appraisal and to the conclusions reached

7. A statement that the appraiser has no present or contemplated future interest in the business being appraised, or a full and complete description of any such interest that may exist

In addition to the requirements for content, there are a number of other requirements that the appraisal report must satisfy in order to fulfill the various functions listed at the beginning of this chapter.

The report must be clear and understandable to the reader. The organization and presentation of ideas and facts should be logical and development of the overall report should be systematic, with good continuity from sentence to sentence, paragraph to paragraph, and section to section of the report.

Everything in the report should be relevant to the matter at hand. Inclusion of material that is not relevant tends to distract the reader and thus to damage the overall effectiveness of the report. The appraiser must avoid the temptation to dwell at length on subjects of only marginal relevance, such as a detailed description of an appraisal approach that was not actually employed and could therefore have been disposed of in a sentence or two.

The language of the appraisal report should avoid, insofar as possible, excessive use of technical or specialized terms that, although they might impress the reader with the appraiser's expertise, also would tend to detract from understanding of the report itself.

While the appraisal report should avoid taking or even suggesting a position of advocacy, it also should demonstrate the appraiser's conviction of the validity of the appraisal methods used and his or her confidence in the correctness of the result.

It is also important—in fact, more so than many appraisers seem to realize— that the appraisal report be free from errors of all kinds. This includes spelling errors, grammatical errors, syntactical errors, typographical errors, and, of course, mathematical errors. The reader of an appraisal report who discovers an error in it, even an error that is inconsequential in terms of its effect on understanding or on the appraiser's conclusions, is likely to wonder, "If the appraiser let this error slip through, how many other errors did he or she make that I am not in a position to detect?" It would be difficult to overemphasize the extent of the negative impact that an error in an appraisal report can have on the reader's confidence in the appraiser's work and in the validity of the value conclusion.

Every appraisal report should be proofread, after it is in final form and ready for reproduction, by someone who is in a position to recognize any errors the report may contain.

Preferably, the appraiser who is responsible for the report and its conclusions, and whose signature will appear in the report, should carefully proofread it himself or herself. If the appraiser is not certain of his or her spelling, for example, then the report also should be read by someone who is a competent speller, or if there are only a few words whose spelling is in doubt, these should be checked with a dictionary. Likewise, the proofreader should be someone whose knowledge of grammar and syntax is adequate.

The mathematical calculations that may be included in the appraisal report should be checked with special thoroughness by someone who is in a position to grasp the significance of the calculations.

The reader of an appraisal report who might choose to go through the calculations himself or herself should be able to duplicate the calculations and the stated result exactly, without having to make allowances, such as for missing signs or symbols, transposed digits, or any of the other kinds of errors that can arise when persons with relatively little mathematical background attempt to copy mathematical calculations.

Preferably, mathematical calculations in the appraisal report should be checked, not just by reading figures from the draft and comparing them with the figures in the final version, but by actually using a calculator. When the various figures appearing in the final copy of the appraisal report have been entered into the calculator and have been subjected to the appropriate mathematical operations, the resulting total shown on the calculator should not merely be compared visually with the correct total shown in the draft report. Rather, the correct total should be entered into the calculator and subtracted from the total resulting from the calculations based on the figures in the final report. The resulting difference should, of course, be zero. If it is not actually zero, this fact will be apparent and will indicate that an error has been made at some point. This procedure of subtracting the correct from the computed total avoids the tendency to see something that is not actually there, which can be a problem when checking agreement of figures by visual comparison.

To be effective in fulfilling all of its functions, the appraisal report also should be professional in appearance. Although the report need not look expensive, except possibly in the case of appraisals resulting from assignments carrying a large fee, it certainly should not look cheap.

All appraisal reports should be typed, of course, if possible on a good quality typewriter making a firm and sharp imprint. If available, a typewriter with a carbon ribbon should be used; otherwise, a fabric ribbon should be well inked, and the type itself should be clean, avoiding unsightly problems such as plugged or fuzzy letters.

With the possible exception of very short letter reports, appraisal reports should be bound. Appraisers who do a substantial number of appraisals may wish to obtain custom-imprinted binders and also possibly to employ special binding techniques such as spiral binding or permanent binding of one kind or another. As an alternative to such custom binding, a variety of manufactured binders of various types can be found in office supply stores.

LETTER REPORTS

A letter report or short-form appraisal report may be appropriate in situations that, for one reason or another, do not require a complete formal report and in which the substantial cost of preparing a formal report is not justified.

The following are examples of situations that may call for a letter report rather than a longer, more formal report:

An appraisal prepared for the owner of a business who is planning to sell and who wants an appraisal to assist in establishing an asking price but does not need a detailed report

An appraisal in connection with a buy–sell agreement between parties who are already in essential agreement about the price but who want written backup for it

A preliminary report of an appraisal, which is to be followed later by a longer, more detailed report

Reports of appraisals made in adversary situations in which the attorney who commissioned the appraisal wishes to avoid making too much information available to the opponent or making such information available too soon

Reports of appraisals that are essentially updates or modifications of previous appraisals, such as reappraisals to investigate value changes that may have occurred in a business or other property as a result of passage of time, changes in the nature or scope of the business, and so on

Even brief letter-type appraisal reports, however, should have at least the minimum content listed in the preceding section of this chapter. The following is an example of a letter report on an appraisal.

EXAMPLE OF LETTER REPORT

Zed Appraisers
123 Fourth Avenue
West Southville, Indiana

December 11, 19X1

John Smith
ABC Distributors, Inc.
789 Tenth Street
West Southville, Indiana

Dear Mr. Smith:

In accordance with your instructions, I have made an appraisal to estimate the fair market value of ABC Distributors, Inc.

For the present purpose, *fair market value* is defined as "the price, in cash or equivalent, that a buyer could reasonably be expected to pay and a seller could reasonably be expected to accept, if the property were exposed for sale on the open market for a reasonable period of time, both buyer and seller being in possession of the pertinent facts, and neither being under compulsion to act."

In the present appraisal the term *property* in the foregoing definition consists of 100% of the capital stock of ABC Distributors, Inc.

The appraisal was based on information obtained by the appraiser during visits to ABC Distributors, including conversations with you and other key personnel, copies of financial statements for the five most recently completed fiscal years as furnished by you, and the appraiser's personal observations. The appraisal also included consideration of other information, such as that related to competition, markets, and general economic conditions, as gathered by the appraiser.

Appraisal methods employed in arriving at the final conclusion of value included the replacement cost approach and the investment value approach. The market data approach was not employed because of unavailability of information on sales of businesses comparable to ABC Distributors, Inc. In addition to the replacement cost approach and investment value approach, the justification for purchase test was used to verify the validity of the final value estimate.

As a result of the appraisal, it is my conclusion that the fair market value of ABC Distributors, Inc., as of October 31, 19X1, was approximately two hundred sixty-five thousand dollars($265,000).

The foregoing estimate of value assumes that all information obtained from you and other employees of ABC Distributors, Inc., including information in the financial statements, is substantially correct, and that there are no undisclosed situations or circumstances that would materially affect the value of the business.

I certify that I have no present or contemplated future interest in ABC Distributors, Inc., and that my fee for this appraisal is independent of the value reported.

Sincerely,

X. Y. Zed, Appraiser

FORMAL APPRAISAL REPORTS

A formal or long-form appraisal report is required in situations that call for more detail in the report than is contained in a letter or short-form report.

The following are examples of some situations in which a formal appraisal report is required:

Appraisal of a closely held business that is to be offered for sale and whose owner wishes to have a detailed appraisal report that can be presented to potential buyers to help justify the price of the business

An appraisal to support a loan application, the report being needed to provide the lending institution with justification for granting the requested loan

Appraisals in connection with condemnation (eminent domain) proceedings, in which the appraisal is used to help determine the amount of compensation

Feasibility studies, particularly those made for large companies, in which the purpose of the appraisal is to explore the desirability of a proposed major undertaking, such as acquisition of another business or other substantial change in the client company's business. (In such situations, a detailed report can provide the necessary information about the proposed undertaking to the company officials who must make the decision, and can also provide at least part of the basis for responding to stockholders and others who may raise questions about it.)

Appraisals in connection with employee stock ownership plans (ESOPs), in which it is desirable to have as complete written justification as possible for stock values as established for purposes of the plan

Various types of governmental filings, such as tax filings, in which the person or company making the filing considers it desirable to support his or her position in detail

Property settlements, such as in connection with division of property in a dissolution of marriage or among the heirs to an estate, in which detailed support for the appraised values may contribute to acceptance of the proposed settlement by the parties involved

Any other situation calling for more detail than is contained in a letter report

In length, a formal appraisal report may vary from as few as 8 or 10 pages to as many as 50 to 100 pages, and sometimes even more.

The report should be broken down into sections according to the manner in which the subject matter is organized. Although the number, content, and sequence of these report sections will depend on both the nature of the appraisal and the appraiser's own inclinations, the following could be considered a typical arrangement of sections in a formal appraisal report:

Letter of transmittal

Cover sheet

Table of contents

Summary and conclusions

Purpose and function of appraisal

Definition of value estimated

Effective date of value estimate

Description of property appraised

Highest and best use

Description of appraisal process

Summary of facts

Statement of conclusions reached

Assumptions and conditions applicable to the appraisal

Appraiser's certification

Supporting data

The *letter of transmittal* may be bound as part of the appraisal report, or it may be a separate document accompanying the report when it is submitted to the client. In either case, the letter of transmittal will be brief, frequently not more than one page or at the most two pages. It is addressed to the person who commissioned the appraisal and serves primarily as a record that the appraisal was completed and the report submitted. The letter of transmittal frequently will include a statement of the appraiser's value conclusion but will contain little or no other information about the appraisal process and results.

The *cover sheet* will be the kind that appears at the beginning of most bound documents. It usually will contain the title of the appraisal report (such as, "Report of Appraisal of ABC Distributors, Inc."), the name of the client for whom the report was prepared, the appraiser's name, the date of the report, and other appropriate information, such as the appraiser's address, the appraiser's report or project number as assigned, and so on.

The *table of contents* will be a listing of the individual sections of the report and the page number on which each begins.

The report section on *summary and conclusions* is optional but is considered desirable by many appraisers. Its purpose is to provide the reader of the report with a convenient summary of the salient conclusions reached, either as an introduction and orientation before reading the complete report or for the benefit of a person who may not intend to go through the complete report in detail. The section on summary and conclusions should be limited to a simple statement of the major results of the appraisal, leaving explanations about the basis for these results to the remainder of the report. Depending on the appraiser's preference, the section on summary and conclusions may appear near the beginning of the report where it serves as an introduction to the material to come, or near the end where it represents a summary of what has gone before.

The section on *purpose and function of appraisal* is a simple set of statements of the purpose and function of the appraisal along the lines of the discussion of appraisal purpose and function in Chapter 4. It states the type of value estimated, together with the appraiser's understanding of the use to be made of the appraisal results. This section usually will be quite short, frequently not more than two or three sentences in length.

The section dealing with *definition of value estimated* will contain an explicit definition of value of the type estimated, using one of the value definitions given in Chapter 2 or some other appropriate definition of value. This section of the report will be quite short, usually consisting of no more than one or two sentences.

The report section on *effective date of value estimate* is a brief statement, usually only one sentence, of the date as of which the value estimate applies.

The report section on *description of property appraised* must, as a minimum, provide the reader of the report with an accurate and unambiguous statement of exactly what it was that was appraised, and to which the value estimate and other conclusions apply. Thus, if an incorporated business has been appraised, it must be clear from this section of the report whether the appraisal was of the capital stock of the corporation or of its assets and liabilities. If the latter, it must be clear from the report just which assets and liabilities were included in the appraisal. Similarly, if a business in the form of a proprietorship or a partnership is appraised, the report section on description of property should include sufficient information so as to leave no reasonable doubt about what was included in the appraisal and what was excluded. A more detailed discussion on the subject of defining property to be appraised appears in Chapter 4.

In addition to defining the property appraised, the appraisal report should make it apparent what property rights were appraised. In most business appraisals, the rights appraised consist of 100% ownership of the property, free from liens and encumbrances other than those specifically stated in the report ("ownership in fee simple"). However, this is not always the case, as there are many other kinds of rights that can pertain to a given property. These include, for example, ownership of only a partial interest in the property, rights to use of the property (as under a lease or rental agreement), various kinds of options, and so on. Accordingly, the nature of the rights appraised should be apparent from the appraisal report.

In addition to a definition of the property and of the rights appraised, the section of a formal appraisal report on description of property appraised also may include other information. This other information can include, for example, a description of the business itself, which may be either brief or detailed depending on the circumstances. If it is anticipated that the appraisal report will be used primarily or exclusively by persons who are already well acquainted with the business, then the description of the business must be sufficient only to demonstrate that the appraiser has familiarized himself or herself with the business as a basis for the appraisal, possibly also including any information about the business that is especially important from the standpoint of the appraisal and the resulting value estimate. If it is anticipated that the appraisal report will be read by persons who are not already familiar with the business, then a more detailed description of the business may be in order. Such a detailed description may include, for example, a description of the principal products and markets, a narrative history of the business, discussion of the backgrounds of key personnel, and whatever other information about the business may be especially useful to readers of the report from the standpoint of grasping the full significance of the appraisal and of the value estimates.

The *highest and best use* of property that has been assumed in estimating its value should always be apparent from the content of the appraisal report. In most business appraisals, the highest and best use of property consists of a continuation of the existing use. In such cases, a formal statement about highest and best use sometimes is omitted from the appraisal report, on the basis that highest and best use is implicitly apparent from the remainder of the report. In some cases, however, the appraiser will conclude that the highest and best use of a business or other property differs from its existing use, in which case this fact must be stated clearly in the appraisal report. Even in cases in which the highest and best use is a continuation of existing use, it is desirable to state that fact in the appraisal report.

The section on *description of appraisal process* is intended primarily to give the reader, who is assumed to have little or no background in appraising, a basic understanding of appraisal concepts and, at least to a limited extent, the actual appraisal process. This section of the report could appropriately begin with a statement of the Principle of Substitution, followed by a brief—possibly not more than one or two paragraphs each—summary of each of the principal approaches to estimating economic value.

Depending on the particular situation, this section of the report also may include material that is especially pertinent to the appraisal at hand, such as an explanation of why one or more of the conventional approaches was not actually applied, a discussion of the nature of goodwill, and so on. The report section dealing with description of the appraisal process itself ordinarily will include little or no specific information about the property being appraised, this information and its effect on the appraisal results being left for other sections of the report.

Following the report section that describes the appraisal process, the section on *summary of facts* presents, in summary form, the pertinent factual information that was gathered during the appraisal and upon which the appraiser's value conclusion is based. This includes both financial and non-financial internal information about the business or other property appraised and external information such as that relating to competition, sales of comparable businesses, local and national economic and other influences, industry outlook, and so on.

In most cases, this section of the report also will include at least a summary of the calculations leading to value estimates by the various approaches, together with related information such as the choice of capitalization rate for application of the investment value approach. This section of the report may conclude with a restatement of the value estimate reached by each appraisal approach that was used, followed by at least a brief summary of the logic employed by the appraiser in the reconciliation process leading to the final value estimate.

Whatever its length and the amount of detail it includes, the report section on summary of facts is a key part of the report from the standpoint of giving the reader an understanding of the appraisal process applied by the appraiser and of the factual basis for the final value conclusion. Accordingly, preparation of this section of the report deserves the utmost in thought and care from the appraiser.

The *statement of conclusions reached* is a brief section of the report, containing a statement of the amount of the appraiser's final value estimate, together with any other conclusions that may be important from the stand-point of the function of the appraisal or the significance of the final value estimate. Brief though it usually is, this report section is the focal point of the entire report, since it presents the ultimate result of the appraisal assignment.

The report section on *assumptions and conditions applicable to the appraisal* consists of an enumeration of at least the major assumptions that were made by the appraiser during the course of the assignment, together with any conditions or limitations on the appraisal results or the report itself. Assumptions may include, for example, that the information obtained from various sources (including the information obtained from the owner or other representative of the business being appraised) is reliable, and that there are no undisclosed facts or circumstances that would affect the appraisal results significantly. If the appraiser has reason to doubt the accuracy or validity of some of the information used in the appraisal, this point should receive special attention in the report section on assumptions and conditions.

In addition to assumptions, this section of the report also may include statements relative to applicable limitations and conditions. These may include, for example, restrictions on publication of the report or on use of information from the report for purposes other than the original purpose. Some appraisers also include a disclaimer regarding matters of a legal nature affecting the property appraised. In situations in which the appraiser may be concerned about the degree of his or her exposure in a legal sense, he or she may wish to consult an attorney regarding the content and wording of this section of the appraisal report.

The purpose of the *appraiser's certification* is to emphasize the appraiser's conviction regarding the appraisal and its results, together with his or her status as an independent, objective professional. This section of the report usually will include statements to the effect that the appraiser has no other interest in the business or other property appraised (or a disclosure and description of such other interest if one exists), together with a statement that the fee for the appraisal is not in any way dependent on the results.

The appraisal report concludes with a collection of *supporting data*, sufficiently important to the appraisal to be included in the report but of such nature that its inclusion in the body of the report was not warranted. The report section on supporting data may include, for example, detailed financial information (such as financial statements covering a period of years) on the business or other property appraised, adjustments to financial information such as in connection with formulation of economic balance sheets or economic income/expense statements, maps and photographs as appropriate, detailed information on comparable sales, and so on. This section of the report also may include a bibliography or list of information sources used by the appraiser in connection with the appraisal. And, of course, a summary of the appraiser's professional background and qualifications usually will be included in the appraisal report.

Chapter 14 is an example of a formal, written appraisal report.

LETTERS OF REPRESENTATION

A letter of representation is not, as the phrase might suggest, a letter authorizing the appraiser to take some action on behalf of a client. Rather, it is a letter or other document in which a person who has provided important information for use in an appraisal confirms (represents) that it is accurate to the best of his or her knowledge and belief, and that there are no other known facts or circumstances that would materially affect the appraisal.

The letter of representation is addressed to the appraiser (and frequently is prepared by the appraiser) and signed by the person who furnished the information in question. In instances in which key information was obtained from several different persons, such as several key executives of a company being appraised, it may be advisable to obtain a letter of representation from each of them.

Letters of representation are used, in fact, in only a relatively small proportion of appraisals. In cases in which a letter of representation is appropriate, however, its importance is such that the appraiser may wish to have legal assistance in formulating the language of the letter.

EXPERT TESTIMONY

Appraisers sometimes are called on to provide expert testimony regarding appraisals they have performed or even regarding the work of other appraisers.

Effectiveness as a witness involves a number of considerations, ranging from good advance preparation to behavior under cross-examination, and is beyond the scope of this book. However, the appraiser who is faced with an assignment to provide appraisal-related testimony will find helpful information in the following sources.

"Court Testimony," in *Valuing a Business*, by Shannon Pratt. Dow Jones–Irwin, 1818 Ridge Rd., Homewood, IL 60430. Chapter 16.

"Is the Appraisal Witness Qualified?" Society of Real Estate Appraisers, 645 N. Michigan Ave., Chicago, IL 60611. Pamphlet.

"A Short Course in Survival Techniques for Expert Witnesses," by George A. Brugger. *Valuation*, November 1981. American Society of Appraisers, P.O. Box 19265, Dulles International Airport, Washington, DC 20041.

14
Formal Appraisal Report

There is no such thing as a typical appraisal assignment. There is a wide variation from assignment to assignment in the nature and circumstances of the assignment, in the methods and techniques used by the appraiser in gathering and analyzing the pertinent facts, in arriving at value estimates, and in reporting the results.

The appraisal report presented in this chapter is one example of a formal written report. Except that names, locations, and so on, have been changed as necessary to preserve confidentiality, the report that follows represents the results of an actual appraisal assignment.

Determination of Fair Market Value
of
Wilson's Fine Things

Report number N–163

March 26, 19X9

SUMMARY AND CONCLUSIONS

An appraisal was performed to determine the fair market value, as of December 31, 19X8, of certain assets of the partnership known as Wilson's Fine Things.

Fair market value is defined as "the price, in cash or equivalent, that a buyer could reasonably be expected to pay and a seller could reasonably be expected to accept, if the property were exposed for sale on the open market for a reasonable period of time, buyer and seller each being in possession of the pertinent facts, and neither being under compulsion to act."

Because of limitations on availability of information, assets included in the appraisal consisted only of merchandise inventory, store furniture and fixtures, leasehold improvements, and commercial goodwill.

Values of merchandise inventory, furniture and fixtures, and leasehold improvements were estimated by the replacement cost approach. The value of goodwill was estimated by the excess earnings method.

For reasons including unavailability of certain information on the results of Wilson's Fine Things's business operations during 19X8, the appraisal made extensive use of internal records of Wilson's Fine Things. These internal records included (1) sales slips, which are the primary source document for information on sales volume and for inventory control, (2) a transaction ledger that contains daily and monthly totals for sales and related transactions, and (3) an inventory ledger that contains a perpetual record of merchandise inventory.

To confirm the validity of the various records and to explore the extent of certain inconsistencies that came to the appraiser's attention, the internal records were reviewed and were tested for accuracy by comparing similar information from different sources.

The review and testing of internal records resulted in the following conclusions:

1. Information on sales volume determined from analysis of a three-month sample of sales slips agreed reasonably well with total sales figures for the corresponding months as shown in the transaction ledger. Accordingly, sales totals shown in the transaction ledger were accepted as valid for the purpose of the appraisal.

2. Comparison of information from sales slips with entries in the inventory ledger showed that recordkeeping procedures related to these two kinds of records were being followed carefully, and , accordingly, the inventory ledger was accepted as an accurate record of the current value of inventory of items listed in the inventory ledger.

3. However, the review of sales slips also disclosed that a substantial portion of total sales volume consists of sales of merchandise that is not listed in the inventory ledger. Sales volume attributable to such uninventoried merchandise was estimated by two methods. These estimates indicated that sales of uninventoried merchandise amounts to between 30% and 75% of sales of inventoried merchandise as shown in the inventory ledger. Accordingly, it is apparent that total merchandise inventory of Wilson's Fine Things is substantially greater than that shown in the inventory ledger.

The appraisal resulted in the following estimates of value, as of December 31, 19X8, of the assets of Wilson's Fine Things as included in the appraisal:

Inventory

    Merchandise included in inventory ledger, approximately $354,859

    Other merchandise inventory, approximately   106,458

    Total merchandise inventory, approximately $461,317

    Furniture and fixtures, and leasehold improvements, approximately   20,000

    Commercial goodwill   0

Total estimated value, as of December 31, 19X8, of appraised assets of Wilson's Fine Things $481,317

Accordingly, it is concluded that *the total fair market value, as of December 31, 19X8, of the assets appraised, is approximately $480,000.*

As previously stated, the appraisal was necessarily limited to those assets of Wilson's Fine Things with respect to which the appraiser had access to the necessary information. To arrive at a figure for the total value of all assets of Wilson's Fine Things, the foregoing estimate should be adjusted (1) upward in an amount equal to the value of assets, including cash, accounts receivable, and any other assets not included in the appraisal process, and (2) downward to the extent of any applicable liabilities of the business.

PURPOSE AND FUNCTION OF APPRAISAL

The purpose of the appraisal was to estimate the fair market value, as of the appraisal effective date, of the property described herein.

The information is to be used in connection with a property settlement related to a dissolution of marriage.

DEFINITION OF VALUE ESTIMATED

For the purpose of this appraisal, *fair market value* is defined as "the price, in cash or equivalent, that a buyer could reasonably be expected to pay and a seller could reasonably be expected to accept, if the property were exposed for sale on the open market for a reasonable period of time, buyer and seller each being in possession of the pertinent facts, and neither being under compulsion to act."

EFFECTIVE DATE OF VALUE ESTIMATE

Value is estimated as of December 31, 19X8.

This date was selected because it is the end of an accounting period, which is important from the standpoint of availability of various kinds of information on which the appraisal is based. Any changes in value between the appraisal effective date and the date of this report will be primarily the result of changes in inventory. Such changes can be expected to be of relatively small magnitude in comparison with the value of inventory as of the appraisal effective date.

DESCRIPTION OF BUSINESS

History

The business known as Wilson's Fine Things was started by Ralph Wilson and was purchased from him by Robert Ross in 19X0. Mr. Ross operated the business as a proprietorship until January 1, 19X2, at which time it was reorganized as a partnership between Robert Ross and Mary Ross, his wife.

Location

The business is located at 612 West Central Avenue, Paradise City, Florida.

Paradise City is a predominantly residential community located on the west coast of Florida, approximately midway between Fort Myers and Naples.

The incorporated community of Paradise City has a 19X8 estimated population of 40,000, many of whom are relatively affluent. Recent population growth is estimated as approximately 10% per year. Greater Paradise City, including areas outside the city limits but within the Paradise City shopping area, has a total population of more than 100,000. In addition to permanent residents, the Paradise City area enjoys a substantial seasonal increase in population, with many of the visitors and seasonal residents also being relatively affluent.

The location of Wilson's Fine Things is on the principal east–west thoroughfare and in the downtown business district of Paradise City.

General Description of Wilson's Fine Things

The store premises are leased under a lease agreement that expires December 31, 19X9, but that includes an option provision for one five-year renewal, that is, until December 31, 19X4. Rent is $1,100 per month, with the lease providing for rent escalation in the form of annual adjustments based on the Consumer Price Index.

The store is well arranged and tastefully decorated, and it presents an appearance, both externally and internally, that is consistent with the high quality of merchandise offered for sale.

The number of personnel working in the store fluctuates somewhat with the level of business, averaging approximately six persons, some of whom are part-time.

Mr. Ross works in the store full-time. Mrs. Ross previously worked in the store on a part-time or casual basis but has not done so far at least several months, since the divorce became imminent.

The store handles a better line of china, silverware, and related items. There is also some sale of other items, including bric-a-brac and antiques, some of which are taken on consignment and sold for the owners' accounts.

Sales are made for cash, check, or charge to bank credit card. Wilson's Fine Things does not ordinarily maintain store charge accounts for customers. However, there is a lay-away procedure, whereby a customer may make a deposit on an item, which is then put aside pending one or more additional payments until the item is paid for in full.

Competition

In addition to Wilson's Fine Things, there are two other stores in Paradise City that offer a more or less similar line of merchandise.

One of these other stores is at a location and offers merchandise such that it can be assumed to represent direct competition to Wilson's Fine Things. This store is Paradise Gifts, at 604 West Central Avenue. Paradise Gifts is a relatively new store, having been established within the past several months.

As for the other store offering merchandise similar to Wilson's Fine Things, it would appear to be no more than indirect competition, inasmuch as it handles a lower grade of merchandise and is at a less desirable location than Wilson's Fine Things.

Trend of Business

Figures reported by Wilson's Fine Things on U.S. Partnership Return of Income (form 1065) show the following trend of sales and net income since the business was organized as a partnership:

Year	Net Sales	Net Income	Change from Previous Year Sales	Income
19X2	$188,824	$34,334		
19X3	$303,546	$53,337	+61%	+55%
19X4	$272,260	$44,109	−10%	−17%
19X5	$444,747	$46,907	+63%	+ 6%
19X6	$341,119	$70,373	−23%	+50%
19X7	$430,397	$63,448	+26%	−10%
19X8	$358,402	*	−17%	*

*19X8 tax return not available at time of appraisal; net sales figure determined from monthly totals as shown in Wilson's Fine Things's transaction ledger.

Recordkeeping Procedures—General

The fiscal year of the business coincides with the calendar year.

Wilson's Fine Things employs an accounting firm to prepare income tax returns and other financial reports needed for external purposes. However, the detailed records on which these reports are based are kept by Wilson's Fine Things, which supplies monthly totals and other information from these internal records to the accounting firm as a basis for tax returns and other financial reports.

This internal recordkeeping is based on a system of documentation, principal elements of which include tags attached to individual items of merchandise, sales slips for transactions with customers, a transaction ledger to which various total figures are posted on a daily or monthly basis, and a perpetual inventory ledger. Because of their importance to the appraisal, these internal records and the manner in which they are used are described in some detail in this report.

Recordkeeping—Merchandise Tags

With some exceptions, each item of merchandise has attached to it a tag containing most or all of the following information:

Retail price of item

Original cost of item, entered in an alphabetic code

Inventory (stock) number (applies to inventoried items only; see subsequent discussion of inventory records)

Possible additional information, such as source of item, especially if obtained from a source such as purchase from a private owner (source information, if given, is entered on the merchandise tag in abbreviated or coded form)

During examination of some of the merchandise of Wilson's Fine Things, the appraiser observed that several of the items bore merchandise tags that, in addition to other information, included the notation "SH–NT." It was explained by store personnel that this notation meant "second-hand, no tax," and that the merchandise in question had been acquired from private sources, no tax having been paid or payable. It was the appraiser's understanding that items whose merchandise tags bore the "SH–NT" notation were not listed in the inventory ledger.

Recordkeeping—Sales Slips

Transactions with customers are recorded on individual sales slips. Sales slips are prenumbered and are dispensed one at a time from dispensers placed at various locations in the store.

Sales slips are used to record transaction types including sales of merchandise (regular sales), repairs, deposits by customers (such as on lay-aways), various other kinds of transactions such as refunds, and credits.

The sales slips are the primary source document for information on sales volume and also for inventory control.

Information entered on sales slips includes:

Date of transaction

Customer's name (frequently omitted from sales slip, especially on transactions of smaller amount)

Sold by (usually indicated by initials)

Type of payment (cash, COD, and so on)

Description of item

Price of item

Amount of sales tax

Total amount of transaction

Sales slip number (preprinted at bottom of slip)

If the item sold has an inventory number, this inventory number is entered on the sales slip as part of the description of the item. Also, the merchandise tag with the inventory number may be removed from the item and physically attached to the sales slip, such as by means of adhesive transparent tape.

Recordkeeping—Transaction Totals

Daily transaction totals are calculated from sales slips for the day and are entered in a ledger that accumulates totals by month. For the purpose of this report, this ledger will be referred to as the transaction ledger.

The transaction ledger includes columns for income from sales, income from repairs, cash expenses, and refunds. There are also columns for net cash, tax, and central bank. At the end of each month, the daily entries for regular sales and income from other sources are totaled. A separate entry is made for what are termed nontax sales, and the resulting totals are reported to Wilson's Fine Things's accountants for use in compilation of annual operating figures for the income tax return and other financial reports as applicable.

Recordkeeping—Inventory Ledger

A perpetual inventory record is maintained in a separate ledger book, which for the purpose of this report will be referred to as the inventory ledger.

The inventory ledger consists of a large number of preruled ledger sheets of the type used by accountants, contained in a post binder. Each line of each ledger sheet contains information on one item of inventory.

The inventory ledger is divided into sections according to kind of item. Within each section, individual items are listed serially by inventory number. This inventory number consists of from one to three letters (generally the initial letters of words descriptive of the kind of item), followed by either three or four digits, starting with the number 100 and thence assigned sequentially for each kind of item. Thus, inventory item CCS109 might apply to a complete china set, number 109 in the section of the inventory ledger devoted to china in sets. Similarly, CA206 would represent candlestick number 209 in the section of the inventory book for candlesticks.

The heading for each page in the inventory ledger is filled out when the page is started. Although format tends to vary somewhat from page to page, the inventory ledger generally includes the following information about each item:

Inventory number

Date of purchase

Description of item, typically including manufacturer's name, style or pattern, and so on

Cost of item

Retail price of item (retail price shown in the inventory ledger will not necessarily be the price for which an item is eventually sold; instead, actual selling price frequently will be less than the nominal retail price)

Date sold

At or shortly after the time an item is sold, the date of sale is entered in the inventory ledger on the line for the item in question. Thus, the inventory ledger provides a permanent record of inventory, including purchases, sales, and unsold items still in inventory.

The appraiser's examination of the inventory ledger was based on photocopies made on January 7, 19X9. At that time, the inventory ledger contained more than 300 pages, with line entries for roughly 10,000 items, approximately 2,800 of which were unsold. The earliest entries in the inventory ledger showed purchase dates early in 19X2, the year the business was reorganized as a partnership. The most recent entries were for purchases of inventory early in January 19X9. Sale dates of inventoried items had been entered in the inventory ledger only up to December 18, 19X8, sales after that date not having been entered in the ledger at the time the copies were made for examination.

During the appraisal, it was determined that notwithstanding the large number of items that it did include, the inventory ledger did not include all of Wilson's Fine Things's inventory of merchandise. Significant omissions from the inventory ledger included:

Merchandise acquired other than through established channels of supply, including so-called second-hand, no tax items as previously mentioned.

Various items of nominal value, such as individual items of plated tableware

Materials and parts held primarily for use in making repairs

Possibly other items that, for one reason or another, are not listed in the inventory ledger

DEFINITION OF PROPERTY APPRAISED

In appraising any property, it is important to define, as unambiguously as possible, the property being appraised. This is particularly important in appraisals of unincorporated businesses. When the business to be appraised is a partnership, there should be agreement between the partners about which items are the property of the partnership and which are owned personally by one of the partners.

In the appraisal of Wilson's Fine Things, determination of property to be appraised was influenced by difficulty in obtaining useful access to certain property or records, together with evident problems in obtaining agreement about ownership of certain items.

Accordingly, the appraisal encompassed those items (1) whose existence could be determined either from physical observation or from business records, and (2) whose nature or presence on the store premises was such that they could reasonably be assumed to be the property of the partnership.

Thus, the property appraised consisted of the following:

Inventory (to the extent that its existence was evident from the inventory ledger or could be inferred from other business records, such as sales slips or monthly transaction totals)

Furniture and fixtures

Leasehold improvements

Commercial goodwill

Consideration was given to the possibility of including the lease on the store premises as part of the property appraised. However, it was concluded that the amount of the rental essentially reflected market rents and, accordingly, that the lease had no significant market value apart from the other assets of the business.

The circumstances of the appraisal were such that it was not feasible to include in the value estimates assets falling in the following categories:

Cash on hand or in banks or other financial institutions (the amount of bank balances as of a given date should be determinable by appropriate inquiry to the bank; however, the appraiser lacked the necessary authority to obtain this information)

Accounts receivable (on the basis of Wilson's Fine Things's stated policy of making sales only for cash, check, or credit card, it can be assumed that the total of any accounts receivable from customers is relatively small)

Any inventory whose existence or value is not reflected in the inventory ledger or other business records of Wilson's Fine Things

For reasons similar to those applicable to the above assets that were excluded from the value estimates, the appraisal also excluded consideration of liabilities of the business.

HIGHEST AND BEST USE

It is an axiom of appraising that the value of property is estimated in anticipation of its being used for its highest and best use.

Highest and best use can be defined as "the legally permissible and reasonably feasible present use, or series of future uses, that will result in the greatest economic benefit to the owner of the property."

In the case of present appraisal, the highest and best use of the property appraised consists of a continuation of the existing use in connection with the business of Wilson's Fine Things. Values as estimated in this appraisal are based on this highest and best use.

APPROACHES TO ESTIMATING VALUE

Essentially, all appraisals to determine economic value have their basis in the Principle of Substitution, which states that "the value of a thing tends to be determined by the cost of acquiring an equally desirable substitute."

There are a number of recognized methods, or approaches, for applying the Principle of Substitution to estimate the economic value of given property. Principal among these recognized approaches are:

Market data approach

Replacement cost approach

Investment value approach (sometimes called income approach)

Although there are a number of other recognized approaches to appraising businesses and business assets, essentially all of them are variations of one or more of the principal approaches listed above.

In applying the *market data approach* to appraising businesses or business assets, the appraiser attempts to identify other businesses or assets, generally similar to those being appraised, that have actually been sold. The appraiser then uses information on these other sales as a basis for estimating the value of the property being appraised.

Although the market data approach is powerful when appraising property such as residential real estate, its use for appraising businesses is severely hampered by lack of availability of sufficient and reliable information on actual sales of businesses. In the case of the majority of business appraisals, this lack of information on actual sales of similar businesses makes it impossible to apply the market data approach effectively.

Accordingly, the market data approach is generally not useful for appraising businesses as a whole. Instead, the market data approach is commonly limited to estimating the value of individual assets, such as items of inventory for which there is an established market.

In the *replacement cost approach,* it is recognized that one form of equally desirable substitute for the property being appraised would be a duplicate of the property itself. Accordingly, the replacement cost approach arrives at an estimate of total value by estimating the cost of duplicating (replacing) the individual elements of the business or other property being appraised, item by item, asset by asset.

In practice, the replacement cost approach is essentially limited to providing the appraiser with an estimate of the cost of replacing or duplicating the tangible assets of the business or other property. This is because there is usually no reasonable way of arriving at an estimate of the cost of replacing intangibles, such as business goodwill.

Accordingly, when the replacement cost approach is used to appraise a business, the value of any intangibles must be estimated by some other means and then must be added to the estimated value of tangible assets (as determined by the replacement cost approach) to arrive at a figure for the total estimated value of the complete business or other group of assets.

In the *investment value approach* to appraising a business or business asset, the property to be appraised is viewed primarily from the standpoint of its investment characteristics. Thus, the investment value approach assumes that an equally desirable substitute for the property being appraised would be one that had similar investment characteristics, not necessarily one that was similar to the property being appraised from a physical, operational, or other standpoint.

These investment characteristics, which provide the basis for comparing property to be appraised with other forms of investment, include principally:

Return on investment, expressed as a percentage of the amount invested (rate of return)

Economic risk associated with the investment

Liquidity of principal amount invested

Expectation of future growth or shrinkage of principal amount

Burden of management

In applying the investment value approach to estimating the value of a business or business asset, the sequence of steps is:

1. Determine the amount of return (typically, profit) attributable to the property to be appraised.
2. Identify other types of investment that are similar to the property to be appraised with regard to investment criteria including liquidity, expectation of future growth or shrinkage of principal amount, burden of management, and especially risk.
3. Use the rate of return actually provided by comparable investments to capitalize the amount of return from the property to be appraised, thus arriving at an estimate of the value of the property.

In appraising businesses, the investment value approach is sometimes used to estimate the value of an entire business by capitalizing the total return produced by the business. However, such an application of the investment value approach frequently poses a number of practical problems, including the difficulty of arriving at an appropriate capitalization rate to be applied to whatever type of income (such as net profit before tax, net profit after tax, net operating profit, net cash flow, etc.) may be selected or available as a basis for the capitalization process.

A more effective application of the investment value approach in appraising businesses is its use to estimate the value of individual assets, including some kinds of intangible assets, whose value cannot readily be determined by other means.

APPROACH TO APPRAISAL OF WILSON'S FINE THINGS

Choice of Appraisal Approach

The various appraisal approaches described in the preceding section of this report were considered from the standpoint of their applicability to the appraisal of Wilson's Fine Things.

A search for information that could be used in connection with the market data approach resulted in identifying only one actual sale of a similar business.

This sale was of a chain of stores, whose volume of business (in excess of $8 million per year) was substantially larger than that of Wilson's Fine Things. Also, information regarding the sale was incomplete in several respects, including omission of information on profitability. Neither the quantity nor the quality of information on sales of similar businesses was considered adequate, and, accordingly, it was determined that the market data approach could not be applied meaningfully to the appraisal of Wilson's Fine Things.

As explained in the preceding section of this report, it is difficult to apply the investment value approach to determine the total value of a complete business, this approach instead being useful primarily in estimating the value of individual assets whose values cannot readily be determined by other means.

Accordingly, it was determined that the best approach to estimating the value of the assets of Wilson's Fine Things was the replacement cost approach, with the investment value approach being used to supplement the replacement cost approach as the means for determining the value of commercial goodwill.

Application of Replacement Cost Approach to Appraisal of Wilson's Fine Things

A common technique for applying the replacement cost approach to estimate the value of tangible assets of a business is to begin with information as shown in financial statements or tax returns, and to adjust the figures to reflect differences between the book values that appear in the financial statements or tax returns and the market values that are the objective of the appraisal process.

Financial statements, specifically so-called income/expense or profit/loss statements, also provide the starting point for estimating the value of intangibles, in this instance commercial goodwill, by means of a form of the investment value approach termed the excess earnings method (also known as the IRS method).

U.S. income tax returns for businesses include, in addition to other information, figures for net income (profit), inventory, and book values of various other items, including fixed assets. Such information from tax returns ordinarily can be used, with adjustments as previously mentioned, for appraisal purposes.

At the time the appraisal assignment was accepted, it was anticipated that tax return information for 19X8 would be available to the appraiser for use in the appraisal. Accordingly, it was planned to use such 19X8 tax return information as a starting point for the estimate of asset values.

However, 19X8 tax return information did not become available as anticipated, and the lack of this information necessitated substantial modifications to the appraisal process as compared to the original plan. (Further modifications to the appraisal process were necessitated by discovery, during the appraiser's investigation, of apparent discrepancies between ostensibly similar information obtained from different sources.)

The appraiser did, however, obtain copies of U.S. Partnership Returns (form 1065) for Wilson's Fine Things for the years 19X2 through 19X7, inclusive. These partnership returns had been prepared by the outside accounting firm from information furnished by Wilson's Fine Things. In addition to the copies of the partnership tax returns, the accountants also furnished the appraiser with certain related information, including month-by-month sales figures and details of the computation of book values of fixed assets.

Approach to Appraisal of Inventory

When using the replacement cost approach to appraise a business or business assets, inventory is valued at the current wholesale cost of replacing existing inventory, less any unsaleable portion. With the exception of possible adjustments for price inflation, the cost of replacing saleable inventory is essentially equal to its original acquisition cost.

When financial statements or tax returns for a business to be appraised are available, the least time-consuming and therefore least expensive method of estimating inventory replacement cost is to use figures for inventory value as· given in the financial statements, adjusting as applicable, such as for changes in wholesale price levels between the time the inventory was acquired and the effective date of the appraisal. This is the method of estimating inventory value that was originally intended for use in the present appraisal.

However, the unavailability of 19X8 tax return information made it necessary to seek an alternative method.

Given the fact that 19X8 tax return information was not available for use in the appraisal, one alternative possibility would have been to conduct an actual physical inventory of merchandise in the store, first identifying each item and then estimating the value of each item, or at least each item of significant value, individually.

With more than 2,800 inventoried items (that is, merchandise listed in the inventory ledger) unsold, and with an unknown quantity of other merchandise not listed in the inventory ledger, such a physical inventory would have been a task of prohibitive magnitude. Merely to catalog the several thousand items of inventory would have required an estimated 75 to 100 hours for a two-person team, and arriving at an actual estimate of the value of the individual items would have required an additional 100 hours or more on the part of a team at least one member of which was a specialist in appraising china and silver.

Accordingly, determination of inventory value on the basis of a physical inventory would have been prohibitive from the standpoint of both cost and time, as well as from the standpoint of the accompanying disruption to the normal business of Wilson's Fine Things.

It was therefore necessary to select another method for estimating the value of inventory.

One other possible method of estimating the value of inventory was to use the figure for total inventory value at the end of 19X7 as shown on the 19X7 tax return, and to adjust this figure to reflect (1) purchases for inventory during 19X8, and (2) cost of merchandise sold during 19X8.

Thus, inventory at end of 19X7, plus cost of additional inventory purchased during 19X8, less cost of inventory sold during 19X8, equals inventory at end of 19X8.

As previously explained in the report section on "Recordkeeping—Inventory Ledger," information on items purchased for inventory appears in the form of detailed entries in the inventory ledger. Likewise, information on items sold from inventory appears in the sales slips that record individual transactions with customers and also in entries in the inventory ledger showing dates of sale of inventoried items.

Accordingly, the alternative method for determining the value of inventory involved use of detailed entries in the inventory ledger to update total inventory as shown in the 19X7 tax return, thus arriving at a figure for total inventory at the end of 19X8.

However, certain discoveries during the appraisal process suggested that the contemplated alternative method, while theoretically sound, might not actually provide a true indication of total inventory value.

In particular, it was discovered (1) that information in the inventory ledger was in substantial disagreement with total inventory as reported in the tax return for 19X7, and (2) that not all merchandise held for sale is included in the inventory ledger. These and related discoveries resulted in formulation of still another method for estimating the value of inventory.

This second method involved (1) calculating the value of inventoried items directly from detailed information in the inventory ledger, and then (2) supplementing the resulting figure for total value of inventoried items with estimates, as determined from other internal records of Wilson's Fine Things, of the value of merchandise not shown in the inventory ledger.

The final approach to estimating the value of inventory of Wilson's Fine Things involved use of both of the previously described methods, in the manner and with the results described in the section of this report entitled "Estimated Values of Assets of Wilson's Fine Things."

Approach to Appraisal of Furniture, Fixtures, and Leasehold Improvements

The market value (replacement cost basis) of furniture, fixtures, and leasehold improvements was estimated using (1) information from the accountants about acquisition cost, age, and tax-related depreciation for individual items, together with (2) discussion with Robert Ross and J.J. Alexander of Alexander and Bartlett, P.A., the accounting firm used by Wilson's Fine Things. Details of this appraisal of furniture, fixtures, and leasehold improvements, and the resulting estimated values, are given in the section of this report on "Estimated Values of Assets of Wilson's Fine Things."

Approach to Appraisal of Commercial Goodwill

Goodwill is an intangible asset consisting of the expectation of continued public patronage of an established going business.

Commercial goodwill (as distinct from personal goodwill) is defined as consisting of those elements of a business that cause customers to return and that usually result in the business earning profits beyond a reasonable return on all other assets of the business.

Such profits beyond a reasonable return on all other assets of the business are customarily accepted as evidence of the existence of goodwill value and are the basis for its measurement by the excess earnings method. The excess earnings method is the most common method for estimating the value of goodwill and is the method chosen for use in the present appraisal.

The results of applying the excess earnings method to estimate the value of the commercial goodwill of Wilson's Fine Things are summarized in the section of this report on "Estimated Values of Assets of Wilson's Fine Things."

ANALYSIS OF INTERNAL RECORDS OF WILSON'S FINE THINGS

Scope of Analysis

As described in the preceding section of this report, appraisal of the assets of Wilson's Fine Things, and particularly the estimate of the value of inventory, required substantial use of internal business records.

These internal business records include, as principal elements:

Sales slips, on which are recorded individual transactions with customers and which provide the primary source information on sales volume and for inventory control

A transaction ledger, containing daily and monthly totals for various kinds of transactions, including sales figures

An inventory ledger, which provides a perpetual record of those items of merchandise included in the ledger

Before information from internal records of Wilson's Fine Things was used to estimate values of assets, the various records were subjected to certain tests, including comparisons with similar information from other records. This was done to confirm the accuracy of the information in the records and to explore the extent of certain inconsistencies that had come to the appraiser's attention during the early part of the appraisal assignment.

Review and Analysis of Sales Slips

Sales slips for 19X8 were made available to the appraiser by Wilson's Fine Things.

The sales slips for the complete year's transactions numbered approximately 3800, and it was concluded that a detailed analysis of sales slips for the entire year would be prohibitive from the standpoint of both cost and time required.

Accordingly, a sample of sales slips representing three months of the year was selected as a basis for detailed analysis.

The sales slips that were studied were for the months of February, October, and December 19X8. The total number of sales slips involved was 1075.

The information from these 1075 sales slips was entered into a computer. With the aid of the computer, information from the sales slips, representing transactions with customers during the months of February, October, and December 19X8, was analyzed for the purpose of determining the following:

1. The relationship between total amount of customer transactions as shown on the individual sales slips and total sales figures for the corresponding months as shown in the transaction ledger and as reported to the outside accountants

2. The relationship between total sales and sales of inventoried items

3. The relationship between the sales slips, as the primary information source on all sales, and entries in the inventory ledger showing sales of inventoried items

4. Any other indications that might be available about whether the sales slips actually represented a complete record of Wilson's Fine Things's transactions with customers.

Comparison of Sales Slips with Transaction Ledger

·The analysis of information from the sales slips indicated that the transaction totals as shown on the sales slips for the three months studied were, in fact, sensibly related total sales figures for the corresponding months as shown in the transaction ledger and as reported to the accountants.

Although the total figures from the sales slips did not agree exactly with the total figures in the transaction ledger, the discrepancies were of relatively small magnitude and could be explained reasonably in such terms as human error, occasional illegibility of sales slip entries, and uncertainty in classifying certain kinds of transactions.

Sales of Inventoried versus Uninventoried Merchandise

Of the 1075 sales slips representing transactions with customers during February, October, and December 19X8, 443 sales slips were for regular sales.

The remaining 632 sales slips were for other customer transactions, such as deposits, refunds, and so on.

Of the 443 sales slips for regular sales, 158 were for items listed in the inventory ledger and included the inventory number as part of the description on the sales slip. The remaining 285 sales slips did not reference inventory numbers and were accordingly categorized as representing sales of uninventoried merchandise—that is, items not listed in the inventory ledger.

Using the computer, the sales slips representing regular sales were analyzed to determine what proportion of regular sales volume represented sales of inventoried merchandise and what proportion represented sales of uninventoried merchandise.

The following table summarizes the results of this analysis:

Analysis of Regular Sales—February, October, and December, 19X8

	Sales Slips	Selling Price
Sales of inventoried items	158	$ 61,827
Sales of uninventoried items	285	45,766
Three-month total	443	$107,593

Sales of univentoried items as percentage of total sales = 42.5%

Sales of uninventoried items as percentage of sales of inventoried items = 74.0%

It is apparent from the table that sales of uninventoried items constitute a substantial portion of total sales. In terms of dollar volume, sales of uninventoried items appear to be approximately 74% as large as sales of inventoried items, and to make up approximately 40% of total sales.

Another indication of the possible relationship between sales of inventoried and uninventoried merchandise can be found in the transaction ledger.

The monthly total of regular sales as reported by Wilson's Fine Things to the accounting firm is made up of two separate subtotals from the transaction ledger. One of these subtotals consists of the total of daily entries in the column "income—sales." The other subtotal is a single entry, "nontax sales."

The following table summarizes information in the transaction ledger relative to the relationship of nontax sales to total regular sales for all 12 months of 19X8.

Analysis of Regular Sales—Twelve Months 19X8

Nontax sales	$ 64,661
Other regular sales	226,081
Total regular sales	$290,742

Nontax sales as percentage of total regular
sales = 22.2%

Nontax sales as percentage of other regular
sales = 28.6%

If nontax sales in the transaction ledger refers to inventory in the category "second-hand, no tax" as previously mentioned, then the above analysis would appear to indicate that approximately 20% of total regular sales is made up of sales of such items.

Comparison of Sales Slips with Inventory Ledger

As a test of recordkeeping procedures relative to the inventory ledger, the computer was used to match information from the 158 sales slips reflecting sales of inventoried items against information for the corresponding items as shown in the inventory ledger.

As previously stated, examination of the inventory ledger had indicated that, at the time the ledger pages were copied for study, sales information had been posted for sales up to December 18, 19X8. Of the 158 sales slips reflecting regular sales of inventoried items, 104 were for sales that took place before December 18, and the remaining 54 were for sales on and after December 18.

Comparison of sales slips for the 104 sales that took place before December 18 with the corresponding items in the inventory ledger disclosed that the inventory ledger had been posted, without a single exception, to show that each of the 104 items had been sold.

Accordingly, it was concluded that recordkeeping procedures with respect to the inventory ledger had been followed scrupulously and that the information in the inventory ledger with regard to items remaining unsold was, therefore, an accurate reflection of the actual inventory of such items.

Analysis of Internal Records—Conclusions

As a result of the various tests of records and recordkeeping procedures just described, the following conclusions were reached:

1. Information regarding sales volume shown on sales slips for the three sample months was in reasonably close agreement with figures for total sales volume as shown in the transaction ledger for the corresponding months. Accordingly, sales volume totals shown in the transaction ledger, and reported to the accountants as a basis for preparation of tax returns and other financial reports, were accepted as accurate.

2. Recordkeeping procedures relative to posting of sales information to the inventory ledger appear to have been followed scrupulously, and, accordingly, information on unsold inventory shown in the inventory ledger was accepted as accurate.

3. A substantial portion of total volume of regular sales was found to consist of sales of merchandise not listed in the inventory ledger. The study suggested that sales of uninventoried items might add from approximately 30% to as much as 75% to sales volume as indicated solely by sales of items listed in the inventory ledger.

ESTIMATED VALUES OF ASSETS OF WILSON'S FINE THINGS

Estimated Value of Inventory

The value of inventory as of December 31, 19X8, was estimated by two different methods:

1. Inventory value as of December 31, 19X7, as reported on the U.S. Partnership Return of Income for 1981, was adjusted to reflect (1) purchases for inventory during 19X8, and (2) cost of sales from inventory during 19X8, thus arriving at a figure for the value of inventory as of December 31, 19X8.

2. The total value of unsold inventoried items as of December 31, 19X8,

was determined directly from the perpetual record in the inventory ledger, and an adjustment was added for the estimated value of merchandise not listed in the inventory ledger. As for the value of uninventoried merchandise, the previously described analysis of sales slips indicated that total sales of uninventoried merchandise were roughly 75% of sales of inventoried items. Figures from the transaction ledger, on the other hand, suggest that sales of uninventoried items are roughly 30% of sales of inventoried items. For the present purpose, the lower and therefore more conservative of the two figures will be used as the basis for estimating the amount of merchandise inventory that is not listed in the inventory ledger.

In both methods, the value of items in inventory as of the appraisal effective date was assumed to be equal to the original acquisition cost of the items without explicit provision for the effect of price inflation. Because the general trend of prices has been upward, the absence of adjustments for inflation when estimating present value will tend to produce a conservative result.

Inventory value as estimated by the first method is as follows:

Total inventory as of December 31, 19X7 (from 19X7 tax return)	$185,000
Plus purchases for inventory during 19X8 (from inventory ledger)	224,746
	$409,746
Less cost of items sold from inventory January 1 through December 17, 19X8 (from inventory ledger)	137,263
	$272,483
Less cost of items sold from inventory December 18 through December 31, 19X8, inclusive (sales not recorded in inventory ledger at time of appraiser's examination)	15,077
Net estimated value of inventory as of December 31, 19X8	$257,406

As estimated by the second method, inventory value as of December 31, 19X8, is as follows:

Total original cost of inventoried items on hand as of December 31, 19X8 (from inventory ledger)	$369,936
Less cost of items sold December 18 through December 31, 19X8, inclusive (sales not posted to inventory ledger as of date of appraiser's examination)	15,077
Net original cost of inventoried items unsold as of December 31, 19X8	$354,859
Plus estimated value of merchandise on hand as of appraisal effective date but not listed in inventory ledger (estimated as 30% of value of inventoried items)	106,458
Total estimated value of inventory as of December 31, 19X8	$461,317

Regarding the two different estimates for inventory value as of the appraisal effective date, it is apparent that the first method is itself based on an estimate (note that the value of inventory as given in the 19X7 tax return is a rounded figure), which estimate is in disagreement with information shown in the inventory ledger for inventory as of the date in question. The second method, on the other hand, is based directly on information from the inventory ledger, the accuracy of which was confirmed by the appraiser's tests as described in the preceding section, "Analysis of Internal Records of Wilson's Fine Things."

Accordingly, the second of the two methods is considered to be the more accurate and is the basis for the final estimate of the value of inventory.

The estimated total value, as of the appraisal effective date, of the inventory of Wilson's Fine Things is approximately $460,000.

Estimated Value of Furniture, Fixtures, and Leasehold Improvements

As a basis for estimating the value of furniture, fixtures, and leasehold improvements, the appraiser reviewed information provided by the accounting firm regarding original cost, age, and depreciation applied for tax purposes, of the individual fixed assets of Wilson's Fine Things. He also made a brief visual inspection of the assets in question, and discussed their value with Robert Ross and J.J. Alexander, the latter a member of the accounting firm Alexander and Bartlett, P.A.

On the basis of information furnished by the accountants, fixed asset values as of the appraisal effective date can be estimated as follows:

Total original acquisition cost of all items of furniture, fixtures, and leasehold improvements	$36,431
Less depreciation applied for tax purposes through December 31, 19X7	23,039
Net book value as of December 31, 19X7	$13,392
Less provision for additional depreciation during 19X8 (appraiser's estimate)	4,750
Estimated net book value as of December 31, 19X8	$ 8,642

With regard to the foregoing estimate, it should be noted that book values of fixed assets tend to be lower than actual market values, for reasons including:

1. Calculations to determine book values are based on original cost without provision for subsequent price inflation
2. Depreciation is applied on the basis of depreciation allowable for tax purposes, which is almost always somewhat greater than the actual loss of market value of the assets.

Accordingly, book values of fixed assets tend to be somewhat lower than actual market values in most cases.

As a further indication of market value of furniture, fixtures, and leasehold improvements, the value of these items was discussed with Ross and Alexander during a visit to Wilson's Fine Things on October 12, 19X8. As a result of this discussion, it was concluded that a reasonable figure for the total market value of furniture, fixtures, and leasehold improvements would be approximately $20,000.

The estimated total value, as of the appraisal effective date, of the furniture, fixtures, and leasehold improvements of Wilson's Fine Things is approximately $20,000.

Estimated Value of Commercial Goodwill

The value of the commercial goodwill of Wilson's Fine Things was estimated by the excess earnings method (also sometimes called the IRS method).

Use of the excess earnings method to estimate goodwill value involves the following steps:

1. Determine a figure for reasonably probable future net income (profit) of the business. (All values are anticipations of the future).

2. Make any applicable adjustments to the figure for expected future net income. In the present instance, a downward adjustment was made as an allowance for reasonable salaries, at estimated market, for the services performed for Wilson's Fine Things by the partners themselves.

3. Estimate the total market value of net tangible assets of the business.

4. Considering investment characteristics including liquidity and degree of economic risk, select an appropriate rate of return on net tangible assets, and use this rate of return to calculate the profit attributable to return on net tangible assets.

5. Subtract the profit attributable to return on net tangible assets (as determined in step 4) from the total adjusted profit (as determined in step 2) to arrive at a figure for the excess earnings attributable to goodwill.

6. Considering factors especially including degree of economic risk, select an appropriate rate of return on intangible assets (in this case commercial goodwill), and use this rate of return to capitalize the excess earnings determined in step 5. The result is the estimated value of goodwill.

In the present instance, the calculations are as follows:

1. Noting the year-to-year variations in annual net income as shown on tax returns for prior years, and in the absence of a figure for net income for 19X8, anticipated future annual net income was estimated as approximately equal to the average for the years 19X5, 19X6, and 19X7, as shown on the tax returns for those years. The net annual income for these three years is:

19X5	$ 46,907
19X6	70,373

19X7	63,448
Three-year total	$180,728
Three-year average	$ 60,243

Accordingly, future net annual income is estimated as approximately $60,000 per year.

2. The estimated future net annual income as determined in the preceding step includes the salaries of the partners. Accordingly, the figure for total net annual income was adjusted downward to reflect provision for the estimated market value of the services performed for the business by the partners.

   According to a survey conducted by the trade association, China and Gift Retailers of America, managers' salaries in retail china and gift stores with sales volume in the same range as Wilson's Fine Things average approximately $15 per hour, which is equivalent to roughly $30,000 per year. Accordingly, the services performed for Wilson's Fine Things by its partners are estimated to have a market value of approximately $30,000 per year per partner full-time. This leads to the following:

Estimated future net annual income (from step 1)	$60,000
Less estimated market value of services performed by Robert Ross	30,000
	$30,000
Less estimated market value of services performed by Mary Ross (estimated as approximately quarter-time)	7,500
Net expected future annual income after adjustment	$22,500

3. Value of net tangible assets is estimated as the sum of estimated value of inventory and estimated value of furniture, fixtures, and leasehold improvements, both as previously determined. Thus:

Estimated market value of inventory, approximately	$460,000

Estimated market value of furniture,
fixtures, and leasehold
improvements, approximately   20,000

Estimated total value of net tangible
assets, approximately $480,000

4. Considering investment criteria including liquidity and degree of eco-
    nomic risk, it is concluded that a reasonable rate of return on tangible
    assets would be approximately 15% per year. Thus, profit attributable
    to return on net tangible assets can be calculated as:

Estimated total market value of
tangible assets (from step 3) $480,000
Times rate of return   × 0.15

Profit attributable to return on
tangible assets $ 72,000

5. The next step in estimating goodwill value by the excess earnings
    method is to subtract profit attributable to return on tangible assets as
    determined in step 4 from expected future annual income after adjust-
    ment as determined in step 2. In the present instance, profit attribut-
    able to return on tangible assets at the selected rate of return ($72,000)
    is greater than expected future annual income after adjustment
    ($22,500). In other words, excess earnings attributable to goodwill are
    nonexistent.

Accordingly, it is concluded that, as measured by the excess earnings
method, *the commercial goodwill of Wilson's Fine Things has zero value.*

Estimated Total Value of Assets of Wilson's Fine Things

In the absence of goodwill value, the total fair market value of the assets of
Wilson's Fine Things is equal to the sum of the estimated values of inventory
and of furniture, fixtures, and leasehold improvements:

Estimated total fair market value of
inventory, approximately $460,000

Estimated fair market value of
furniture, fixtures, and leasehold
improvements, approximately   20,000

$480,000

Thus, *the estimated total fair market value, as of the appraisal effective
date, of the assets of Wilson's Fine Things as appraised, is approximately
$480,000.*

ASSUMPTIONS AND LIMITING CONDITIONS

This appraisal incorporates the following assumptions and limiting conditions:

1. This appraisal was made, and this report has been prepared, for the purposes stated in the report section, "Purpose and Function of Appraisal." Neither the report nor the information it contains should be used for any other purpose, and they are invalid if so used.

2. This appraisal is based upon information obtained from sources that, with exceptions as noted herein, the appraiser believes to be reliable. However, the appraiser has not had opportunity to confirm the validity of all of the information, and, accordingly, it cannot be guaranteed.

3. The appraiser assumes no responsibility for matters of a legal nature affecting the property appraised, nor is any opinion of title rendered. The appraisal assumes a marketable title, with ownership in fee simple absolute, and the property has been appraised as though free and clear of liens and encumbrances.

4. The distribution of total value among the various elements of the property applies only for the purposes of this appraisal, and the separate value estimates for the individual elements of the property should not be used for any other purpose, and are invalid if so used.

5. Neither this appraisal nor any part of it shall be used in connection with any other appraisal.

6. The appraiser, by reason of performing this appraisal and preparing this report, is not to be required to give testimony nor to be in

attendance in court or at any governmental hearing with reference to the matters herein, unless prior arrangements have been made with the appraiser relative to such additional employment.

APPRAISER'S CERTIFICATION

I hereby certify:

1. That the statements and opinions expressed in this report are correct to the best of my knowledge and belief, subject to the assumptions and conditions stated.
2. That my engagement to perform this appraisal, and my compensation therefor, are independent of the value reported.
3. That I have no present or contemplated future interest in the property appraised.
4. That this appraisal has been performed in accordance with the Code of Ethics of The Institute of Business Appraisers, Inc.
5. That it is my opinion that the value of the property appraised is as stated in this report.

_____

J. J. MARTIN, APPRAISER

April 29, 19X9

APPRAISER'S QUALIFICATIONS

J.J. Martin is a business appraiser and consultant specializing in business valuations and appraisals, business acquisitions and divestitures, and related fields.

His formal education includes degrees from East Western University and the Midwest Central College. He has also had special training in financial management and analysis, appraisal techniques, and other subjects.

Martin's employment history includes various managerial positions in commerce and industry. He is a former officer of Technological Products, Inc.

He is accredited by The Institute of Business Appraisers as a Certified Business Appraiser.

PRINCIPAL INFORMATION SOURCES AND REFERENCES

Interview with J.J. Alexander, Alexander and Bartlett, P.A., September 30, 19X8. Telephone conversations with Alexander, various dates.

Visit to Wilson's Fine Things and interview with Robert Ross and J. J. Alexander, October 12, 19X8.

Visits to Wilson's Fine Things and interviews with Robert Ross, November 18, 19X8; January 6, 19X9; February 14, 19X9; March 21, 19X9.

Transcript of deposition of Robert Ross, April 13, 19X8.

Transcript of deposition of Robert Ross, September 14, 19X8.

U.S. Partnership Return of Income (form 1065), Wilson's Fine Things, for calendar years 19X2, 19X3, 19X4, 19X5, 19X6, and 19X7.

Depreciation schedules, Wilson's Fine Things, as prepared by Alexander and Bartlett, P.A.

Monthly sales totals, Wilson's Fine Things, years 19X6, 19X7, and 19X8 (part), as compiled by Alexander and Bartlett, P.A.

Sales slips of Wilson's Fine Things, months of February, October, and December 19X8.

Pages from Wilson's Fine Things transaction ledger, months of January through December 19X8, inclusive.

Wilson's Fine Things inventory ledger, perpetual inventory record book.

Partnership Agreement between Robert Ross (husband) and Mary Ross (wife), April 6, 19X2.

Telephone conversation with John Moore, China and Gift Retailers of America, Inc., New York, NY 10020, October 4, 19X8.

"Analysis of Retail China and Gift Sales and Operating Statistics," 19X7, China and Gift Retailers of America, Inc., New York, NY 10020.

"Paradise City," publication of Greater Paradise City Chamber of Commerce, 19X8.

Paradise City Yellow Pages, United Telephone Company, 19X7 and 19X8.

"19X8 Annual Statement Studies," Robert Morris Associates, Philadelphia, PA 19107.

U.S. Internal Revenue Service, Revenue Ruling 59–60.

"How to Determine the Value of a Business," by Dr. Walter Jurek, Quality Services, Inc., 1977.

Business Valuation Handbook, by Desmond and Kelley, Valuation Press, Inc., 1977.

Valuing a Business, by Shannon Pratt, Dow Jones–Irwin, 1982.

"Basic Business Appraisal," The Institute of Business Appraisers, Inc., 1982.

15

Small Business Appraisal Report

This chapter illustrates a business appraisal and reporting technique that is useful in appraising small businesses when the function of the appraisal neither requires nor justifies a full formal investigation by the appraiser. In this case, the appraisal was needed by the owners of the business to assist them in arriving at a proposed selling price for it.

In this appraisal, the appraiser relied on information provided by the owners of the business, without attempting to verify this information through independent investigation. This limitation of the appraisal results is brought out in the report section on "Conditions and Limitations." This is also the reason for omission from the report of the customary appraiser's certification.

Notwithstanding the limitations resulting from reliance on information furnished by the owner, this type of appraisal has a major advantage in that, by reducing the amount of work the appraiser is required to perform, it makes a professional appraisal available at a price the owner should be able to afford, and which is much lower than the cost of a full, formal appraisal such as that illustrated in Chapter 14.

Small Business Appraisal Report Walter's Furniture, Inc.

Report no. SBAR-S-924

June 19X9

Walter's Furniture, Inc.

ESTIMATE OF FAIR MARKET VALUE—PROCEDURE

Using information furnished by Mr. and Mrs. Walter Vandevier, including information compiled by their accountant, an estimate was made of the fair market value of Walter's Furniture, Inc.

The business as appraised consists of all tangible assets as shown on the economic balance sheet of Exhibit A, together with intangible assets consisting of commercial goodwill. Inventory is assumed to be constant at the reported value as of August 31, 19X8; any variation in inventory will be reflected dollar for dollar in the estimated market value of the business.

Fair market value is defined as "the price, in cash or equivalent, that a buyer could reasonably be expected to pay and a seller could reasonably be expected to accept, if the business were exposed for sale on the open market for a reasonable period of time, both buyer and seller being in possession of the pertinent facts, and neither being under compulsion to act."

The procedure used to estimate the fair market value of Walter's Furniture, Inc. was as follows:

1. An accountants' balance sheet was prepared from information furnished by Mr. and Mrs. Walter Vandevier, including information compiled by their accountant. This accountants' balance sheet was then reviewed for adjustments leading to an economic balance sheet that would reflect the actual fair market value of the various assets and

liabilities as of the date of the balance sheet. The accountants' balance sheet, the adjustments, and the resulting economic balance sheet are shown in Exhibit A.

2. Income/expense information furnished by Mr. and Mrs. Walter Vandevier, including information compiled by their accountant for the three most recent fiscal years, was reviewed in order to arrive at a basis for forecasting the future financial performance of the business. ("All values are anticipations of the future.") Exhibit B is a three-year comparison of income/expense statements, also including three-year average figures. Then, proceeding from the historical data of Exhibit B, Exhibit C shows the development of, first, a pro forma accountants' income/expense forecast and, finally, an economic income/expense forecast.

3. Next, an estimate was made of the value of goodwill associated with the business. For appraisal purposes, *goodwill* is defined as "the expectation of continued patronage of an established, going business," and usually results in the business earning profits beyond a reasonable return on all other assets of the business. Thus defined, goodwill has the following characteristics:

   a. Goodwill is an intangible asset, which does not usually appear on a business balance sheet prepared according to conventional accounting practice.

   b. Goodwill may be either commercial (attached to or associated with a business enterprise) or personal (associated with a person rather than with the business enterprise of which that person may be a part).

   c. Goodwill requires time to create.

   d. Goodwill is nonseverable from the business enterprise (commercial goodwill) or person (personal goodwill) with which it is associated.

   e. Commercial goodwill may include the elements of (1) goodwill of location, (2) goodwill of product or service (quality, reputation, etc.), and (3) general business goodwill.

In the case of Walter's Furniture, Inc., the value of goodwill was estimated by the so-called excess earnings method (also sometimes known as the IRS method). With this method, annual pretax profit is determined from an economic income/expense statement. This pretax profit is then reduced by the profit attributable to return on net

Exhibit A
BALANCE SHEET ADJUSTMENTS
Balance sheet information as of August 31, 19X8

	Accountants' Balance Sheet	Adjustments	Economic Balance Sheet
ETS			
▮	51,091	−51,091[a]	0
▮unts receivable	64,969		64,969
▮ntory	139,883		139,883
▮d assets:			
▮iture and tures	23,121		23,121
▮cles	10,205		10,205
▮r fixed assets	10,737		10,737
	44,063	0	44,063
▮ depreciation	23,230		23,230
fixed assets	20,833	0	20,833
▮r assets	2,386		2,386
▮l assets	279,162	−51,091	228,071
▮BILITIES			
▮unts payable	13,353		13,353
▮ries payable	509		509
▮osits	7,171		7,171
▮s payable	13,259		13,259
▮r liabilities	848		848
▮l liabilities	35,140	0	35,140
▮ OF ASSETS ▮ESS LIABILITIES	244,022	−51,091	192,931

▮sh not included in business as appraised.

tangible assets, as calculated by applying an appropriate rate of return to the net tangible assets as determined from an economic balance sheet. The remaining pretax profit is considered to be the excess earnings attributable to the goodwill of the business.

These excess earnings attributable to goodwill are then capitalized at

Exhibit B
THREE-YEAR COMPARISON OF INCOME/EXPENSE STATEMENTS

	FY 19X6	% Chg	FY 19X7	% Chg	FY 19X8	Three-Year Average	% of Total
NET SALES	524,515	−9	479,890	39	668,045	557,483	100.00
COST OF SALES							
Inventory at beginning	104,399		108,062		124,384	112,282	20.14
Purchases	278,499		286,645		411,699	325,614	58.41
Freight and duty	6,358		5,252		6,175	5,928	1.06
	389,256		399,959		542,258	443,824	79.61
Less end inventory	108,358		124,436		139,883	124,226	22.28
Net cost sales	280,898	−2	275,523	46	402,375	319,599	57.33
GROSS PROFIT	243,617	−16	204,367	30	265,670	237,885	42.67
Less OH, G & A							
Office salaries	54,500		34,400		40,000	42,967	7.71
Other salaries	44,029		41,673		35,736	40,479	7.26
Advertising	9,320		1,882		3,698	4,967	0.89
Travel and entertainment	829		679		2,110	1,206	0.22
Commissions	16,393		13,957		38,835	23,062	4.14
Rent	17,472		17,472		17,528	17,491	3.14

Depreciation and amortization	2,231		2,281		2,125	2,212	0.40
Insurance	23,595		32,464		33,861	29,973	5.38
Telephone	5,284		4,702		5,204	5,063	0.91
Utilities	4,165		5,165		4,837	4,722	0.85
Professional services	1,800		1,800		1,850	1,817	0.33
Office expense	1,532		1,746		2,426	1,901	0.34
Payroll taxes	8,419		7,066		5,949	7,145	1.28
Auto expense	3,169		4,187		5,356	4,237	0.76
Interest	65		275		275	205	0.04
Other taxes	2,032		751		4,030	2,271	0.41
Maintenance	1,053		2,152		1,465	1,557	0.28
Supplies	702		943		1,104	916	0.16
Dues and subscriptions	1,128		1,351		1,310	1,263	0.23
Profit sharing	10,571		11,334		8,424	10,110	1.81
Other and miscellaneous	1,578		2,452		1,311	1,780	0.32
TOTAL OH, G and A	209,867	−10	188,732	15	217,434	205,344	36.83
NET OPERATING PROFIT	33,750	−54	15,635	209	48,236	32,540	5.84

Exhibit C

DEVELOPMENT OF ECONOMIC INCOME/EXPENSE FORECAST

	Accountants' Three-Year Average Income/Expense Statement		Pro forma Accountants' Income/Expense Forecast		Adjustments	Economic Income/Expense Forecast	
	Dollars	Percent of Sales	Dollars	Percent of Sales		Dollars	Percent of Sales
NET SALES	557,483	100.00	500,000[a]	100		500,000	100
COST OF SALES							
Inventory at beginning	112,282	20.14					
Purchases	325,614	58.41					
Freight and duty	5,928	1.06					
	443,824	79.61					
Less end inventory	124,226	22.28				0	0.00
Net cost sales	319,598	57.33	286,644	57.33		286,644	57.33
GROSS PROFIT	237,885	42.67	213,356	42.67		213,356	42.67
Less OH, G&A							
Office salaries	42,967	7.71	38,537	7.71	−8537[b]	30,000	6.00
Other salaries	40,479	7.26	36,305	7.26		36,305	7.26
Advertising	4,967	0.89	4,455	0.89		4,455	0.89
Travel and entertainment	1,206	0.22	1,082	0.22		1,082	0.22
Commissions	23,062	4.14	20,684	4.14		20,684	4.14
Rent	17,491	3.14	15,687	3.14	−3687[c]	12,000	2.40

368

Depreciation and amortization	2,212	0.40	1,984	0.40		1,984	0.40
Insurance	29,973	5.38	26,882	5.38		26,882	5.38
Telephone	5,063	0.91	4,541	0.91		4,541	0.91
Utilities	4,722	0.85	4,235	0.85		4,235	0.85
Professional services	1,817	0.33	1,630	0.33		1,630	0.33
Office expense	1,901	0.34	1,705	0.34		1,705	0.34
Payroll taxes	7,145	1.28	6,408	1.28		6,408	1.28
Auto expense	4,237	0.76	3,800	0.76		3,800	0.76
Interest	205	0.04	184	0.04	-184^d	0	0.00
Other taxes	2,271	0.41	2,037	0.41		2,037	0.41
Maintenance	1,557	0.28	1,396	0.28		1,396	0.28
Supplies	916	0.16	822	0.16		822	0.16
Dues and subscriptions	1,263	0.23	1,133	0.23		1,133	0.23
Profit sharing	10,110	1.81	9,068	1.81	-9068^d	0	0.00
Other and miscellaneous	1,780	0.32	1,596	0.32		1,596	0.32
TOTAL OH, G&A	205,344	36.83	184,171	36.83	−21476	162,695	32.54
NET OPERATING PROFIT	32,541	5.84	29,186	5.84	21476	50,662	10.13

[a] Estimated future sales volume.
[b] Reduction of officers' salaries with change of ownership.
[c] Reduction of rent as result of reduced size of store area.
[d] Interest expense treated as cost of capital.
[e] Assumes discontinuance of profit sharing plan at time of ownership change.

a selected capitalization rate to arrive at a figure for the estimated value of goodwill. In applying the excess earnings method to estimate the value of goodwill, rate of return on net tangible assets, and separately a capitalization rate to be applied to excess earnings, are selected on the basis of rates of return currently available from investments of various types, giving consideration to risk aspects of the various types of investments, including the business that is the subject of the value estimate.

The computations leading to the estimate of the value of goodwill of Walter's Furniture, Inc., are shown in Exhibit D.

4. Finally, the total estimated fair market value of Walter's Furniture, Inc., was determined as the sum of the estimated replacement cost of the tangible assets, net of liabilities, and the estimated value of goodwill.

ESTIMATE OF FAIR MARKET VALUE—CONCLUSIONS

As a result of the foregoing procedure, the following conclusions were reached:

1. The total estimated replacement cost of the tangible assets, net of liabilities, of Walter's Furniture, Inc., is approximately $192,931 as of the date of the value estimate (from Exhibit A, Economic Balance Sheet).

2. The estimated annual pretax profit, after provision for reasonable owner–manager's salary, is approximately $50,662 (from Exhibit C, Economic Income/Expense Forecast).

3. The estimated value of the goodwill of Walter's Furniture, Inc., is approximately $30,190 as of the date of the value estimate (from Exhibit D).

4. The total fair market value of Walter's Furniture, Inc., as of the date of the value estimate is approximately $225,000 (sum of estimated replacement cost of tangible assets less liabilities, and estimated value of goodwill).

Exhibit D
ESTIMATE OF GOODWILL VALUE BY EXCESS EARNINGS METHOD

Adjusted net profit before income tax (from economic income/expense statement)		$ 50,662
Less profit attributable to return on tangible assets:		
Net of assets less liabilities (from economic balance sheet)	$ 192,931	
Times rate of return on tangible assets 20%	× 0.2	
Profit attributable to return on tangible assets		38,586
Net excess earnings attributable to goodwill		$ 12,076
Capitalization rate for excess earnings = 40% equivalent to multiplier of 2.5		× 2.5
Estimated value of goodwill		$ 30,190

FINANCIAL COMPARISON WITH OTHER COMPANIES IN SIMILAR BUSINESS

Using information from financial reports prepared by 349 other retail furniture dealers, statistical comparisons were made between balance sheet and income/expense statement information for Walter's Furniture, Inc., and composite data for the 349 other companies.

These comparisons are shown in Exhibits E, F, and G.

APPLICATION OF MARKET DATA APPROACH— SALES OF OTHER COMPANIES

A search of available sources failed to disclose any usable information on actual sales of businesses similar to Walter's Furniture. Accordingly, it was not possible to apply the market data approach in arriving at an estimate of the market value of Walter's Furniture.

Exhibit E
BALANCE SHEET COMPARISON
Walter's Furniture, Inc. as of August 31, 19X8, versus Other Companies in Similar Busine
(All data are in percentages)

	Walter's Furniture, Inc.	Average of 349 other companies SIC code 5712 (retail furniture dea
ASSETS		
Cash and equivalent	18.3	5.6
Accounts receivable	23.3	20.0
Inventory	50.1	53.6
Other current assets	0.8	1.7
Total current assets	92.5	80.9
Fixed assets—net	7.5	13.2
All other tangible assets		5.2
Intangible assets—net		0.7
TOTAL ASSETS	100.0	100.0
LIABILITIES		
Accounts payable	4.8	18.3
Notes and loans payable—short-term		10.3
Accrued expenses	0.2	4.7
All other current liabilities	7.6	10.7
Total current liabilities	12.6	44.1
Long-term debt	0.0	15.1
All other noncurrent liabilities		3.1
TOTAL LIABILITIES	12.6	62.3
NET OF ASSETS LESS LIABILITIES	87.4	37.7
	100.0	100.0

RULE OF THUMB PRICING INFORMATION

According to one recognized source, a rule of thumb that is sometimes used
by business brokers in pricing retail furniture stores is "sale price should be

based on . . . value of equipment and inventory. . . . If . . . profit will return the down payment in two years, goodwill should be worth 10% of the annual gross."*

If applied to Walter's Furniture, this rule of thumb would result in a price of approximately $240,000, assuming that terms of sale include a down payment of no more than $100,000.

In applying any rule of thumb, however, it must be borne in mind that rules of thumb are, at best, only approximations and cannot be expected to be valid for application over a wide range of situations, each involving more or less unique conditions and circumstances, such as are found in actual practice.

JUSTIFICATION FOR PURCHASE TEST

The justification for purchase test is sometimes called by other names, including the business broker's method, the acid test, and the ability formula.

Exhibit F

INCOME/EXPENSE STATEMENT COMPARISON
Walter's Furniture, Inc. versus Other Companies in Similar Business
(All data are in percentages)

	Walter's Furniture, Inc. Three-year Average (unadjusted figures)	Average of 349 other companies in SIC code 5712 (retail furniture dealers)
Net sales	100.0	100.0
Cost of goods or services	57.3	61.2
Gross profit	42.7	38.8
OH, sales, G and A expense	36.8	36.0
Operating profit	5.8	2.7
All other expenses/income		−1.1
Profit before taxes	5.8	1.6

* *Guide to Buying or Selling a Business*, by James M. Hansen. Grenadier Press, 1979.

Exhibit G

RATIO COMPARISON

Walter's Furniture, Inc. as of August 31, 19X8, versus Other Companies in Similar Business

	Walter's Furniture	349 Other Companies in SIC Code 5712 (retail furniture dealers)		
		Lower Quartile	Median	Upper Quartile
Current ratio	7.3	1.4	1.9	2.8
Quick ratio	3.3	0.2	0.5	1.1
Sales/receivables	10.3	6.9	16.4	58.1
Cost of sales/inventory	2.9	1.6	2.4	3.8
Sales/working capital	3.0	12.8	6.3	3.3
Earnings before interest and taxes/interest	174.4	0.4	1.9	4.8
Cash flow/current maturity long-term debt	(infinite)	−0.1	1.1	3.0
Fixed assets/net worth	0.1	0.7	0.3	0.1
Debt/net worth	(infinite)	4.3	1.7	0.7
Percent profit before taxes/tangible net worth	19.7	−1.0	10.2	27.7
Percent profit before taxes/total assets	17.3	9.0	3.5	−1.5
Sales/net fixed assets	32.1	11.4	32.6	69.9
Sales/total assets	2.4	1.4	2.2	2.9
Percent depreciation and amortization/sales	0.3	1.5	0.9	0.6
Percent lease and rental expense/sales	2.6	5.3	3.7	2.4
Percent officer's comp./sales	6.0	7.9	5.0	3.2

The justification for purchase test is not, strictly speaking, a method for estimating the value of a business or other property, as are the replacement cost approach, the market data approach, and other recognized appraisal methods. Rather, the justification for purchase test provides a means to test the reasonableness of a value estimate that has been made by one or more of the other approaches. An especially important application of the justification for purchase test is to determine the reasonableness of a proposed selling price for a business or other property that is actually to be offered for sale.

In essence, the justification for purchase test consists of (1) assuming that the business or other property is actually purchased by a buyer who pays a price equal to the appraised value (or some other price such as a seller's asking price), and then (2) examining the transaction from the buyer's viewpoint to determine whether the purchase was, in fact, an economically sound move.

Generally speaking, the purchase of a business or other income-producing property can be considered to be economically sound if the income produced is sufficient to permit the property to pay for itself over a reasonable period of time and if the buyer's rate of return on investment compares favorably with rates of return available on other, comparable, investments.

Exhibit H shows the results of applying the justification for purchase test to Walter's Furniture, assuming:

A total purchase price of $225,000

A down payment of 45%

Payment of the balance of the purchase price in equal monthly installments over a period of five years with 12% annual interest on the unpaid balance

With annual profits and other assumptions as indicated

The final row of figures in Exhibit H is the cash flow a buyer could expect, given the indicated assumptions.

CONDITIONS AND LIMITATIONS

1. The small business appraisal summarized in this report was performed, and this report was prepared, solely for the personal information and use of the client in arriving at a proposed selling price for the business,

and neither this report nor the information it contains should be used for any other purpose, and are invalid if so used.

2. The analysis and conclusions in this report are based in large part on information furnished by Mr. and Mrs. Walter Vandevier, including information compiled by their accountant. No attempt has been made to verify the accuracy or completeness of this information, and any significant errors in or omissions from the information furnished will have a corresponding effect on the analysis and on the conclusions reached. No inspection of the business or of any of the assets has been made, and no responsibility is assumed in connection with matters that an inspection might disclose.

3. Other information used in the analysis and report was obtained from sources believed to be reliable, but the validity of this information and of the conclusions therefrom are in no sense warranted by the appraiser, her agents, or employees.

4. No responsibility is assumed for matters of a legal nature affecting the property analyzed, nor is any opinion of title rendered. The analysis assumes a marketable title and has been made as though the property is free and clear of liens and encumbrances except as specifically provided for in the analysis.

5. This analysis and report do not constitute a formal appraisal as the term is commonly understood, and they should not be used as a substitute for a formal appraisal in situations or circumstances such that a formal appraisal, including inspection of the business and verification of information furnished by the client, is in order.

6. The client, by accepting this report, agrees that neither the appraiser nor any of her agents or employees will be required to give testimony, nor to be in attendance in court or at any governmental hearing with reference to the matters herein, unless prior arrangements have been made relative to such additional services.

JUSTIFICATION FOR PURCHASE TEST*

PURCHASE ASSUMPTIONS

Total price	$225,000
Down payment	45%
Balance financed	$123,750
Number monthly installments	60
Interest on balance	12%
Annual profit	
First year	$ 50,000
Annual growth	0%
Owner's salary	$ 15,000
Effective tax rate	35%

nnual Data	Year 1	Year 2	Year 3	Year 4	Year 5	Year 6
pening principal	123,750	99,000	74,250	49,500	24,750	0
yment on principal	24,750	24,750	24,750	24,750	24,750	0
osing principal	99,000	74,250	49,500	24,750	0	0
terest	13,365	10,395	7,425	4,455	1,485	0
ofit pretax	50,000	50,000	50,000	50,000	50,000	50,000
us owner's salary	15,000	15,000	15,000	15,000	15,000	15,000
tal	65,000	65,000	65,000	65,000	65,000	65,000
ess interest	13,365	10,395	7,425	4,455	1,485	0
xable income	51,635	54,605	57,575	60,545	63,515	65,000
timated tax	18,072	19,112	20,151	21,191	22,230	22,750
et after tax	33,563	35,493	37,424	39,354	41,285	42,250
ess payment on principal	24,750	24,750	24,750	24,750	24,750	0
et cash flow	8,813	10,743	12,674	14,604	16,535	42,250

Copyright © 1983 by Raymond C. Miles.

16

Appraisal Problem

16

Appraisal Problem

Readers who would like to try their skill at appraising may find the following problem of interest.

This problem is part of the written examination that must be completed by members of The Institute of Business Appraisers as part of the procedure for achieving accreditation as a Certified Business Appraiser.

SUMMARY OF APPRAISAL ASSIGNMENT

You have been retained by S. S. Smith, a local attorney, to appraise a local business, Superior Metal Products, Inc.

Superior Metal Products is a closely held corporation, 100% of whose stock is owned jointly by Mr. and Mrs. J.J. Jones. Mr. and Mrs. Jones are in the process of getting a divorce, and the appraisal of Superior Metal Products is needed in connection with a proposed property settlement.

It is contemplated that the property settlement will include either (1) purchase of Mrs. Jones's interest in the business by Mr. Jones, who will then continue to own and manage the business, or (2) sale of the business, with the proceeds of the sale being divided between Mr. and Mrs. Jones.

The attorney who has retained you is representing Mrs. Jones in the divorce action. She has asked you to appraise the business and to provide her with a formal written report that can be submitted to the court as part of the basis for the property settlement.

BACKGROUND INFORMATION ON SUPERIOR METAL PRODUCTS

At your request, Mr. Jones has provided you with the accompanying general information on Superior Metal Products, including a three-year income/expense statement and a balance sheet for the most recently ended fiscal year. Mrs. Jones has reviewed this information and says that, as far as she can tell, it is correct.

After having reviewed the attached general information and financial statements, you interviewed Mr. Jones and obtained the following additional information from him.

Mr. and Mrs. Jones bought the business 15 years ago, paying the former owner $100,000 in a combination of cash and notes. All of the notes have been paid off, and Mr. and Mrs. Jones now own the business free and clear with the exception of normal business indebtedness as shown on the balance sheet.

When Mr. and Mrs. Jones bought the business, it was doing a total volume of $400,000 per year. Last year, it did almost $1 million in business, which is an increase of about 25% from the previous year. This was an exception to what had been a relatively modest growth trend (with exceptions in individual years) during the previous 14 years.

Mr. Jones believes that the increase in Superior Metal Products sales volume between 19X7 and 19X8 is a direct result of more effective marketing efforts, which produced substantial increases in volume of orders from two existing customers. He expressed the opinion that the favorable trend of sales volume is likely to continue in the future.

Mr. Jones is president and general manager of Superior Metal Products, and Mrs. Jones is vice-president and treasurer of the corporation. However, Mrs. Jones has not been active in the business on a day-to-day basis.

Of the amounts shown on the accompanying income/expense statements as officers' salaries, $60,000 is Mr. Jones's salary, and $20,000 is Mrs. Jones's salary.

Mr. and Mrs. Jones also own personally the building in which Superior Metal Products is located. It was recently appraised, for insurance purposes, as having a value of $300,000. Insurance on the building costs $22,000 per year, and taxes are $6,000 per year.

There is a mortgage on the building in the amount of $200,000, with interest at 8.5%. Mr. and Mrs. Jones rent the building to Superior Metal Products for $56,000 per year, from which they net $4,366 in cash (or $11,000 including the portion of the mortgage payments that reduce principal) after paying the building's expenses.

Mr. and Mrs. Jones have the usual business owner's perquisites. These include Mr. Jones's use of a Lincoln Mark IV that is leased by the company. Mrs. Jones drives a Cadillac, also leased by Superior Metal Products. Three or four times a year, Mr. and Mrs. Jones attend conventions, with the cost paid by the company.

INFORMATION AVAILABLE FOR APPRAISAL

As a basis for appraising Superior Metal Products, you have gathered the following information:

General information on Superior Metal Products, as furnished by Mr. Jones and as shown in Exhibit A.

Three-year income/expense statements on Superior Metal Products, as shown in Exhibit B.

Balance sheet for Superior Metal Products, as of the end of the most recent fiscal year, as shown in Exhibit C.

Composite financial statistics on other jobbing and repair machine shops, as shown in Exhibits D, E, and F. (You obtained this information from the publication, "Annual Statement Studies," by Robert Morris Associates, P.O. Box 8500, S-1140, Philadelphia, PA 19178.)

Information as shown in Exhibit G on actual sales of other companies whose line of business is generally similar to Superior Metals Products. (This information was furnished by The Institute of Business Appraisers as one of its member services.)

The information listed above and shown in the exhibits may or may not be all the information you will need to complete the appraisal assignment. If you find that you need additional information, you will be expected to obtain it from appropriate sources. This applies to information that should be available from sources such as in the local community, government agencies, industry, libraries, and so on.

If you use additional information from printed sources, identify the information and the sources in your appraisal report.

Should you find that you need additional information of such nature that it could only be obtained from Superior Metal Products, you should set up an interview with Mr. Jones and, putting yourself temporarily in Mr. Jones's position, record such information as (1) Mr. Jones might reasonably be in a position to provide, and (2) would be consistent with the other known facts in the situation. Any such additional information, of course, should be identified in the appraisal report as having been obtained through interviews with Mr. Jones.

Financial Information

The attached three-year income/expense statement (Exhibit B) has been prepared by the company's accountant and reflects sales, costs, profits, and so on, as reported on the company's federal income tax returns (Subchapter S) for the corresponding years. The attached balance sheet (Exhibit C) also has been prepared by the accountant.

Exhibit A
GENERAL INFORMATION
Location

The office and factory of Superior Metal Products are located at:

> 1234 Fifth Street
> Your City
> Your State or Province

Products

Various machined and fabricated metal products are manufactured in small to moderate quantities on special orders from various customers, who incorporate them in end items that the customers manufacture and sell.

Manufacturing

The company owns the required equipment to manufacture the products it produces. This equipment includes lathes, screw machines, milling machines, and sheet metal equipment. Materials, consisting primarily of sheet metal and standard bar stock, are purchased from outside sources. Approximately eight months ago, the machinery was appraised, for insurance purposes, by an outside appraiser specializing in machinery and equipment appraisals. This appraisal resulted in an estimated total market value for all machinery and equipment of approximately $235,000.

Marketing

Superior Metal Products serves customers within a radius of approximately 50 miles of your city. Approximately three-fourths of total sales volume involves customers who have previously placed orders with Superior Metal Products. This relationship tends to be relatively constant from year to year. The company has a list of approximately 120 customers whom it considers regular customers. Of these 120 customers, there is one that accounts for approximately 35% of total sales volume; the nine largest customers account for a total of approximately 85% of total sales volume. To ensure repeat business from existing customers, and to develop as many new customers as possible, Superior Metal Products maintains a full-time sales force consisting of a sales manager and two salespeople.

Personnel

Total personnel complement consists of:

1	General manager (Mr. Jones)
1	Secretary to Mr. Jones (also serves as secretary to sales manager)
1	Mrs. Jones, vice-president and treasurer (not active in day-to-day business)
1	Office manager (also serves as purchasing agent)
1	Payroll and billing clerk
1	Sales manager
2	Salespeople
1	Factory foreman
9	Production workers, two of whom function as working leadmen
1	Inspector
1	Packing, shipping, and receiving clerk
20	Total personnel

Exhibit B
THREE-YEAR INCOME/EXPENSE STATEMENT
FOR YEAR ENDING DECEMBER 31

	19X6	19X7	19X8
INCOME—NET SALES	$768,624	$766,543	$957,136
EXPENSES:			
Production materials	$181,681	$185,804	$236,592
Officers' salaries	80,000	80,000	80,000
Sales department salaries and commissions	54,697	56,217	67,698
Other salaries and wages	168,432	176,984	189,824
Advertising	13,618	13,697	16,954
Travel and entertainment	16,584	14,037	14,953
Rent	56,000	56,000	56,000
Depreciation and amortization	9,684	9,684	9,684
Insurance	20,683	22,687	24,620
Telephone	3,360	3,331	3,621
Utilities	6,769	7,692	9,730
Accounting	4,800	4,800	4,800
Vacation pay	9,751	10,219	11,041
Payroll taxes	43,569	45,653	48,879
Automobile expense	15,698	15,302	17,651
Interest expense	15,098	15,330	23,598
Key man life insurance on Mr. Jones	8,000	8,000	8,000
Repairs	9,198	8,697	9,254
Office supplies	2,331	2,158	2,365
Factory supplies	7,198	5,841	5,651
Miscellaneous	2,687	2,490	2,981
Total expenses	$729,838	$744,623	$843,896
PROFIT BEFORE INCOME TAX	$ 38,786	$ 21,920	$113,240

Exhibit C
BALANCE SHEET AS OF DECEMBER 31, 19X8

ASSETS

Cash		$ 42,518	
Accounts receivable		110,764	
Inventory		64,423	
Prepaid expenses		6,911	
Fixed assets:			
Machinery and equipment	$ 87,930		
Office equipment	19,608		
Vehicles	12,044		
	$119,582		
Less accumulated depreciation	77,472		
		42,110	
Other assets		13,257	
Total assets			$279,983

LIABILITIES

Accounts payable		$ 45,911	
Notes and loans payable		140,150	
Accrued expenses		612	
Other liabilities		—	
Total liabilities			186,673

OWNERS' EQUITY $ 93,310

[a] Inventory is valued at lower of cost or market.
[b] Fixed assets are depreciated on a straight-line basis over the estimated useful life of the asset.
[c] Notes and loans payable to local banks and are secured by accounts receivable and inventory.
[d] The company is the owner of a key man life insurance policy, consisting of term insurance in the face amount of $400,000 on the life of the owner.

Exhibit D
COMPOSITE INCOME/EXPENSE STATEMENT INFORMATION
191 Jobbing and Repair Machine Shops with
Assets between $250,000 and $1,000,000

	(All data are in percentages)
Net sales	100.0
Cost of goods or services	66.4
Gross profit	33.6
OH, sales, G&A expense	24.7
Operating profit	9.0
All other expenses	1.7
Profit before taxes	7.2

Exhibit E
COMPOSITE BALANCE SHEET INFORMATION
191 Jobbing and Repair Machine Shops with
Assets between $250,000 and $1,000,000

	(All data are in percentages)
ASSETS	
Cash and equivalent	8.3
Accounts receivable	26.4
Inventory	17.2
Other current	1.4
Total current	53.2
Fixed assets—net	39.7
All other tangible	0.6
Intangibles—net	6.5
Total assets	100.0
LIABILITIES	
Accounts payable	11.2
Notes and loans payable—short-term	12.3
Accrued expenses	8.9
All other current	4.9
Total current	37.2

	(All data are in percentages)
Long-term debt	20.5
All other noncurrent	0.8
Total liabilities	58.5
NET OF ASSETS LESS LIABILITIES	41.5

Exhibit F
OPERATING RATIOS OF 191 JOBBING AND REPAIR MACHINE SHOPS WITH ASSETS BETWEEN $250,000 AND $1,000,000

	Lower Quartile	Median	Upper Quartile
Current ratio	1.0	1.4	2.0
Quick ratio	0.6	1.0	1.4
Sales/receivables	6.4	8.1	10.6
Cost of sales/inventory	5.4	9.9	27.3
Sales/working capital	83.3	13.6	7.8
Earnings before interest and taxes/interest	2.7	5.3	10.0
Cash flow/current maturity long-term debt	1.6	2.5	5.0
Fixed assets/net worth	1.7	1.0	0.6
Debt/net worth	2.7	1.5	0.7
Percent profit before taxes/ tangible net worth	17.9	34.3	51.4
Percent profit before taxes/ total assets	6.5	13.1	20.0
Sales/net fixed assets	3.2	4.9	8.7
Sales/total assets	1.6	1.9	2.5
Percent depreciation and amortization/sales	5.8	3.3	2.0
Percent lease and rental expense/sales	2.7	1.5	0.9
Percent officers' comp./sales	10.1	6.8	4.7

Exhibit G

DATA FOR MARKET COMPARISON

THE INSTITUTE OF BUSINESS APPRAISERS, INC.

P. O. BOX 1447, BOYNTON BEACH, FL 33435   PHONE 305-433-0908

Date: _____

To IBA Member:

The information below is supplied in response to your request for data to be used in applying the "market data approach" to business appraisal. Because of the nature of the sources from which the information is obtained, we are not able to guarantee its accuracy. Neither do we make any representation as to applicability of the information to any specific appraisal situation.

Following is an explanation of the column headings in the data table:

"Seller & Type of business" = Name of seller, and principal line of business.

"SIC#" = Principal Standard Industrial Classification number applicable to business sold.

"AnnGr." = Reported annual sales volume of business sold.

"AnnNet" = Reported annual net (profit) of business sold. In most cases, the figure given will be net after income tax; however, in some cases pre-tax profit may be reported.

"SlgPr." = Reported price paid by buyer.

"Pr/Gr" = Ratio of price paid to reported annual sales.

"Pr/Net" = Ratio of price paid to reported annual net of company sold.

"Buyer" = Name of purchaser.

"Mo/Yr" = Month and year during which transaction was consummated.

Abbreviations: "K" = X 1,000;   "M" = X 1,000,000

DATA FOR MARKET COMPARISON

Seller.&.Type.of.business..	SIC#	AnnGr.	AnnNet	SlgPr.	Pr/Gr	Pr/Net	Buyer	Mo/Yr
Venture Ride Metal fabrication	3400	$ 1.5M	$ 180K	$ 1.1M	0.73	6.1	Cochrane	11/80
Dahlstrom Mfg. Co. Metal fabricator	3400	$ 20M	Unknwn	$ 1.6M	0.08	Unkn	Powers Regulator Co.	--/73
Fanstell, Inc Metal products	3400	$87.2M	$ 1.3M	$28.7M	0.33	22.1	H. K. Porter Co., Inc.	--/76
Creech Metal Fabricator Inc Metal fabrication	3400	$ 1.2M	$ 350K	$ 1.4M	1.17	4.0	Blanco	01/80
S. E. Steel Metal fabrication	3400	$ 450K	$ 75K	$ 315K	0.70	4.2	Nall	08/79
Will's Co Inc	3400	$ 131M	$ 6.1M	$23.5M	0.18	5.7	Superior Tube Co	--/76

390

Index

Basic Business Appraisal gives professional appraisers, brokers, accountants, lawyers, and bankers—anyone in the "business-watching" business—a practical working guide to the principles and applications of business appraisals.

The most comprehensive source available.

Raymond C. Miles, a professional business appraiser and consultant, provides proven, step-by-step procedures for determining the market value of any business, for a variety of professional needs. Miles goes beyond the common "peripheral" coverage generally given to business appraisal, to zero in on a range of truly state-of-the-art techniques, including—

● a complete discussion of several little-known approaches to valuing businesses—for example, the "Justification for Purchase Test," a technique never before described in any book
● an examination of the various conditions that call for having a business appraised—acknowledging the completely different perspectives of a banker, a lawyer, and an accountant
● an entire chapter devoted to preparing the appraisal report—the key to actually using the appraisal, yet a subject rarely mentioned in other books
● numerous references to the most helpful business and legal resources
● definitions of all value-related terms
● a "Practice Appraisal Problem" to test your understanding of procedure
● a detailed explanation of "Choosing the Capitalization Rate"—an invaluable tool for any business appraiser.

Plus two actual business appraisal reports.

To help you apply the principles of appraisal, Miles provides two appraisals taken from actual practice, which illustrate exactly how business appraisal theory works on paper. There are two forms: One for a small business appraisal report—important because small businesses are often appraised using methods designed for large-scale appraisals, which are beyond the affordability of owners or potential purchasers of small businesses. The other business appraisal form is one commonly used to appraise businesses with gross earnings of over $1 million.

Featuring a checklist of over 200 questions to ask when appraising a business, together with an extensive bibliography of the appraisal literature, **Basic Business Appraisal** is the one desktop reference you need—whether you're on the buying or selling side—for hands-on mastery of the business appraisal.

About the author

Raymond C. Miles is Vice President of Business Sales Associates, Inc., and Executive Director of The Institute of Business Appraisers, Inc. The author of **How to Price a Business** (Institute for Business Planning), Mr. Miles is a Certified Business Appraiser. He holds an MS in science from Pennsylvania State University.